YOUR PERFECT
DOG

First edition for the United States published in 2014
by Barron's Educational Series, Inc.

All inquiries should be addressed to:
Barron's Educational Series, Inc.
250 Wireless Blvd.
Hauppauge, NY 11788
www.barronseduc.com

ISBN-13: 978-0-7641-6638-9
Library of Congress Control Number: 2012956070

Conceived, edited, and designed by
Marshall Editions
The Old Brewery
6 Blundell Street
London N7 9BH
www.marshalleditions.com

Editorial Director   Sorrel Wood
Design   Paul Turner, Stonecastle Graphics
Editorial Assistants   Philippa Davis, Lucy Kingett
Production   Nikki Ingram

Originated in Singapore by Pica Digital Pte Ltd
Printed and bound in China by 1010 Printing
International Ltd.

9 8 7 6 5 4 3 2 1

Front cover: Erik Lam/Shutterstock.com; back cover:
Eric Isselee/Shutterstock.com

YOUR PERFECT
DOG

DAVID ALDERTON

BARRON'S

Contents

Introduction

There's more to choosing a dog that's right for you than looks alone. It's just as important to find out about the unique character and personality of each breed.

The successful pairing of a dog and owner provides a partnership of unconditional love, trust, and companionship. On the other hand, a mismatched dog and owner is a recipe for an unhappy household, and accounts for the three million purebred dogs that are made homeless each year in the United States alone.

Your Perfect Dog invites you to become actively involved in discovering more about yourself as a potential dog owner, before you choose a new or additional pet. It tells you everything you need to know about the wildly different doggy personalities out there. Its unique system throws up a number of potential matches—each dog is graded out of ten against various characteristics that are important to you, the owner. Once you've considered the range of dogs that might suit you best, you are then free to make the final selection on your own terms. This book profiles 174 of the most popular breeds of dog in the world, plus one extra: the mongrel or mutt (see page 23). Although a complete catalogue of dog breeds is beyond the scope of this book, you will find a broad and general representation across the categories of dogs, from working dogs to toy dogs. With 175 different dogs to choose from, you are sure to find the breed that is just right for you.

Havanese

Part One: Find Your Human Profile

This chapter analyzes you as the owner: Will you be bringing your new canine friend into a noisy household of young children, or the arms of a retired couple who love traveling? If you travel a lot, for example, will your dog have the temperament to deal with change while he stays in temporary accommodation?

19 human profiles focus on owner age, family life, work situation, housing, finance, and hobbies and lifestyle.

There is a flowchart on pages 9–11 to help you pick the perfect profile.

Each profile lists the key considerations for an owner with this profile when choosing a dog.

Part Two: Review the Dog Profiles

The heart of the book covers 175 of the most popular breeds, plus 75 designer dogs, organized into groups of similar breeds in color-coded sections: gundogs, hounds, terriers, companion dogs, herding dogs, and working dogs. The most similar dogs are arranged on facing pages for easy comparison. Each dog is profiled in depth, with plenty of details about the breed: physical attributes, origins/background, likes, and breed-specific requirements.

Health issues related to a particular breed are highlighted in the main text when they are likely to have a significant impact on the owner. Any new puppy should be screened for potential inherited ailments by the breeder. Regardless of breed, a new owner should have a pet checked over by a veterinarian as soon as possible.

Side panels introduce new "designer dogs"—crossbred dogs that combine aspects of two different purebreds.

Height and weight are given for each dog, based on the average male (bitches tend to be slightly smaller, especially in the larger breeds). Measurements given are for the standard size of the breed unless otherwise stated. You may find that other sizes, such as toy or giant, are available for some breeds.

Flick through the pages of the book to see where your profile scores highest. This dog is your ideal match! Each dog is rated out of ten, with ten being the best match.

Part Three: Find Your Perfect Dog

At the back of the book, you'll find a roundup of the top picks for your profile.

1 Human Profiles

To find your perfect dog, you first need to know what kind of owner you are—what's your "human profile"?

The entries in this section are not necessarily mutually exclusive—you may find that several human profiles apply to you. You can track two or more profiles, taking into consideration your living circumstances, lifestyle, and interests, and use them to find your perfect match.

How to Find the Right Profile for You

The flowchart questionnaire on pages 9–11 is designed to identify the main human profile you should be looking for throughout the book. Alternatively, simply browse the profiles on pages 12–17 to see which one seems most appropriate to you.

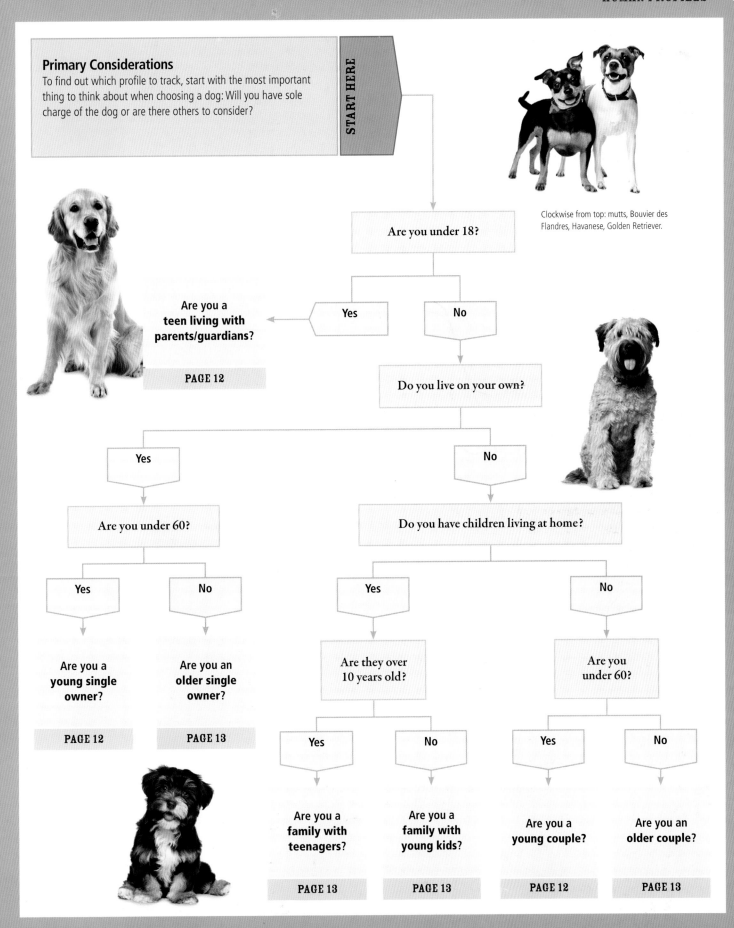

Primary Considerations

To find out which profile to track, start with the most important thing to think about when choosing a dog: Will you have sole charge of the dog or are there others to consider?

START HERE

Clockwise from top: mutts, Bouvier des Flandres, Havanese, Golden Retriever.

Are you under 18?

Yes → **Are you a teen living with parents/guardians?** PAGE 12

No → **Do you live on your own?**

Yes → **Are you under 60?**

Yes → **Are you a young single owner?** PAGE 12

No → **Are you an older single owner?** PAGE 13

No → **Do you have children living at home?**

Yes → **Are they over 10 years old?**

Yes → **Are you a family with teenagers?** PAGE 13

No → **Are you a family with young kids?** PAGE 13

No → **Are you under 60?**

Yes → **Are you a young couple?** PAGE 12

No → **Are you an older couple?** PAGE 13

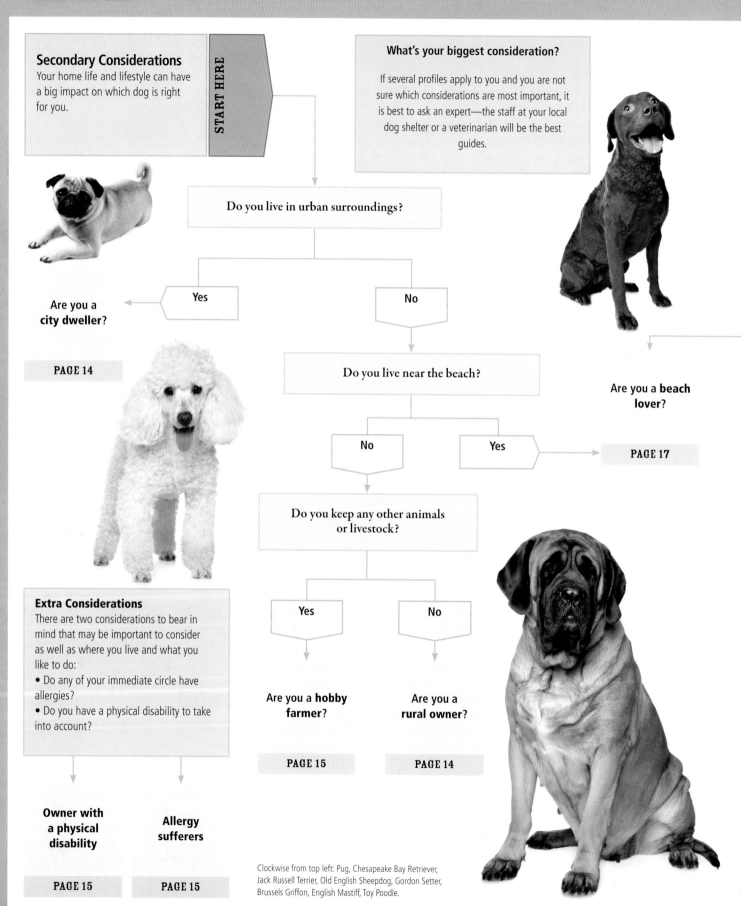

Secondary Considerations
Your home life and lifestyle can have a big impact on which dog is right for you.

START HERE

What's your biggest consideration?

If several profiles apply to you and you are not sure which considerations are most important, it is best to ask an expert—the staff at your local dog shelter or a veterinarian will be the best guides.

Do you live in urban surroundings?

Yes

No

Are you a **city dweller**?

PAGE 14

Do you live near the beach?

Are you a **beach lover**?

No

Yes → PAGE 17

Do you keep any other animals or livestock?

Yes

No

Extra Considerations
There are two considerations to bear in mind that may be important to consider as well as where you live and what you like to do:
• Do any of your immediate circle have allergies?
• Do you have a physical disability to take into account?

Are you a **hobby farmer**?

Are you a **rural owner**?

PAGE 15

PAGE 14

Owner with a physical disability

Allergy sufferers

PAGE 15

PAGE 15

Clockwise from top left: Pug, Chesapeake Bay Retriever, Jack Russell Terrier, Old English Sheepdog, Gordon Setter, Brussels Griffon, English Mastiff, Toy Poodle.

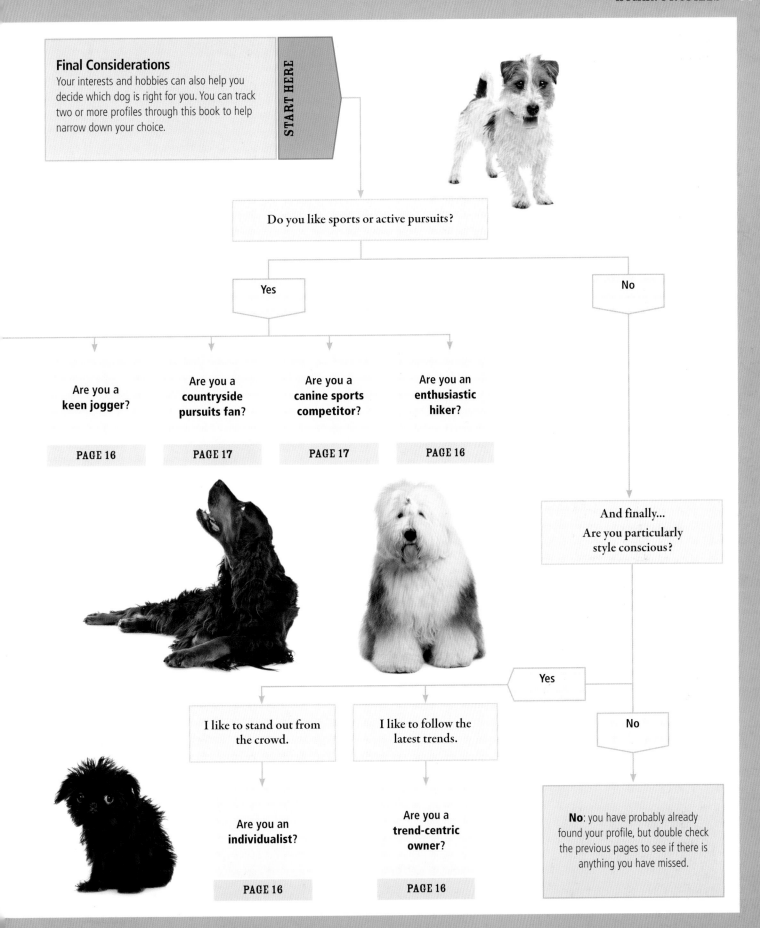

Final Considerations
Your interests and hobbies can also help you decide which dog is right for you. You can track two or more profiles through this book to help narrow down your choice.

START HERE

Do you like sports or active pursuits?

Yes

No

Are you a
keen jogger?

PAGE 16

Are you a
**countryside
pursuits fan?**

PAGE 17

Are you a
**canine sports
competitor?**

PAGE 17

Are you an
**enthusiastic
hiker?**

PAGE 16

And finally...
Are you particularly
style conscious?

Yes

No

I like to stand out from
the crowd.

I like to follow the
latest trends.

Are you an
individualist?

PAGE 16

Are you a
**trend-centric
owner?**

PAGE 16

No: you have probably already
found your profile, but double check
the previous pages to see if there is
anything you have missed.

Basic Profiles

These profiles will help you make crucial decisions about finding a dog that is compatible with your lifestyle. For each profile there are key things to consider before you get a dog.

Golden Retriever

Teen living with parents

Living in this situation, you will be dependent to a great extent on the cooperation and understanding of parents/guardians, who may or may not share your enthusiasm for a canine companion. Their attitude must be considered when choosing a breed, so be prepared to compromise on your choice of dog in these circumstances. That said, dogs that have been chosen for this profile are generally "one-person" dogs rather than family dogs (compared to the family with teenagers, opposite).

KEY CONSIDERATIONS

* If you have elderly parents, do not select a large, active breed and expect them to look after your pet when you are away—particularly if you are heading off for relatively long periods, for example, to study at college.
* Think ahead: Your life is likely to be changing rapidly at this stage. What will happen if you need to move elsewhere for work but can only afford to rent an apartment?
* You may form various relationships and have children during your pet's lifetime, which are other factors to bear in mind.

Young single owner

In this category, your dog's day-to-day care will be exclusively your responsibility, which affects both budget and training. Much also depends on where you are living and how much time you have to look after your dog. If you are out of the house for much of the day, you may need to organize care for your pet. Also, if you lead an active lifestyle and enjoy activities such as running or hiking, it is a good idea to choose a correspondingly active breed that you can take with you.

KEY CONSIDERATIONS

* Bear in mind that larger dogs eat more, and therefore cost more to keep. That said, if you are looking for an active pet, middle-sized to large dogs tend to have better stamina.
* Remember that training your pet will be solely your responsibility. Strong breeds need firm training to prevent them from becoming liabilities as they mature. Neutering is highly recommended, helping to calm the temperament of male dogs especially.
* Much will depend on your home surroundings. A large, active dog cooped up in a small house or yard will soon become bored.

Young couple

It is great to share the companionship of a dog, but you may both find yourselves working hard—and playing hard, too—so you need to be sure that you can devote sufficient time to your pet. Ideally, one of you needs to be able to get back home at lunchtime to exercise your pet. Otherwise, your dream dog will soon become unruly, bored, and destructive.

KEY CONSIDERATIONS

* If you are both out all day, be prepared to pay for a dog sitter, who will come in and spend time with your pet, and/or a dog walker.
* Consider an older, house-trained rescue dog, which could be ideal for your situation. A useful starting point is to contact a breed rescue organization.
* Your budget will be impacted if you are both working, given the additional care costs. They will be greater than just the typical care costs of food and veterinary care or health insurance.

Family with young kids

There is indisputable evidence that having a dog in a family can be very beneficial in terms of encouraging children's emotional development, as well as helping to prevent allergies. But you need to choose very carefully to ensure that your dog is compatible in this situation. Obtaining an older dog that is not used to children is not recommended.

* Large dogs are not a good choice to keep alongside toddlers—their size means they are capable of inadvertently knocking a child over.
* Young children need to be taught to be gentle with dogs. A small or frail breed is not a good choice, and terriers can be short of patience. It is better to focus on a true companion breed.
* Good hygiene is vital with children crawling or playing on the floor—and be sure that your dog is regularly dewormed.

Family with teenagers

A lively lifestyle calls for an active dog, which enjoys running and playing with teenage members of the household. Such activities will reinforce the bond between humans and their pets. You may want to avoid breeds with more demanding grooming requirements, as time is likely to be at a premium. Parents still need to be prepared to take overall responsibility for the family pet. In comparison to the teenager profile opposite, here dogs are chosen to bond with the whole family.

* A friendly breed that will interact well with both family members and friends is an ideal choice.
* A particularly large or strong breed is not the best choice—such dogs will not be so easy for teenagers to control on the leash, especially if they have relatively little previous experience of dogs.
* Some teenagers will be eager to participate with their pets in one or more of the canine sports, such as dog agility or flyball.

Older single owner

Age is generally no barrier to owning a dog, but some breeds are more suitable for senior owners than others because of their size and exercise and grooming needs. Consider finding an older dog at this stage, rather than an exuberant puppy that is likely to be more problematic to integrate into the home.

* A dog provides companionship and reassurance for older people on their own, helping to deter potential break-ins at home, too.
* Studies have confirmed the health benefits for such owners who keep dogs. In general, dog owners remain fitter, because of the need to exercise their pets every day.
* Keeping a dog helps older people living alone to feel less isolated in their communities, and also enables them to socialize more easily.
* See also, considerations below.

Older couple

Because long-haul, overseas vacations may not appeal as they once did, this means that domestic, dog-friendly trips can be arranged instead. With any children having left home, a pet dog can help to fill the void as well. Depending on your situation, it may be wise to choose a breed that is likely to accept the presence of young grandchildren without problems.

* Care costs are likely to be important if you are on a fixed budget. Unsurprisingly, smaller dogs are more economical to feed.
* A mixed-breed from a shelter may be a better choice than an expensive purebred puppy.
* Looking to the future, dogs may be permitted in assisted-living accommodation, but in such surroundings, the choice of a relatively quiet canine companion will be essential, to avoid any risk of upsetting the neighbors.

Secondary Profiles

These profiles will help you narrow down your choices. You may find that where you live and what hobbies you like doing are more important when it comes to choosing a dog than other aspects of your lifestyle (see also pages 16–17).

City dweller

With more and more people living in urban surroundings, choosing a dog suited to this lifestyle is increasingly important. Few people can drive out into the countryside once or twice a day to exercise a pet, and will be reliant on using city parks for this purpose. Finding the right dog is especially challenging if you live in an apartment with no backyard.

KEY CONSIDERATIONS

* It is especially important to ensure that your dog is well socialized and used to meeting other dogs and people from an early age.
* Small breeds with medium- to low-exercise needs that are also quiet by nature are ideal for city life, as frequent barking can lead to complaints from neighbors.
* Keeping your dog fully immunized is especially important in city surroundings where lots of dogs are being exercised together in parks, and strays especially can spread diseases.

Rural owner

Virtually any type of dog can be considered for these surroundings, but do not forget to consider lifestyle factors as well. Many active breeds that were originally developed for working purposes thrive in this type of environment. Bear in mind, though, that they will still need plenty of exercise in order to prevent them from becoming bored and destructive around the home.

KEY CONSIDERATIONS

* It is not just the type of environment where you live that is important. The length of time that you can commit to your pet is also significant.
* Do train your dog to return to you when you call. Hounds in particular are likely to instinctively run off when in a rural environment.
* Anticipate the unexpected. Retrievers may plunge into stretches of water where there might be strong currents, while terriers may venture underground into burrows and get trapped.
* Even in homes with ample private land, make sure the borders of your property are secure to prevent your dog running off.

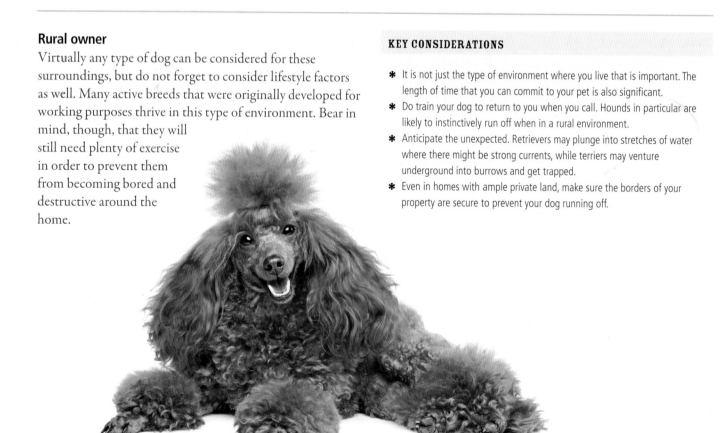

Toy Poodle; Boxer (opposite)

Hobby farmer

When farming on a small scale, either working the land or keeping livestock, you are likely to want a canine companion that will not only be a pet, but will also contribute to your chosen way of life, essentially working as a farm dog. Stock herding is an obvious area where a dog can be of value—breeds that have evolved to form close bonds with their handlers are best suited to this type of lifestyle.

KEY CONSIDERATIONS

* Although collies are best known for herding sheep, they can work with a variety of other livestock, and some have even been known to herd flocks of chickens and ducks.
* Additional training will be necessary if you want your dog to work alongside you. Remember that it will take time and effort for your pet to master the requisite skills.
* Some stock-herding dogs will also prove to be alert guardians, warning you of the approach of strangers or possible predators.

Owner with physical disability

Dogs have long proved themselves as companions, but can also be trained successfully to provide vital assistance for people with physical disabilities—acting as seeing-eye dogs, hearing dogs, and even being able to warn vulnerable owners of impending epileptic attacks.

KEY CONSIDERATIONS

* If you have a physical weakness, it is very important to select a dog that will be easy for you to control and will not pose a danger in terms of pulling you over.
* If you have a weakness affecting your hands, choose a short-coated breed, which will have very minimal grooming needs compared with a long-haired or even a wire-coated dog.
* If mobility is an issue, always take a cell phone with you when out for a walk, so that you can contact help easily in case your dog runs off.

Allergy sufferers

Unfortunately, allergies of all types are becoming more common, and the symptoms themselves tend to be quite nonspecific. Itchy eyes, repeated sneezing, and a tight-chested feeling are all typical indicators. If you suspect that you or a family member may be allergic to dogs, ask your doctor to check this out, as there could be a different cause—it might even be something like grass pollen brought in on your dog's coat.

KEY CONSIDERATIONS

* It tends to be skin particles—or "dander"—rather than dog hair that causes the problem, although breeds that tend not to shed their hair are generally regarded as hypoallergenic.
* Many designer dogs have poodle ancestries and are promoted as being hypoallergenic, but this does not apply in every case.
* It is possible to take medication to help in overcoming the worst of the symptoms, and in some cases the condition may improve on its own over time.

More About You

What you like to do and things that you think are important should also influence your choice of dog. These profiles really help focus your options after you have covered the considerations related to your daily life.

Papillon

Trend-centric owner

If you like to keep up with the latest trends and fashions, you may find you are particularly drawn to certain types of dog by virtue of their appearance. This can be linked with their movement, too, with many of the sight hounds especially being very elegant, seemingly running with minimal effort.

KEY CONSIDERATIONS

* Don't lose sight of the fact that there is more to a dog than the way it looks—be sure a dog fits with all aspects of your own home and lifestyle.
* Bear in mind that many dogs likely to appeal to trend-centric owners require considerable grooming to look their best.
* Overbreeding can be a problem in the most stylish and popular breeds, so be particularly careful when buying a dog of this type.

Individualist

Finding a pet dog that stands out from the crowd can be tricky. Purebred dogs have a uniformity of appearance, as they are bred and judged against a breed standard—and not each other. Their temperaments, too, are generally quite similar across a breed. Other than choosing a particularly unusual breed, you may find what you are looking for in a mutt or crossbred designer dog.

KEY CONSIDERATIONS

* There is variety in the case of some purebred dogs, in terms of their coat patterning, so you can still have an individual that is very distinctive.
* You might want to choose a designer dog for your companion, as such dogs are much more varied in appearance than purebreds.
* As with the profile above, remember that the dog's appearance is of far less significance in terms of its suitability as a pet than its ancestry.

Keen jogger

Some dogs are better suited to running than others in terms of their build. These tend to be hound breeds that were originally developed to run, along with other breeds such as the Dalmatian, whose working ancestry demanded pace and stamina. Avoid running with your pet when the sun is at its hottest, as dogs cannot sweat effectively and are vulnerable to heatstroke.

KEY CONSIDERATIONS

* It is very important not to overexercise young dogs of bigger breeds, as their bodies take time to mature and this can do serious damage.
* Just like people, a dog needs to build up its stamina over time. An unfit individual can suffer injuries, so devise a suitable training schedule.
* Choose an area away from traffic and be aware of the surface on which you are running. Hard surfaces can injure dogs' paws.

Enthusiastic hiker

Hiking is ideal for many dogs, but young dogs must be exercised with caution to protect their joints. Heading off into rural areas gives you the chance to allow your dog off the leash so that it can run for periods as well, probably covering more ground than you do over the course of a hike.

KEY CONSIDERATIONS

* Don't think that a marathon hike each weekend will allow you to keep an active dog in urban surroundings for the remainder of the week.
* Always take a bottle of water and a bowl with you so your pet can have a drink along the way.
* Beware of native wildlife, such as venomous snakes, not to mention ticks that can spread potentially deadly Lyme disease to your pet.

Countryside pursuits fan

A number of different breeds of dog were originally developed to participate in activities such as hunting and retrieving shot game. Although the original purpose behind their development may no longer apply, you can enter these breeds in various competitions to keep their working skills alive. Many of these sporting companions will excel at lure coursing (chasing a plastic lure across open ground).

KEY CONSIDERATIONS

* There is a distinct difference in some cases between the working and show forms of the same breed. If you are interested in participating in field sports, choose a puppy from working stock.
* Be aware that even pet dogs may react in a way more expected of their working ancestors, putting them—and potentially you—in danger, with retrievers jumping into water, for example.
* If you want your dog to develop into a good sporting companion, there are specialist training courses that you can sign up for together.

Beach lover

Certain breeds traditionally work in and around the sea, helping fishermen land catches safely. Many more dogs of all types like to play on the beach though, where they can chase after balls, run around, play in the surf, and even swim. Owners should be wary in areas with strong currents, as even dogs who are good swimmers can get into difficulty in such conditions, especially if they have been bred in calmer freshwater areas. Some water-loving dogs have been marked under 10 because of this, or if they are likely to be affected by sand (due to prominent eyes), require shade due to a heavy coat, or need grooming after a visit to the beach.

KEY CONSIDERATIONS

* Dogs are often banned from popular beaches in summer, and if you take your pet onto the beach, it is vital to ensure that it will be well behaved and will not annoy other beach users.
* Be certain to take fresh water and a drinking bowl; otherwise, your pet may be inclined to drink seawater that, with its high salt content, is likely to be harmful if consumed in any quantity.
* Beware when taking a dog onto a pebbly beach. Puppies may try to chew the pebbles, cracking their teeth, or may even swallow them, which will require veterinary intervention.

Canine sports competitor

There is now a wide range of different fun competitive activities that you can participate in with your dog, irrespective of its type, although certain breeds are instinctively better at certain activities than others. Sports include: agility, flyball, terrier racing, sledding, sheepdog trials, and "heelwork to music" (canine dancing). A search on the Internet can guide you to clubs in your area.

KEY CONSIDERATIONS

* Good basic training is essential to allow your dog to take part in sports, to keep it from becoming distracted or simply running off after another dog.
* Young dogs particularly will enjoy sports such as flyball, and there is the added benefit that you will also stay fit while running alongside your pet during training and at competitions.
* It helps if you can use part of your yard for less formal training of your dog on a regular basis, in order to reinforce the lessons taught at club training sessions.

Border Collie

2Dog Profiles

Every dog breed in the directory is rated from one to ten according to how well it is suited to the different human profiles—ten is a perfect match.

Which Dog Is Right for You?

Choosing to get a dog is a happy occasion, but it is not a decision to be taken lightly. You are deciding on a companion who will be part of your daily life for 10–16 years. It is therefore very important to consider not only your domestic circumstances now, but also how your life may change over this period. Try not to be swayed by fashion—what suits someone else's lifestyle may not be applicable to yours, and bear in mind that all puppies are just as cute as each other, but some get to be very big dogs in a short space of time.

The Importance of Ancestry

The ancestry of a particular breed will be far more significant, in terms of whether it will work with your lifestyle, than the way it looks as a puppy. Dogs retain strong behavioral instincts that reflect their breed's origins.

While some breeds were developed specifically as companions over the course of centuries, the majority were intentionally bred to undertake tasks such as hunting or guarding livestock and property. Their past will impact significantly on their behavior today, and also influence other aspects of their care, such as their grooming and exercise needs. Some breeds are more energetic than others, while those with long coats are likely to need more grooming than their short-coated cousins.

It is hard to predict the personality of your pet, as each dog is an individual. Generally, the temperament of purebred dogs is relatively consistent across the breed. It can be much harder to predict the temperament of rescue dogs, especially if they have been badly treated in the past. Staff at the rescue center may be able to give you some insight, based on their own observations (perhaps the dog prefers women and is reserved around men, for example). The only way that you can really build up an understanding is to live with your new pet for a trial period. It may take a little longer to win the confidence and trust of a rescue dog, depending on its background, but in time your patience will be rewarded.

Rescued puppies are far easier to get to know, and will probably have a better temperament than adult rescue dogs, as puppies are less likely to have been the victims of lasting abuse. A puppy's temperament will probably be influenced more directly by their parent breeds' disposition.

Ordinary crossbred dogs (called mongrels or "mutts," see page 23) are generally easygoing and instinctively friendly, provided they have been socialized early in life. This is something that is critically important for all dogs, but particularly in the case of breeds like terriers that tend to be naturally less well disposed toward others of their own kind.

Your Responsibilities

Effective training is very important. It is worth bearing in mind that some breeds—particularly those, such as retrievers, developed to work on a one-to-one basis with people—are instinctively likely to respond more effectively to training than others. It is a good idea to sign up for dog-training classes, giving you access to the support and advice of a professional trainer. Your veterinarian may be able to help by ruling out any underlying medical problems and referring your pet to a canine behaviorist if necessary. Always remember that the sooner you seek advice, the easier it should be to overcome the problem.

If you are unsure of your new dog's temperament, it is a good idea to fit your pet with a muzzle when out in public. Muzzling is also recommended for sight hounds like greyhounds that can mistake a small dog for a hare. Staffordshire Terriers and other instinctively dominant breeds may also need muzzling if they are intolerant of other dogs, because you may not be physically able to separate your dog if a fight does break out.

QUESTIONS TO ASK YOURSELF BEFORE YOU GET A DOG

Am I out all day?

If **YES**, then a dog is really not a suitable companion unless you can make arrangements for its care.

Do I live in an apartment or in the city?

If **YES**, you should choose a small, quiet dog.

Do I have an active lifestyle, and enjoy mountain biking, running, and hiking?

If **YES**, and you want a dog to join in, select a suitably athletic dog, such as a hound (pages 52–77).

If **NO**, choose a more placid companion, such as a toy breed (see companion dogs, pages 112–135).

Do I have children?

If **YES**, it is crucial to choose a child-friendly breed.

If you have older children, remember that dogs can live 10–16 years, and your circumstances will change—will you care for the dog once your children leave home?

Am I worried that I may not be able to cope with my dog as I get older?

If this is a concern, then why not approach a local dog rescue shelter about fostering dogs? This arrangement could benefit you both.

Do I often go on vacation?

If **YES**, and you will be traveling abroad in particular, you may need to factor in the cost of a dog sitter or kennel.

Alternatively, there are plenty of opportunities for you to take your pet with you on vacation, particularly if you are happy to travel shorter distances.

Am I particularly house-proud or living in rented accommodation?

If you have just redecorated, or don't like vacuuming every day, be sure to pick a breed that will not shed. Crucially, you can also seek out an older, house-trained individual that is less likely to cause damage around the home. Even when your landlord allows pets, damage to your home can become very expensive.

Are veterinary fees a worry?

If your dog is involved in an accident, the cost of the emergency care and orthopedic surgery is likely to be eye-wateringly high. Look into insuring your pet, but bear in mind that routine costs such as vaccinations and neutering will not be covered. Read the small print carefully, particularly with regard to exclusions, excesses, and claims.

Insured or not, it would be worthwhile saving a small amount each month to create an emergency fund.

Where to Start?

The dogs are organized according to type, so that similar breeds are next to each other. Each breed references the American Kennel Club (AKC) group. You can browse the whole book, look up your favorite breed in the index, or use these family groups as a starting point. You may also like to consider whether you want a purebred dog at all—perhaps you should consider a mutt, or even a designer crossbreed (see pages 22–23).

Scale
★ Least (required) / Shortest / Simplest
★★★★★ Most / Longest / Hardest

Gundogs

Bred to work closely with people, gundogs are athletic, energetic, and good-natured. Relatively large in stature, they need plenty of exercise to prevent them from becoming bored around the home. Gundogs would live well on a farmstead. They are generally very eager to learn, and they will form a close bond with family members. Closely linked to the AKC sporting group.
Turn to page 24.

Irish Red Setter

Height:	★★★★★
Training:	★
Grooming:	★★★
Bark factor:	★★
Placidity:	★★
Exercise:	★★★★
Lifespan:	★★★
Upkeep costs:	★★★★

Hounds

There are two categories of hounds. Scent hounds use their noses to locate their quarry, while sight hounds rely on their keen eyesight for this purpose. Both groups have good stamina, and will prove to be energetic and generally genial, although sight hounds are normally somewhat shyer by nature. Dogs from the AKC hound group can be found here.
Turn to page 52.

Borzoi

Height:	★★★
Training:	★★★★
Grooming:	★★
Bark factor:	★★★
Placidity:	★★★
Exercise:	★★★★★
Lifespan:	★★★
Upkeep costs:	★★★★

Terriers

Terriers form a group of typically small yet very determined dogs. They tend not to be especially social with their own kind, but make alert and lively companions. They can be quite vocal, and often display an independent streak—so beware, as they may decide to disappear underground on occasions when out for a walk. Closely linked to the AKC terrier group.
Turn to page 78.

Fox Terrier

Height:	★
Training:	★★★★
Grooming:	★★★★
Bark factor:	★★★★★
Placidity:	★★★★
Exercise:	★★★
Lifespan:	★★★★★
Upkeep costs:	★★

Companion Dogs

These are friendly, small breeds that thrive on human company. They are ideal for urban life, but must not be left alone for long periods. They possess determined personalities, and know almost instinctively how to beg for tidbits, so be prepared to have a hard heart at times, as these little dogs can be prone to obesity. This section includes dogs from the AKC non-sporting and toy groups.

Turn to page 112.

Lhasa Apso

Height:	★
Training:	★★
Grooming:	★★★
Bark factor	★★★
Placidity:	★★
Exercise:	★★
Lifespan:	★★★★★
Upkeep costs:	★★

Herding Dogs

Usually split into two subgroups. There are smaller breeds, developed to help farmers herd stock, who retain strong working instincts that must be catered to if you choose one as a companion. Flock guardians are larger dogs that will be suspicious of strangers. Independent by nature, these dogs will be harder to train. These dogs fall under the AKC herding group.

Turn to page 136.

German Shepherd Dog

Height:	★★★★★
Training:	★
Grooming:	★★★★
Bark factor:	★★
Placidity:	★★★
Exercise:	★★★★★
Lifespan:	★★★★
Upkeep costs:	★★★

Working Dogs

A very mixed group of breeds, each of which has its own character. You really need to examine the ancestry and relationships of these dogs with particular care before making any choice. Some are much more relaxed in the company of strangers than others, but they generally have pretty active natures. This section includes AKC working group and non-sporting dogs.

Turn to page 164.

Great Dane

Height:	★★★★★
Training:	★★★
Grooming:	★★★
Bark factor:	★★★
Placidity:	★★★
Exercise:	★★★★
Lifespan:	★★★
Upkeep costs:	★★★★

Mutt or Designer Dog?

Designer dogs are crossbreeds in terms of their origins. They are bred from two different purebreds with the intention of combining particular characteristics of these breeds into one dog. There are a growing number of different designer dogs in the world, and a few of these are on the way to becoming breeds in their own right—over time, designer dogs may be paired with each other, establishing a more recognizable appearance or "type."

The designer pairings described in this book are included on the profile pages of their parent breeds, in colored panels. A virtually limitless number of different designer dogs is possible in theory. This practice is new—nearly all designer dog breeds are in their early stages, with a few notable exceptions, such as the internationally popular Labradoodle. This book includes the most popular and widely available crossbreeds, combining breeds that are commonly kept.

The Labradoodle crossbreed, shown on this page, is the best-known member of the designer dogs, and it is no coincidence that many other designer dogs have poodle ancestry. The original aim of the Poodle–Labrador Retriever cross was to create a hypoallergenic guide dog. Unfortunately, it isn't an exact science, and although Poodle-crosses are fairly unlikely to provoke an allergic response, there is no guarantee in this regard, as it depends on the individual dogs involved.

As you can see from the two Labradoodles shown below, physical characteristics within the new breed will be very variable in the early stages of the breeding program, particularly in the case of a first-generation (or "F1") cross. F1 crosses are more variable simply because a stable type (appearance) has not been created at this stage. As the breeding program develops over the generations, a more recognizable type of dog evolves as more and more similar dogs are paired together, gradually reducing the differences between them. This mirrors the way that all breeds were developed originally, and accounts for the standardized appearance of established breeds.

To understand the requirements and probable temperament of a designer dog, take a look at both of its parents. It is likely to have a character that is somewhere between the two.

Name that breed

A tradition has grown up of referring to designer dogs with a name reflecting both ancestral breeds. A **Labradoodle**, for example, is the result of a mating between a Labrador Retriever and a Poodle. The names are quite changeable, so in this book the dogs are also referred to by the names of the parent breeds.

Both dogs pictured here are Labradoodles, but you can see that great variation in terms of appearance is possible—this will be true even of dogs within the same litter.

Mutt

Height	Typically 20 in (51 cm)
Weight	About 31 lb (14 kg)
Country of origin	Worldwide

Also known as a mongrel, the name is given to a puppy resulting from the mating of two other mutts. Such individuals have no immediate purebred ancestry, unlike the "designer" crossbreeds (see opposite). Their appearance is variable; but, generally, most mutts are medium-sized, and are of mixed rather than single ("pure") coloration, because patterning is more common in all domestic dogs, generally. They tend to have smooth coats, but some individuals are wire- or even long-coated. Mutts from different parts of the world may look very distinct. Originally from a typical street-dog background, intelligence and adaptability are critical for survival. While real street dogs are often shy around people, a typical mutt, reared as a pet from puppyhood, should develop into a friendly, well-balanced companion.

LIKES

* Being around people
* Exploring unfamiliar surroundings
* Playing

NEEDS

* Treatment against parasites
* Careful health checks
* Neutering

Is this your perfect dog?

Teen living with parents
●●●●●●●●●●

Owner with physical disability
●●●●○○○○○○

Young single owner
●●●●●●●○○

Allergy sufferers
●●○○○○○○○○

Young couple
●●●●●●●●●

Trend-centric owner
●●○○○○○○○○

Family with young kids
●●●●●○○○○

Individualist
●●●●●●●●●●

Family with teenagers
●●●●●●●●●

Keen jogger
●●●●●●○○○

Older single owner
●●●●●●●○○

Enthusiastic hiker
●●●●●●○○○

Older couple
●●●●●●●○○

Countryside pursuits fan
○○○○○○○○○○

City dweller
●●●●●○○○○

Beach lover
●●●●●●●●○○

Rural owner
●●●●●●●○○

Canine sports competitor
●●●●●●●●●●

Hobby farmer
●●●●●●●○○

American Water Spaniel

Height 18 in (46 cm)
Weight 45 lb (20 kg)
Country of origin United States

For many years, the American Water Spaniel could be seen working on farms in the Midwest, especially in Wisconsin, but it is now more widely kept as a sporting companion. Its curly coat with distinctive brown shades of coloration indicates an ancestry involving the Irish Water Spaniel and the Curly-coated Retriever, and it displays characteristics of both. As its name suggests, the American Water Spaniel takes to water readily. Stand back when your pet emerges from the water, as it will dry itself by shaking much of the moisture out of its coat. Although good swimmers, American Water Spaniels can struggle with waves and strong currents in the sea, so are more suited to swimming in freshwater.

LIKES

* Being in water
* Retrieving games
* Flyball competitions

NEEDS

* Varied training routines
* Calm water
* Supervision near water with strong currents

Is this your perfect dog?

Teen living with parents ●●●●●●○○○○	Family with young kids ●●●●●●○○○○	City dweller ●●●●●●○○○○	Individualist ●●○○○○○○○○
Young single owner ●●●●●○○○○○	Family with teenagers ●●●●●●●○○○	**Rural owner** ●●●●●●●●●●	Keen jogger ●●●●●●●●○○
Young couple ●●●●●●○○○○	Older single owner ●●●●●●○○○○	Hobby farmer ●●●●●●●●○○	**Enthusiastic hiker** ●●●●●●●●●●
	Older couple ●●●●●●○○○○	Owner with physical disability ●●●●●●●○○○	**Countryside pursuits fan** ●●●●●●●●●●
		Allergy sufferers ●●●●○○○○○○	Beach lover ●●●●●●●●○○
		Trend-centric owner ●●●●○○○○○○	Canine sports competitor ●●●●●●●●○○

AKC group: sporting

Irish Water Spaniel

Height 22 in (56 cm)
Weight 55 lb (25 kg)
Country of origin Ireland

There is no mistaking the Irish Water Spaniel, with its curly coat and ratlike tail offset by unique coloration. It exists in one color only—a shade of liver, described as "puce" because of its purple hues. The dog doesn't shed much hair, but will need regular grooming and trimming. The largest of all the spaniels, the Irish Water Spaniel is not a breed that will be content lazing around at home. Bred to work, it retains an energetic nature, and responds very well to positive encouragement during training, always eager to please its handler. Like the American Water Spaniel (opposite), these dogs were developed to work in freshwater areas, and can struggle with sea currents.

Is this your perfect dog?

Teen living with parents
●●●●●●○○○○

Older couple
●●●●●○○○○○

Allergy sufferers
●●●●●●●●○○

Enthusiastic hiker
●●●●●●●●●○

Canine sports competitor
●●●●●●●●●○

Young single owner
●●●●●●○○○○

City dweller
●●○○○○○○○○

Trend-centric owner
●●●●●●●●○○

Countryside pursuits fan
●●●●●●●●●●

AKC group: sporting

Young couple
●●●●●●●●●●

Rural owner
●●●●●●●●●●

Individualist
●●●●●●●●●○

Beach lover
●●●●●●●●●○

Family with young kids
●●●●●●○○○○

Hobby farmer
●●●●●●●●●●

Keen jogger
●●●●●●●○○○

Family with teenagers
●●●●●●●●●○

Owner with physical disability
●●○○○○○○○○

Older single owner
●●●●○○○○○○

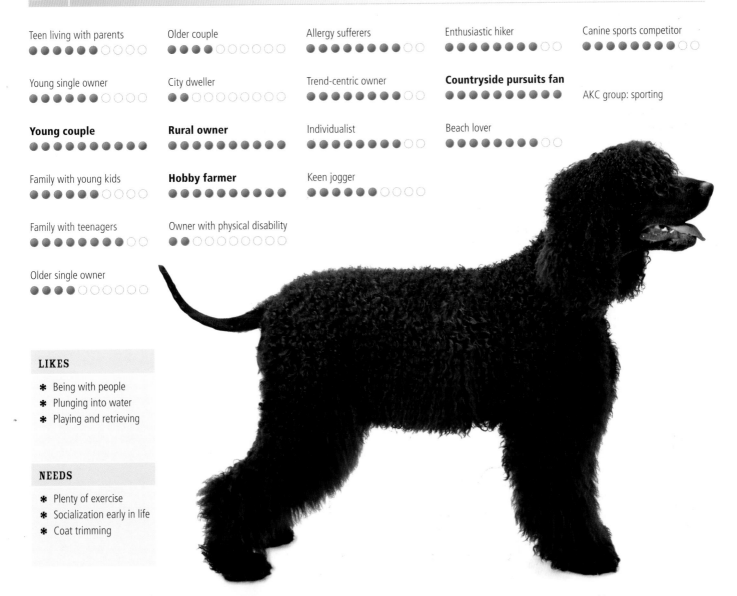

LIKES

* Being with people
* Plunging into water
* Playing and retrieving

NEEDS

* Plenty of exercise
* Socialization early in life
* Coat trimming

Welsh Springer Spaniel

Height	18 in (46 cm)
Weight	35 lb (16 kg)
Country of origin	United Kingdom

The Welsh Springer Spaniel is highly valued as a working gundog. The breed is defined by its coloration, being exclusively tan and white. It loves going in water—something to remember when you are in the countryside. In terms of temperament, the Welsh Springer is typically enthusiastic, and makes an energetic and eager companion. Training tends to be quite straightforward, but make sure you involve all members of the family in the process to avoid any risk of your spaniel becoming a one-person dog. Welsh Springer Spaniels thrive on positive encouragement from their handler, and are instinctively eager to please.

LIKES

* Being around people
* Playing and retrieving
* An active lifestyle

NEEDS

* Plenty of attention
* Watching around water
* Lots of exercise

 Is this your perfect dog?

Teen living with parents
●●●●●●○○○○

Owner with physical disability
●●○○○○○○○○

Young single owner
●●●●●●○○○○

Allergy sufferers
●●○○○○○○○○

Young couple
●●●●●●●●○○

Trend-centric owner
●●●○○○○○○○

Family with young kids
●●●●●●○○○○

Individualist
●●●●○○○○○○

Family with teenagers
●●●●●●●●●●

Keen jogger
●●●●●●●○○○

Older single owner
●●●●●●○○○○

Enthusiastic hiker
●●●●●●●●○○

Older couple
●●●●●●○○○○

Countryside pursuits fan
●●●●●●●●●●

City dweller
●●○○○○○○○○

Beach lover
●●●●●●○○○○

Rural owner
●●●●●●●●●●

Canine sports competitor
●●●●●●○○○○

Hobby farmer
●●●●●●●●●●

AKC group: sporting

English Springer Spaniel

Height 20 in (51 cm)
Weight 55 lb (25 kg)
Country of origin United Kingdom

The English Springer Spaniel has changed noticeably in appearance over the past century: dogs that are descended from show stock tend to be heavier than their working cousins. All English Springers are active, and need regular exercise. If these dogs are allowed to become bored at home they will soon turn destructive, chewing and scratching furnishings. Owners need to pay particular attention to the area surrounding the dog's close-lying ears, extending into the ear canal, as this is prone to infection. The breed's unusual name stems from the way these dogs will head through vegetation when working, flushing or "springing" game for the waiting guns.

Is this your perfect dog?

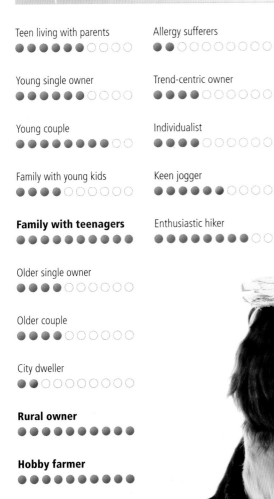

Teen living with parents
●●●●●●○○○○

Young single owner
●●●●●●○○○○

Young couple
●●●●●●●●○○

Family with young kids
●●●●○○○○○○

Family with teenagers
●●●●●●●●●○

Older single owner
●●●●○○○○○○

Older couple
●●●●○○○○○○

City dweller
●●○○○○○○○○

Rural owner
●●●●●●●●●●

Hobby farmer
●●●●●●●●●○

Owner with physical disability
●●○○○○○○○○

Allergy sufferers
●●○○○○○○○○

Trend-centric owner
●●●●●○○○○○

Individualist
●●●●○○○○○○

Keen jogger
●●●●●●○○○○

Enthusiastic hiker
●●●●●●●●○○

Countryside pursuits fan
●●●●●●●●●●

Beach lover
●●●●●●○○○○

Canine sports competitor
●●●●●●○○○○

AKC group: sporting

LIKES

* Being active
* Walking in wooded areas
* Lots of attention

NEEDS

* Regular ear checks
* Space for exercise
* Opportunity to explore

English Springer Spaniel and German Shepherd Dog

Spanierd puppies tend to be black and tan in coloration—like the German Shepherd Dog (page 157)—and their coats are relatively long. Training your Spanierd should be reasonably straightforward.

Sussex Spaniel

Height 15 in (38 cm)
Weight 45 lb (20 kg)
Country of origin United Kingdom

This rare breed has undergone something of a revival, as more owners discover its undeniable charms—it is a very friendly breed with a relaxed personality. It is named after the county of Sussex in southern England, where it was created in the late 1700s. Hounds were involved in the breed's development, which you can hear in the way these spaniels call, allowing their handlers to track them as they move through dense vegetation, flushing game. They have a thick, golden-liver colored coat to protect them from thorns, and a very distinctive rolling gait.

Is this your perfect dog?

Teen living with parents	Allergy sufferers	Keen jogger	Beach lover
●●●●○○○○○○	●●●●○○○○○○	●●●●○○○○○○	●●●●●●○○○○
Young single owner	Trend-centric owner	Enthusiastic hiker	Canine sports competitor
●●●●●●○○○○	●●●●●○○○○○	●●●●●●●●○○	●●●●○○○○○○
Young couple	Individualist	**Countryside pursuits fan**	
●●●●●●●●○○	●●●●●●●●○○	●●●●●●●●●●	AKC group: sporting

Family with young kids
●●●●●●○○○○

Family with teenagers
●●●●●●●●●●

Older single owner
●●●●●●○○○○

Older couple
●●●●●●○○○○

City dweller
●●○○○○○○○○

Rural owner
●●●●●●●●●●

Hobby farmer
●●●●●●●●●●

Owner with physical disability
●●○○○○○○○○

LIKES

* Exploring countryside areas
* Relaxing at home
* Being with its owner

NEEDS

* Long daily walks
* Regular ear checks
* A backyard environment

Clumber Spaniel

Height	19 in (48 cm)
Weight	50 lb (23 kg)
Country of origin	United Kingdom

The Clumber is one of the largest spaniels, and is named after the estate of the Duke of Newcastle in northern England, where it was first kept in the 1700s. The Clumber Spaniel is large and has relatively short legs, which means that it is neither as agile nor as fast as similar breeds, and, unusually, it is very quiet when working in undergrowth seeking out game. Another uncommon feature is that Clumbers traditionally worked in packs rather than individually. Quiet and slightly reserved, the Clumber Spaniel is sociable with other dogs, and makes a dignified companion.

Is this your perfect dog?

LIKES	NEEDS
✱ Country walks	✱ Plenty of exercise
✱ Other dogs	✱ Sensible feeding
✱ Cool weather	✱ Socialization with people

Teen living with parents
●●●●○○○○○○

Owner with physical disability
●●○○○○○○○○

Young single owner
●●●●○○○○○○

Allergy sufferers
●●●●○○○○○○

Young couple
●●●●●○○○○○

Trend-centric owner
●●●○○○○○○○

Family with young kids
●●●●○○○○○○

Individualist
●●●●○○○○○○

Family with teenagers
●●●●●●○○○○

Keen jogger
●●○○○○○○○○

Older single owner
●●●●○○○○○○

Enthusiastic hiker
●●●●●●●●○○

Older couple
●●●●○○○○○○

Countryside pursuits fan
●●●●●●●●●●

City dweller
●●○○○○○○○○

Beach lover
●●●●●●○○○○

Rural owner
●●●●●●●●●●

Canine sports competitor
●●●●○○○○○○

Hobby farmer
●●●●●●●●●●

AKC group: sporting

English Cocker Spaniel

Height   17 in (43 cm)
Weight   30 lb (13.5 kg)
Country of origin   United Kingdom

The Cocker is the most commonly kept of all the spaniels, thanks to its relatively small size and enthusiastic, friendly nature. It is also kept for sporting purposes, and is used with smaller game. The breed's name comes from a game bird called the woodcock, its traditional quarry.

English Cocker Spaniels appear in a range of colors. Unfortunately, some bloodlines, of solid-colored Cockers in particular, can suffer from "rage syndrome," a genetic problem causing them to be unexpectedly aggressive. Although rare, this possibility should be considered. They can suffer ear infections, but are generally healthy dogs.

LIKES

* Playing regularly
* Being with people
* Lots of attention

NEEDS

* Plenty of exercise
* Walks in the countryside
* Regular ear care

Cocker Spaniel and Poodle

Cockapoos are among the most popular designer dogs, with both Miniature and Toy Poodles (page 126) being used in combination with English or American Cockers. They have tousled hair and enthusiastic natures.

Is this your perfect dog?

Teen living with parents
●●●●●●●●○○

Owner with physical disability
●●●●○○○○○○

Young single owner
●●●●●●○○○○

Allergy sufferers
●●○○○○○○○○

Young couple
●●●●●●●●○○

Trend-centric owner
●●●●○○○○○○

Family with young kids
●●●●●●○○○○

Individualist
●●●●○○○○○○

Family with teenagers
●●●●●●●●●●

Keen jogger
●●●●○○○○○○

Older single owner
●●●●●●○○○○

Enthusiastic hiker
●●●●●●●●○○

Older couple
●●●●●●●●○○

Countryside pursuits fan
●●●●●●●●●●

City dweller
●●●●○○○○○○

Beach lover
●●●●●●○○○○

Rural owner
●●●●●●●●●●

Canine sports competitor
●●●●●●●●○○

Hobby farmer
●●●●●●●○○○

AKC group: sporting

For other Cocker Spaniel crossbreeds, see pages 54 and 182.

Cocker Spaniel

Height 15 in (38 cm)
Weight 26 lb (12 kg)
Country of origin United States

It is descended from its English counterpart, but the Cocker Spaniel is sufficiently different in size and appearance to have developed into a distinct breed. Outside its homeland it is known as the American Cocker Spaniel. In terms of appearance, the Cocker Spaniel is more petite—but be prepared for grooming the long coat. As a result of their shared ancestry, Cocker Spaniels can also unfortunately suffer from "rage syndrome," although, as with the English Cocker Spaniel opposite, bicolored individuals are less at risk. In terms of temperament, these dogs are normally very friendly.

LIKES	NEEDS
* Family life	* Determined brushing and combing
* Exploring	* Ear care
* Playing with toys	* An active lifestyle

Is this your perfect dog?

Teen living with parents
●●●●●●●●○○

Owner with physical disability
●●●●○○○○○○

Young single owner
●●●●●●○○○○

Allergy sufferers
●●○○○○○○○○

Young couple
●●●●●●●●○○

Trend-centric owner
●●●●●●●●○○

Family with young kids
●●●●●●○○○○

Individualist
●●●●●●○○○○

Family with teenagers
●●●●●●●●●●

Keen jogger
●●●●○○○○○○

Older single owner
●●●●●●●○○○

Enthusiastic hiker
●●●●●●●○○○

Older couple
●●●●●●○○○○

Countryside pursuits fan
●●●●●●●●●●

City dweller
●●●●○○○○○○

Beach lover
●●●●●●●○○○

Rural owner
●●●●●●●●●●

Canine sports competitor
●●●●●●●●○○

Hobby farmer
●●●●●●●○○

AKC group: sporting

Field Spaniel

Height 18 in (46 cm)
Weight 45 lb (20 kg)
Country of origin United Kingdom

This particular breed is better known as a working gundog than as a pet, but it will nevertheless make a very friendly and loyal companion. The Field Spaniel is very similar to the English Cocker Spaniel, although larger in size. During the late 1940s, the breed was close to extinction, but crosses with the English Cocker and the Springer Spaniel saved it from extinction. The Field Spaniel was referred to as the Black Spaniel for a time in show circles, simply because this color was most common. Liver and roan variants also exist, and some have tan or small areas of white in their coats.

LIKES

* Exploring
* Regular daily exercise
* Lots of affection

NEEDS

* Country walks
* Going out daily
* Brushing and combing

Is this your perfect dog?

Teen living with parents
●●●●●●○○○○

Young couple
●●●●●●●○○○

Family with teenagers
●●●●●●●●○○

Owner with physical disability
●●●●○○○○○○

Young single owner
●●●●●●○○○○

Family with young kids
●●●●○○○○○○

Older single owner
●●●●●●○○○○

Allergy sufferers
●●●●○○○○○○

Older couple
●●●●●●○○○○

Trend-centric owner
●●●●●○○○○○

City dweller
●●○○○○○○○○

Individualist
●●●●○○○○○○

Rural owner
●●●●●●●●●●

Keen jogger
●●●●●●●○○○

Hobby farmer
●●●●●●●●●○

Enthusiastic hiker
●●●●●●●●○○

Countryside pursuits fan
●●●●●●●●●●

Beach lover
●●●●●●○○○○

Canine sports competitor
●●●●●●○○○○

AKC group: sporting

Brittany

Height	20 in (51 cm)
Weight	40 lb (18 kg)
Country of origin	France

Although known as the Brittany Spaniel for a time, the description of "spaniel" was dropped because this breed—named after the region of Brittany in northwestern France—is actually a multipurpose gundog. It is able to point, set, and track, as well as flush and retrieve game. It looks very much like a Long-legged Spaniel and exists in similar colors, being either brown or black and white, with some individuals being tricolored. Since being introduced to the United States in 1931, the Brittany has developed along slightly different lines, especially in terms of coloration. The only recognized colors in the United States are liver or orange, combined with white. Roan patterning, when the colored coat is mixed in with the white areas, is acceptable too.

LIKES	NEEDS
✳ Plenty of exercise	✳ Consistent training
✳ Family life	✳ Good daily walks
✳ Exploring the countryside	✳ Plenty of praise

 ## Is this your perfect dog?

Teen living with parents
●●●●●●●●○○

Owner with physical disability
●●○○○○○○○○

Young single owner
●●●●●●○○○○

Allergy sufferers
●●○○○○○○○○

Young couple
●●●●●●●●○○

Trend-centric owner
●●●●●●●○○○

Family with young kids
●●●●●●○○○○

Individualist
●●●●●●●○○○

Family with teenagers
●●●●●●●●●●

Keen jogger
●●●●●●●○○○

Older single owner
●●●●●●●○○○

Enthusiastic hiker
●●●●●●●●●●

Older couple
●●●●●●●●○○

Countryside pursuits fan
●●●●●●●●●●

City dweller
●●○○○○○○○○

Beach lover
●●●●●●●○○○

Rural owner
●●●●●●●●●●

Canine sports competitor
●●●●●●●●○○

Hobby farmer
●●●●●●●●●●

AKC group: sporting

Brittany and Labrador Retriever

This combination of two very responsive gundogs results in puppies that are exuberant yet relatively easy to train, either as pets or as working dogs. **Brittadors**, also known as **Labanies**, are smaller than Labradors (page 43).

English Setter

Height 25 in (64 cm)
Weight 55 lb (25 kg)
Country of origin United Kingdom

Setters are a group of relatively large gundogs, bred from spaniel stock, whose function was to "set"—meaning "sit" in Old English—when they had detected game nearby. The English Setter has recently undergone a serious decline in numbers and popularity, which is a great shame, as these are very elegant dogs, attractively colored with soft, silky coats.

English Setters are very responsive to training and are friendly by nature, so they make excellent companions, although they are not suited to urban living. Combing the longer hair on their legs—called "feathering"—is the best way to remove mud from this area, once it has dried.

Is this your perfect dog?

Teen living with parents
●●●●●○○○○○

Older single owner
●●●●●○○○○○

Owner with physical disability
●●○○○○○○○○

Enthusiastic hiker
●●●●●●●●●●

Young single owner
●●●●●●○○○○

Older couple
●●●●●●○○○○

Allergy sufferers
●●○○○○○○○○

Countryside pursuits fan
●●●●●●●●●●

Young couple
●●●●●●●○○○

City dweller
●●○○○○○○○○

Trend-centric owner
●●●●○○○○○○

Beach lover
●●●●●●○○○○

Family with young kids
●●●●○○○○○○

Rural owner
●●●●●●●●●●

Individualist
●●●●●●○○○○

Canine sports competitor
●●●●●●○○○○

Family with teenagers
●●●●●●●●●●

Hobby farmer
●●●●●●●●●●

Keen jogger
●●●●●●●○○○

AKC group: sporting

LIKES
* Human companionship
* Space at home
* Country trails

NEEDS
* Regular grooming
* Good daily walks
* Exercise off the leash

Gordon Setter

Height 25 in (64 cm)
Weight 70 lb (32 kg)
Country of origin United Kingdom

This particular setter is defined by its coloration, sometimes to the extent of being described as the Black-and-Tan Setter. It is a Scottish breed, developed in the late 1600s by the Duke of Gordon, who originally bred other colors, too. The dark coloration of these setters could have been a distinct drawback when they were working in the field, but this combination proved popular in show rings, and, as a result, having tan present only on the extremities of the body became universally accepted. Having evolved in a rugged landscape, the Gordon Setter is a hardy breed, but will also settle well in homes where there is space to accommodate one of these relatively large dogs.

Is this your perfect dog?

LIKES	NEEDS
✱ Space to run	✱ Training to quell
✱ Exploring the countryside	overexcitement
✱ Lots of attention	✱ Brushing and combing
	✱ Plenty of play

Teen living with parents
●●●●○○○○○○

Rural owner
●●●●●●●●●●

Keen jogger
●●●●●●●●○○

Young single owner
●●●●●●○○○○

Hobby farmer
●●●●●●●●●●

Enthusiastic hiker
●●●●●●●●●●

Young couple
●●●●●●●●○○

Owner with physical disability
●●○○○○○○○○

Countryside pursuits fan
●●●●●●●●●●

Family with young kids
●●●●○○○○○○

Allergy sufferers
●●○○○○○○○○

Beach lover
●●●●●●○○○○

Family with teenagers
●●●●●●●●○○

Trend-centric owner
●●●●●●○○○○

Canine sports competitor
●●●●●●○○○○

Older single owner
●●●●○○○○○○

Individualist
●●●●○○○○○○

AKC group: sporting

Older couple
●●●●●●○○○○

City dweller
●●○○○○○○○○

Irish Setter

Height	26 in (66 cm)
Weight	65 lb (29.5 kg)
Country of origin	Ireland

Often inaccurately called the Red Setter, thanks to its stunning chestnut coat, the Irish Setter is strikingly beautiful. Its color has significantly enhanced its popularity, but do not be misled by its refined look—the Irish Setter is also a very active dog and one of the hardest breeds of gundog to train, especially in terms of returning when called. Young dogs in particular can prove wayward if something distracts their attention. Part of the reason may be due to crossings with Borzois (page 71), carried out early in the Irish Setter's development. However, if you can meet the needs of these setters, they make fantastic companions.

Is this your perfect dog?

Teen living with parents
●●●●●○○○○○

Young single owner
●●●●●●○○○○

Young couple
●●●●●●●●○○

Family with young kids
●●●●○○○○○○

Family with teenagers
●●●●●●●●●○

Older single owner
●●●●○○○○○○

Older couple
●●●●●●○○○○

City dweller
●●○○○○○○○○

Rural owner
●●●●●●●●●○

Hobby farmer
●●●●●●●●●○

Owner with physical disability
●●○○○○○○○○

Allergy sufferers
●●○○○○○○○○

Trend-centric owner
●●●●●●●●●●

Individualist
●●●●●●●○○○

Keen jogger
●●●●●●●●●○

Enthusiastic hiker
●●●●●●●●●●

Countryside pursuits fan
●●●●●●●●●●

Beach lover
●●●●●●●○○○

Canine sports competitor
●●●●○○○○○○

AKC group: sporting

LIKES	NEEDS
✱ Running off the leash	✱ Patient, understanding training
✱ Plenty of exercise	✱ An active owner
✱ Toys to play with	✱ Positive encouragement

Irish Setter and Standard Poodle

Irish Doodle Setters tend to range from shades of cream to red, and usually have a tousled coat with a wider head than the Irish Setter. They make very enthusiastic companions.

Irish Red-and-White Setter

Height 27 in (69 cm)
Weight 70 lb (32 kg)
Country of origin Ireland

In the 1700s, there were three different types of Irish Setter. Yet while the Irish Setter itself is now well known, the Irish Red-and-White Setter has become rare. The breed used to be favored by hunters, because its white patches increased its visibility in the field, allowing owners to track the position of their dogs more easily. As it has defined white and red areas, this setter can be easily distinguished from the rare third form—known as the "Shower of Hail" Setter—with its red coat broken with lots of tiny white spots, resembling hailstones. The Irish Red-and-White Setter's energetic nature means these dogs can easily become bored at home.

Is this your perfect dog?

Teen living with parents
●●●●○○○○○○

Young single owner
●●●●●●○○○○

Young couple
●●●●●●●●○○

Family with young kids
●●●●○○○○○○

Family with teenagers
●●●●●●●●●●

Older single owner
●●●●○○○○○○

Older couple
●●●●●●○○○○

City dweller
●●○○○○○○○○

Rural owner
●●●●●●●●●●

Hobby farmer
●●●●●●●●●●

Owner with physical disability
●●○○○○○○○○

Allergy sufferers
●●○○○○○○○○

Trend-centric owner
●●●●●●●●○○

Individualist
●●●●●●●●●●

Keen jogger
●●●●●●●●○○

Enthusiastic hiker
●●●●●●●●●●

Countryside pursuits fan
●●●●●●●●●●

Beach lover
●●●●●●○○○○

Canine sports competitor
●●●●○○○○○○

AKC group: sporting

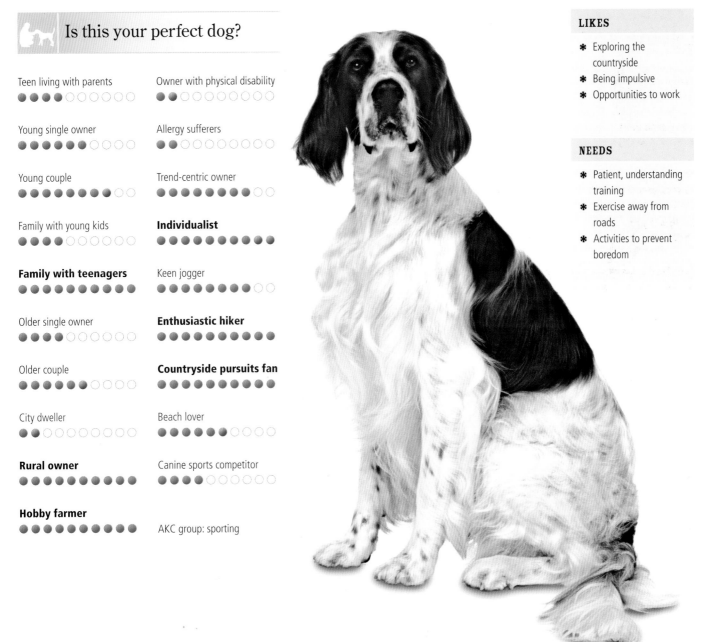

LIKES
* Exploring the countryside
* Being impulsive
* Opportunities to work

NEEDS
* Patient, understanding training
* Exercise away from roads
* Activities to prevent boredom

Finnish Spitz

Height   20 in (51 cm)
Weight   35 lb (16 kg)
Country of origin   Finland

This beautiful Scandinavian breed has eye-catching golden coloration, but delve a little deeper into its origins and you may identify a possible problem with choosing this dog as a pet. Finnish Spitzes have a particular way of hunting birds, using a loud and distinctive bark to alert the huntsman to the presence of their quarry. This trait has earned the breed the name of the "barking bird dog." It is said to have feline attributes, and not just because of its quarry; it has a catlike independent side to its nature. It is a breed of spitz descent, which is reflected in its pricked ears and the tail that curls to one side of the body.

Is this your perfect dog?

Teen living with parents
●●●●○○○○○○

Rural owner
●●●●●●●●●●

Keen jogger
●●●●●●●●○○

Beach lover
●●●●●●○○○○

Young single owner
●●●●●●○○○○

Hobby farmer
●●●●●●●●●●

Enthusiastic hiker
●●●●●●●●●●

Canine sports competitor
●●●●●●●●○○

Young couple
●●●●●●●●○○

Owner with physical disability
●●●●○○○○○○

Countryside pursuits fan
●●●●●●●●●●

Family with young kids
●●●●○○○○○○

Allergy sufferers
●●○○○○○○○○

Family with teenagers
●●●●●●●●○○

Trend-centric owner
●●●●●●●●○○

Older single owner
●●●●●●○○○○

Individualist
●●●●●●○○○○

Older couple
●●●●●●○○○○

City dweller
●●●●○○○○○○

LIKES

* Being the only dog at home
* Barking
* Being with people

NEEDS

* Sensitive training
* Plenty of exercise
* Country walks

AKC group: non-sporting

Spinone Italiano

Height 25 in (64 cm)
Weight 75 lb (34 kg)
Country of origin Italy

The origins of the large, shaggy Spinone Italiano—also known under its anglicized name, the Italian Spinone—lie in the area of northwestern Italy known as Piedmont. Individuals are often quite pale, although darker, tan-colored dogs can be seen, too. Spinones usually have a great temperament, being very friendly, with an exuberant nature. Although they have a deep bark, this is not a guard dog breed. Its rough coat has a functional purpose: when following a scent, the Spinone Italiano can run through undergrowth with minimal risk of being injured. Sharp twigs may break off and become stuck in its wiry coat—perhaps the reason it is named after a very prickly bush.

LIKES	NEEDS
✳ Relaxing indoors	✳ Regular grooming
✳ Praise and attention	✳ Plenty of exercise
✳ Ambling along	✳ Drool to be wiped away

Is this your perfect dog?

Teen living with parents
●●●●○○○○○○

Owner with physical disability
●●●●○○○○○○

Young single owner
●●●●●●●●○○

Allergy sufferers
●●○○○○○○○○

Young couple
●●●●●●●○○○

Trend-centric owner
●●○○○○○○○○

Family with young kids
●●●●●●○○○○

Individualist
●●●●●●○○○○

Family with teenagers
●●●●●●●●●●

Keen jogger
●●●●●●●●○○

Older single owner
●●●●●●○○○○

Enthusiastic hiker
●●●●●●●●●●

Older couple
●●●●●●○○○○

Countryside pursuits fan
●●●●●●●●●●

City dweller
●●○○○○○○○○

Beach lover
●●●●●○○○○○

Rural owner
●●●●●●●●●●

Canine sports competitor
●●●●●●○○○○

Hobby farmer
●●●●●●●●●●

AKC group: sporting

Flat-coated Retriever

Height   23 in (58 cm)
Weight   80 lb (36 kg)
Country of origin   United Kingdom

The appearance of the Flat-coated Retriever's coat, the result of crossbreeding with setters, prompted it to be known as the Wavy-coated Retriever at first. The wavy coat became less conspicuous over time, and so the name was changed.

The Flat-coated Retriever first came to prominence as a gundog in the 1860s, but has never proved very popular as a pet, nor is it widely used as a gundog today. Nevertheless, it has a very good, reliable temperament combined with a stunning, glossy black coat. You may see liver-colored individuals and yellow, too, but they cannot be shown. Sadly, the breed appears to be vulnerable to various cancers. However, on balance, these are excellent—if underrated—companion dogs.

LIKES	NEEDS
* Pleasing people	* Plenty of exercise
* Being active	* Little grooming
* Learning new tasks	* Short training sessions

Is this your perfect dog?

Teen living with parents
●●●●●●○○○○

Hobby farmer
●●●●●●●●●●

Young single owner
●●●●●●○○○○

Owner with physical disability
●●●●○○○○○○

Young couple
●●●●●●●○○

Allergy sufferers
●●○○○○○○○○

Family with young kids
●●●●●●○○○○

Trend-centric owner
●●●●○○○○○○

Family with teenagers
●●●●●●●●●●

Individualist
●●●●○○○○○○

Older single owner
●●●●○○○○○○

Keen jogger
●●●●●●●●●○

Older couple
●●●●●●○○○

Enthusiastic hiker
●●●●●●●●●●

City dweller
●●○○○○○○○○

Countryside pursuits fan
●●●●●●●●●●

Rural owner
●●●●●●●●●●

Beach lover
●●●●●●●●○○

Canine sports competitor
●●●●●●●●○○

AKC group: sporting

Curly-coated Retriever

Height	27 in (69 cm)
Weight	80 lb (36 kg)
Country of origin	United Kingdom

The Curly-coated Retriever's coat consists of small, tight curls that cover the entire body. This is thought to have been a feature inherited from the Irish Water Spaniel (page 25), which contributed to this breed's ancestry. The Curly-coated Retriever is very easy to care for, needing nothing more than brushing once or twice a week to keep the coat from becoming tangled. This grooming can affect the coat's appearance, but spraying with water will keep it looking good. In the face of the overwhelming popularity of other retriever breeds, Curly-coated Retrievers are not often seen today, which is a shame. Aside from their distinctive appearance, they also have a friendly and calm disposition.

LIKES

* Swimming
* Exploring the countryside
* Home life

NEEDS

* Ongoing training
* Plenty of activity
* Play sessions

Is this your perfect dog?

Teen living with parents
●●●●●●○○○○

Hobby farmer
●●●●●●●●●●

Young single owner
●●●●●●○○○○

Owner with physical disability
●●●●○○○○○○

Young couple
●●●●●●●●○○

Allergy sufferers
●●●●●●●●○○

Family with young kids
●●●●●●○○○○

Trend-centric owner
●●●●●●●●○○

Family with teenagers
●●●●●●●●●●

Individualist
●●●●●●●●○○

Older single owner
●●●●●●●○○○

Keen jogger
●●●●●●●●●○

Older couple
●●●●●●○○○○

Enthusiastic hiker
●●●●●●●●●●

City dweller
●●○○○○○○○○

Countryside pursuits fan
●●●●●●●●●●

Rural owner
●●●●●●●●●●

Beach lover
●●●●●●●●●●

Canine sports competitor
●●●●●●●●○○

AKC group: sporting

Golden Retriever

Height   24 in (61 cm)
Weight   75 lb (34 kg)
Country of origin   United Kingdom

Few breeds have proved to be more adaptable than the Golden Retriever, which—although it is still often seen as a working gundog—now undertakes a much wider range of roles. These range from acting as a guide dog through to working as a drug detector, and, of course, it is very popular as a pet. The Golden Retriever's popularity is partly due to its attractive golden coloration, which varies in depth between individuals. There can be confusion between this breed and yellow Labradors (opposite), but Golden Retrievers are easily recognized by their longer coats. They have hearty appetites and will tend to overeat, gaining weight rapidly as a result.

LIKES

* Working with people
* Playing in water
* Chasing after toys

NEEDS

* Plenty of activity
* Careful feeding
* Suitable training

Is this your perfect dog?

Teen living with parents
●●●●●●○○○○

Young single owner
●●●●●●○○○○

Young couple
●●●●●●●●○○

Family with young kids
●●●●●●○○○○

Family with teenagers
●●●●●●●●●●

Older single owner
●●●●●●○○○○

Older couple
●●●●●●●●○○

City dweller
●●●●○○○○○○

Rural owner
●●●●●●●●●○

Hobby farmer
●●●●●●●●●●

Owner with physical disability*
●●●●●●●●●●

Allergy sufferers
●●●●●○○○○○

Trend-centric owner
●●●●●●○○○○

Individualist
●●●●○○○○○○

Keen jogger
●●●●●●●●○○

Enthusiastic hiker
●●●●●●●●●●

Countryside pursuits fan
●●●●●●●●●●

Beach lover
●●●●●●●●●●

Canine sports competitor
●●●●●●●●○○

AKC group: sporting

For a Golden Retriever crossbreed, see page 49.

*Invaluable for the blind, but not suitable for everyone in the profile.

Labrador Retriever

Height 24 in (61 cm)
Weight 75 lb (34 kg)
Country of origin United Kingdom

The most popular breed in the world, the Labrador Retriever makes a very versatile companion. In spite of its name and the show standard, the coloration of the yellow Labrador is surprisingly pale these days, verging on cream. Black is the original color associated with the breed, while chocolate coloring is a more recent introduction to Labrador bloodlines. These dogs can be prone to hip dysplasia, but screening has reduced incidences dramatically. Watching the weight of your pet will help with any hip weakness and its overall health.

Labrador Retriever and Standard Poodle

The **Labradoodle** was the original designer dog, created in the hope of providing hypoallergenic guide dogs. Labradoodles make friendly, intelligent companions. Their coats are usually a single color.

LIKES
* Returning toys
* Human interaction
* Plunging into water

NEEDS
* A lot of exercise
* Strict feeding regime
* Weight monitoring

Is this your perfect dog?

Teen living with parents ●●●●●●●●○○

Young single owner ●●●●●●○○○○

Young couple ●●●●●●●●○○

Family with young kids ●●●●●●○○○○

Family with teenagers ●●●●●●●●●●

Older single owner ●●●●●●○○○○

Older couple ●●●●●●●●○○

City dweller ●●●●○○○○○○

Rural owner ●●●●●●●●●●

Hobby farmer ●●●●●●●●●●

Owner with physical disability* ●●●●●●●●●●

Allergy sufferers ●●●●●○○○○○

Trend-centric owner ●●●●○○○○○○

Individualist ●●○○○○○○○○

Keen jogger ●●●●●●●●○○

Enthusiastic hiker ●●●●●●●●●●

Countryside pursuits fan ●●●●●●●●●●

Beach lover ●●●●●●●●●●

Canine sports competitor ●●●●●●●●○○

AKC group: sporting

*Invaluable for the blind, but not suitable for everyone in the profile.

For another Labrador Retriever crossbreed, see page 169.

Nova Scotia Duck Tolling Retriever

Height	21 in (53 cm)
Weight	51 lb (23 kg)
Country of origin	Canada

The unusual name of this retriever stems from its unique training. When working, it starts by playing along the edge of the water, often chasing a so-called "tolling stick" thrown by its owner. This acts as a lure to draw curious waterfowl within reach of the hidden guns. After the shots have been fired, the Nova Scotia Duck Tolling Retriever then switches to retrieving mode. A wide range of different gundogs contributed to the breed's ancestry, so it looks less like a retriever than other dogs in the gundog group. Its double-layered coat is water-repellent and gives good protection in cold water. Adaptable and quick learners, Nova Scotia Retrievers integrate well into the household.

LIKES

* Entering water
* Interacting with people
* Playing with sticks

NEEDS

* Obedience training
* Plenty of toys
* Supervision near water

 ## Is this your perfect dog?

Teen living with parents
●●●●●●○○○○

Owner with physical disability
●●○○○○○○○○

Young single owner
●●●●●●○○○○

Allergy sufferers
●●○○○○○○○○

Young couple
●●●●●●●●○○

Trend-centric owner
●●●●●●○○○○

Family with young kids
●●●●●●○○○○

Individualist
●●●●●●○○○○

Family with teenagers
●●●●●●●●○○

Keen jogger
●●●●●●●●○○

Older single owner
●●●●●●○○○○

Enthusiastic hiker
●●●●●●●●●●

Older couple
●●●●●●○○○○

Countryside pursuits fan
●●●●●●●●●●

City dweller
●●○○○○○○○○

Beach lover
●●●●●●●●●●

Rural owner
●●●●●●●●●●

Canine sports competitor
●●●●●●○○○○

Hobby farmer
●●●●●●●●●●

AKC group: sporting

Chesapeake Bay Retriever

Height 26 in (66 cm)
Weight 75 lb (34 kg)
Country of origin United States

The Chesapeake Bay Retriever is a powerful swimmer that has developed webbing between its toes, so it can move through water more effectively. Its coat has a slightly oily, water-resistant texture, allowing the dog to shake much of the water out of its coat once back on land.

The Chessie, as the breed is affectionately known, is named after a large sea inlet located on the Eastern Seaboard, south of Washington, D.C., where it came to prominence. This is a strong and very hardy breed of retriever, popularly kept as a companion. The Chessie's physique is powerfully built rather than elegant, compared with many other retrievers, such as the Golden Retriever and Labrador (pages 42 and 43).

LIKES

* Regular swimming
* Working with people
* Being outdoors

NEEDS

* Careful training
* Little grooming
* Plenty of exercise

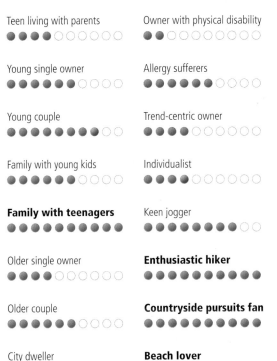

Is this your perfect dog?

Teen living with parents
●●●●○○○○○○

Owner with physical disability
●●○○○○○○○○

Young single owner
●●●●●●○○○○

Allergy sufferers
●●●●●●○○○○

Young couple
●●●●●●●○○○

Trend-centric owner
●●●●●○○○○○

Family with young kids
●●●●●●○○○○

Individualist
●●●●○○○○○○

Family with teenagers
●●●●●●●●●●

Keen jogger
●●●●●●●●●○

Older single owner
●●●●○○○○○○

Enthusiastic hiker
●●●●●●●●●●

Older couple
●●●●●●○○○○

Countryside pursuits fan
●●●●●●●●●●

City dweller
●●○○○○○○○○

Beach lover
●●●●●●●●●●

Rural owner
●●●●●●●●●●

Canine sports competitor
●●●●●●○○○○

Hobby farmer
●●●●●●●●●●

AKC group: sporting

Standard Poodle

Height	15 in (38 cm)
Weight	70 lb (32 kg)
Country of origin	Germany

Poodles' stylized coat trim has practical merit, dating back to when they were used to retrieve game from water. The coat added drag, so clipping the hair made it easier for the dog to swim. Leaving the dog's joints covered with fur protected those areas in freezing water, while the pom-pom on the tail meant that the dog could be seen quite easily when swimming. Keep in mind that these dogs are primarily freshwater swimmers, bred to retrieve in fairly calm stretches of water. The Standard Poodle's coat is hypoallergenic, so they have been used to create a number of crossbreeds, allowing some people who are otherwise allergic to dogs to have a chance of keeping one as a companion. Standard Poodles are playful and responsive pets.

LIKES

* Learning tricks
* Swimming
* Human company

NEEDS

* Coat clipping
* Dental checks
* Good walks

Standard Poodle and Afghan Hound

The long, flowing coat of the Afghan tends to be replaced by a shorter, curly coat in the case of the **Pooghan**. The coloration is often quite variable.

Is this your perfect dog?

Teen living with parents	●●●●●●●●○○	Owner with physical disability	●●●●○○○○○○
Young single owner	●●●●●●●●○○	**Allergy sufferers**	●●●●●●●●●●
Young couple	●●●●●●●●○○	**Trend-centric owner**	●●●●●●●●●●
Family with young kids	●●●●●●●●○○	Individualist	●●●●●●○○○○
Family with teenagers	●●●●●●●●●●	Keen jogger	●●●●○○●○○○
Older single owner	●●●●●●○○○○	Enthusiastic hiker	●●●●●●●●●○
Older couple	●●●●●●●○○○	Countryside pursuits fan	●●●●●●●○○○
City dweller	●●○○○○○○○○	Beach lover	●●●●●●●●○○
Rural owner	●●●●●●●●●●	Canine sports competitor	●●●●●●●●○○
Hobby farmer	●●●●●●●●●●	AKC group: non-sporting	

For other Standard Poodle crossbreeds, see pages 88, 110, 137, 141, 144, 148, 149, 159, 162, and 195.

Wire-haired Pointing Griffon

Height 19 in (48 cm)
Weight 40 lb (18 kg)
Country of origin Netherlands

The affectionate Wire-haired Pointing Griffon has proved to be a reliable gundog, adept at both pointing and retrieving. The French version of its name—griffon d'arrêt à poil dur Korthals—incorporates that of its creator, Edward K. Korthals, but it is often referred to in English simply as the Griff. These gundogs develop a close bond with their owners, so be sure to involve everyone in the household in a puppy's care, to ensure it does not become fixated on one person. The Wire-haired Pointing Griffon's coloration is reasonably distinctive, ideally being steel gray and brown— other variants, including chestnut brown, are accepted in the show ring. The breed sheds far less than many other dogs, meaning it may be tolerated by allergy sufferers.

Is this your perfect dog?

Teen living with parents
●●●●○○○○○○

Owner with physical disability
●●○○○○○○○○

Young single owner
●●●●●○○○○

Allergy sufferers
●●●●●●●●○○

Young couple
●●●●●●●○○

Trend-centric owner
●●○○○○○○○○

Family with young kids
●●●●○○○○○○

Individualist
●●●●●●○○○○

Family with teenagers
●●●●●●●●●●

Keen jogger
●●●●●●●●○○

Older single owner
●●●●●●○○○○

Enthusiastic hiker
●●●●●●●●●●

Older couple
●●●●●●○○○○

Countryside pursuits fan
●●●●●●●●●●

City dweller
●●○○○○○○○○

Beach lover
●●●●●●○○○○

Rural owner
●●●●●●●●●●

Canine sports competitor
●●●●●●○○○○

Hobby farmer
●●●●●●●●●●

AKC group: sporting

LIKES
* Being with people
* Exploring in undergrowth
* Being out in all weather

NEEDS
* Little grooming
* Plenty of exercise
* Country walks

German Pointers

Height	25 in (64 cm)
Weight	70 lb (32 kg)
Country of origin	Germany

Under the heading of German Pointers come three distinct breeds—short-haired, wire-haired, and long-haired—distinguished by their coats. The German Short-haired Pointer was created from various other European pointer breeds during the late 1800s, and contributed to the development of its wire-haired relatives soon afterward. There is a distinct family resemblance, and the two breeds exist in a similar range of colors, ranging from tan and white, to dark brown, and black and white. The least common of the three German pointers is the Long-haired Pointer, whose coat is also the most demanding to care for. Make sure that your yard is well fenced whichever you choose—these dogs can jump well and will try to escape if bored.

LIKES

* Working outdoors
* Being in the countryside
* Human company

NEEDS

* Sensible training
* Variable grooming
* Plenty of activity

German Short-haired Pointer and Nova Scotia Duck Tolling Retriever

A **German Short-hair Toller** is ideal if you are seeking a gundog that enjoys the water. Puppies may resemble their German relative in color, but the chocolate and white areas are more clearly defined.

Is this your perfect dog?

Teen living with parents
●●●●○○○○○○

Owner with physical disability
●●○○○○○○○○

Young single owner
●●●●●●○○○○

Allergy sufferers
●●●○○○○○○○

Young couple
●●●●●●○○○○

Trend-centric owner
●●●●○○○○○○

Family with young kids
●●●●○○○○○○

Individualist
●●●●○○○○○○

Family with teenagers
●●●●●●●●●●

Keen jogger
●●●●●●●●○○

Older single owner
●●●●○○○○○○

Enthusiastic hiker
●●●●●●●●●●

Older couple
●●●●○○○○○○

Countryside pursuits fan
●●●●●●●●●●

City dweller
●●○○○○○○○○

Beach lover
●●●●●●●○○○

Rural owner
●●●●●●●●●●

Canine sports competitor
●●●●●●●○○○

Hobby farmer
●●●●●●●●●●

AKC group: sporting

Pointer

Height	24 in (61 cm)
Weight	66 lb (30 kg)
Country of origin	United Kingdom

Also known as the English Pointer, this breed plays a highly individual role. It is no coincidence that its muzzle is long and deep, as this allows it to pick up the minutest traces of scent. Once it has detected its quarry—game birds such as partridge or woodcock—a Pointer adopts its characteristic stance, indicating the bird's presence by standing with its body extended and one foot raised just slightly off the ground. Pointers are very determined working dogs, and even those kept as pets sometimes behave this way when out in the countryside. Unlike hounds, the Pointer does not chase after quarry, nor will it retrieve game.

Pointer and Golden Retriever

Gointer puppies often look similar to Labradors. Breeding stock must be assessed in advance for hip dysplasia, to which both parent breeds are susceptible.

LIKES

* A countryside environment
* Working opportunities
* Domestic life

NEEDS

* Considerable exercise
* Little grooming
* Encouragement when working

Is this your perfect dog?

Teen living with parents
●●●●○○○○○○

Owner with physical disability
●●○○○○○○○○

Young single owner
●●●●●●○○○○

Allergy sufferers
●●●●○○○○○○

Young couple
●●●●●●○○○○

Trend-centric owner
●●●●○○○○○○

Family with young kids
●●●●○○○○○○

Individualist
●●●●●●○○○○

Family with teenagers
●●●●●●●●●●

Keen jogger
●●●●●●●●○○

Older single owner
●●●●●●○○○○

Enthusiastic hiker
●●●●●●●●●●

Older couple
●●●●●●●○○○

Countryside pursuits fan
●●●●●●●●●●

City dweller
●●○○○○○○○○

Beach lover
●●●●●●○○○○

Rural owner
●●●●●●●●●●

Canine sports competitor
●●●●●●●○○○

Hobby farmer
●●●●●●●●●●

AKC group: sporting

Vizsla

Height	24 in (61 cm)
Weight	62 lb (28 kg)
Country of origin	Hungary

Elegant gundogs, with distinctive chestnut-gold coloration, Vizslas were bred to work on the plains of Hungary, so have plenty of stamina. Like most gundogs developed to work with people, Vizslas make loyal companions— but their exercise needs must be taken into consideration. Vizslas are emphatically not suited to urban living. Two coat types are now recognized, with the Wire-haired Vizsla being rarer than its smooth-coated counterpart. Both are similar in temperament, and are gentle and faithful dogs. The thin fur of the smooth-coated form means these dogs can be vulnerable to the cold, unlike the Wire-haired Vizsla, which has a thicker coat thanks to its German Wire-haired Pointer ancestry.

LIKES

* Playing games
* Household life
* Being active

NEEDS

* Space to run
* Good training
* Long walks

Is this your perfect dog?

Teen living with parents
●●●●○○○○○○

Owner with physical disability
●●○○○○○○○○

Young single owner
●●●●●○○○○○

Allergy sufferers
●●●●○○○○○○

Young couple
●●●●●●○○○○

Trend-centric owner
●●●●●●●●○○

Family with young kids
●●●●○○○○○○

Individualist
●●●●○○○○○○

Family with teenagers
●●●●●●●●●●

Keen jogger
●●●●●●●●●○

Older single owner
●●●●○○○○○○

Enthusiastic hiker
●●●●●●●●●●

Older couple
●●●●●●○○○○

Countryside pursuits fan
●●●●●●●●●●

City dweller
●●○○○○○○○○

Beach lover
●●●●●●○○○○

Rural owner
●●●●●●●●●●

Canine sports competitor
●●●●●●○○○○

Hobby farmer
●●●●●●●●●●

AKC group: sporting

Weimaraner

Height	28 in (71 cm)
Weight	79 lb (36 kg)
Country of origin	Germany

The smooth, sleek, silvery-gray appearance of the Weimaraner—pronounced *vy-me-rah-ner*—is very distinctive, and in recent years it has been joined by a long-haired variant. This longer coat gives the appearance of a silvery setter, with feathering on the back of the legs and underside of the tail. The well-muscled, elegant shape of these dogs reflects the fact that they require plenty of exercise, and, like many gundogs, they are most suited to rural surroundings. Weimaraners are adaptable working dogs, and can swim well, as revealed by their webbed feet. They are responsive to training in general, irrespective of whether or not you want to have a working dog.

LIKES

* Being active
* Hunting game birds
* Getting wet

NEEDS

* Little grooming
* A lot of exercise
* Careful feeding

Weimaraner and German Shepherd Dog

Combining these German breeds typically results in puppies that are darker in color than Weimaraners and lack their sleek profile. **Weimshepherd** puppies will grow into large, intelligent, and responsive companions.

Is this your perfect dog?

Teen living with parents
●●●●○○○○○○

Owner with physical disability
●●○○○○○○○○

Young single owner
●●●●●●○○○○

Allergy sufferers
●●●●○○○○○○

Young couple
●●●●●●○○○○

Trend-centric owner
●●●●●●●●○○

Family with young kids
●●●●○○○○○○

Individualist
●●●●●●○○○○

Family with teenagers
●●●●●●●●●●

Keen jogger
●●●●●●●●○○

Older single owner
●●●●○○○○○○

Enthusiastic hiker
●●●●●●●●●●

Older couple
●●●●●●●○○○

Countryside pursuits fan
●●●●●●●●●●

City dweller
●●○○○○○○○○

Beach lover
●●●●●●●●○○

Rural owner
●●●●●●●●●●

Canine sports competitor
●●●●●●○○○○

Hobby farmer
●●●●●●●●●●

AKC group: sporting

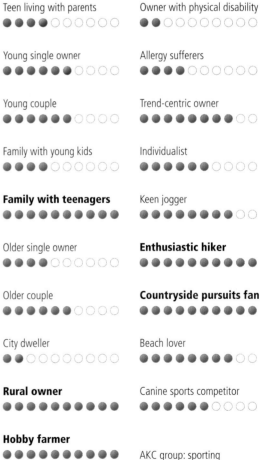

Dachshund

Height	9 in (23 cm)
Weight	25 lb (11.5 kg)
Country of origin	Germany

Don't be fooled by the size of the Dachshund—these brave, determined dogs were originally developed for hunting badgers in their underground lairs. Today, they are one of the most recognizable breeds. The Dachshund has been bred in standard and miniature sizes, and in three coat types—smooth, long-haired, and wire-haired. The coloration can be equally varied. Unusually, even in the case of bicolored Dachshunds, white is not an accepted color for the show ring. Unfortunately, the combination of the breed's long back and short legs can lead to serious back problems, including slipped disks. For this reason, these feisty little dogs must not be encouraged to climb and jump.

LIKES

* A set routine
* Eating
* Exploring burrows

NEEDS

* Careful training
* No climbing
* Strict feeding regime

Is this your perfect dog?

Teen living with parents
●●●●●●○○○○

City dweller
●●●●●●●●○○

Individualist
●●●●○○○○○○

Young single owner
●●●●●●●●○○

Rural owner
●●●●●●●●○○

Keen jogger
○○○○○○○○○○

Young couple
●●●●●●●●○○

Hobby farmer
●●●●●●●●○○

Enthusiastic hiker
●●○○○○○○○○

Family with young kids
●●○○○○○○○○

Owner with physical disability
●●●●●●○○○○

Countryside pursuits fan
●●○○○○○○○○

Family with teenagers
●●●●●●○○○○

Allergy sufferers
●●●●●○○○○○

Beach lover
●●●●●●○○○○

Older single owner
●●●●●●●●●○

Trend-centric owner
●●●●○○○○○○

Canine sports competitor
●●○○○○○○○○

Older couple
●●●●●●●●●○

Dachshund and Pembroke Welsh Corgi

The **Dorgi** is prominently and unusually displayed in the Kennel Club, London, where only purebreds are normally recognized. The crossbreed features in a portrait of Queen Elizabeth II with her dogs.

AKC group: hound

For another Dachshund crossbreed, see page 106.

Portuguese Podengo Pequeno

Height 8 in (20 cm)
Weight 10 lb (4.5 kg)
Country of origin Portugal

The Portuguese Podengo Pequeno is the smallest of the three Portuguese Podengos. In its working role it acts like a terrier, driving out rabbits for its larger relatives to chase down, and historically they were also taken on ships to control rat populations. Its size and friendly nature have made it a popular pet, increasingly outside of Portugal, though you may have to be patient and travel to a breeder in order to acquire one of these puppies. Podengo Pequenos are always bicolored—in typical Mediterranean canine style—being either golden or tan with white markings. You can choose between wire-haired and smooth-coated varieties.

Is this your perfect dog?

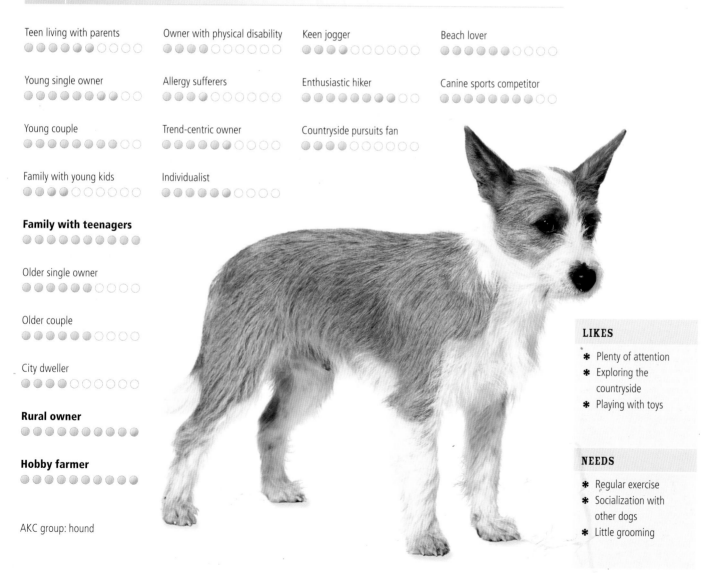

Teen living with parents
●●●●●●●○○○

Young single owner
●●●●●●●●○○

Young couple
●●●●●●●●○○

Family with young kids
●●●●○○○○○○

Family with teenagers
●●●●●●●●●●

Older single owner
●●●●●●●○○○

Older couple
●●●●●●○○○○

City dweller
●●●●○○○○○○

Rural owner
●●●●●●●●●●

Hobby farmer
●●●●●●●●●●

AKC group: hound

Owner with physical disability
●●●●●○○○○○

Allergy sufferers
●●●●○○○○○○

Trend-centric owner
●●●●●●○○○○

Individualist
●●●●●●○○○○

Keen jogger
●●●●●○○○○○

Enthusiastic hiker
●●●●●●●●●○

Countryside pursuits fan
●●●●●○○○○○

Beach lover
●●●●●●○○○○

Canine sports competitor
●●●●●●●●●○

LIKES

* Plenty of attention
* Exploring the countryside
* Playing with toys

NEEDS

* Regular exercise
* Socialization with other dogs
* Little grooming

Beagle

Height 15 in (38 cm)
Weight 30 lb (14 kg)
Country of origin United Kingdom

Be prepared to be patient if you chose this good-natured scent hound as a companion. Beagles love to be outdoors pursuing scents, but training them to return when called can be a frustrating task, particularly with a young dog. Few breeds are more affectionate or enthusiastic, though, particularly when you return home—but watch any shopping you bring with you. Your Beagle will prove very adept at disappearing with tasty items! In fact, Beagles tend to be greedy as far as food is concerned, and it is important not to overfeed them, as they will put on weight very rapidly. The use of treats as part of the training process should be kept to a minimum, too.

Beagle and Cocker Spaniel

This combination may feature English or American Cocker Spaniels (pages 30 and 31). The **Bocker**'s coloration is often more in line with that of the spaniel, rather than reflecting the Beagle's typical hound coloration.

AKC group: hound

Is this your perfect dog?

Teen living with parents
●●●●●●●●○○

Young single owner
●●●●●●●●○○

Young couple
●●●●●●●●○○

Family with young kids
●●●●●●●●●●

Family with teenagers
●●●●●●●●●●

Older single owner
●●●●●●○○○○

Older couple
●●●●●●○○○○

City dweller
●●●●○○○○○○

Rural owner
●●●●●●●●●●

Hobby farmer
●●●●●●●●●○

Owner with physical disability
●●○○○○○○○○

Allergy sufferers
●●●●●○○○○○

Trend-centric owner
●●●●○○○○○○

Individualist
●●●●●●●●○○

Keen jogger
●●●●●●●●○○

Enthusiastic hiker
●●●●●●●●●●

Countryside pursuits fan
●●●●●●●●●●

Beach lover
●●●●●○○○○○

Canine sports competitor
●●●●●●●●○○

LIKES
* Plenty of exercise
* Playing ball
* Being part of the family

NEEDS
* Good training
* To be kept away from small pets
* Weight monitoring

For other Beagle crossbreeds, see pages 55, 140, 146, and 188.

Basenji

Height 17 in (43 cm)
Weight 24 lb (11 kg)
Country of origin Zaire

This African hunting dog is sometimes described as barkless, although in reality, Basenjis can utter yodel-like calls. The breed's origins are something of a mystery. It has been suggested that they could be descended from dogs that were portrayed on ancient Egyptian tombs. The Basenji's original role was to chase game into nets set across forest paths. Its behavior often varies from that of other dogs. For example, Basenjis can uncurl their tails when sprinting to give themselves better balance, and are adept at climbing, with chain-link fences proving no obstacle. Basenjis should always be tested for Fanconi syndrome, a kidney ailment that can be treated if detected early. These dogs naturally look a little worried, thanks to the wrinkled skin on their foreheads.

LIKES

* Warm surroundings
* A cat-free home
* Grooming itself

NEEDS

* A snug-fitting coat
* Cooked vegetables
* Lots of exercise

Basenji and Beagle

Beagles have been widely used in designer dog breeding, but the unusual Basenji breed rarely features. **Baseagles** themselves weigh under 30 lb (14 kg), and have bi- or tricolored markings.

Is this your perfect dog?

Teen living with parents
●●●●○○○○○○

Owner with physical disability
●●●●○○○○○○

Young single owner
●●●●●●○○○○

Allergy sufferers
●●●●○○○○○○

Young couple
●●●●●●●○○○

Trend-centric owner
●●●●●●○○○○

Family with young kids
●●●●●●●○○○

Individualist
●●●●●●●●●●

Family with teenagers
●●●●●●●○○○

Keen jogger
●●●●●○○○○○

Older single owner
●●●●●●●●○○

Enthusiastic hiker
●●●●●●●●●○

Older couple
●●●●●●●●○○

Countryside pursuits fan
●●●●●●●○○○

City dweller
●●●●●●●○○○

Beach lover
●●○○○○○○○○

Rural owner
●●●●●●●●●●

Canine sports competitor
●●●●○○○○○○

Hobby farmer
●●●●●●●●○○

AKC group: hound

For another Basenji crossbreed, see page 139.

Basset Hound

Height 14 in (36 cm)
Weight 60 lb (27 kg)
Country of origin United Kingdom

Low-slung and long-bodied, Basset Hounds have a surprising amount of stamina, although their short legs make it easier to keep up with them than taller hounds. Basset Hounds can be vulnerable to back ailments and for this reason should not be encouraged to jump up. These hounds require plenty of exercise though, and their food intake needs to be strictly controlled so they do not become overweight, which would increase the strain on their backs, leaving them at greater risk of suffering slipped disks. Basset Hounds are very enthusiastic and inquisitive dogs, and are social by nature, especially with their own kind. They possess a deep, resonating, and musical bark.

LIKES

* Lots of attention
* Plenty of exercise
* Investigating scents

NEEDS

* Strict feeding
* Training to return
* Little grooming

Is this your perfect dog?

Teen living with parents
◉◉◉◉◉◉◉○○○

City dweller
◉◉○○○○○○○○

Keen jogger
◉◉◉◉◉○○○○○

Beach lover
◉◉◉◉○○○○○○

Young single owner
◉◉◉◉◉◉◉◉○○

Rural owner
◉◉◉◉◉◉◉◉◉◉

Enthusiastic hiker
◉◉◉◉◉◉◉◉◉◉

Canine sports competitor
◉◉◉◉○○○○○○

Young couple
◉◉◉◉◉◉◉◉○○

Hobby farmer
◉◉◉◉◉◉◉◉◉○

Countryside pursuits fan
◉◉◉◉◉◉◉◉◉○

AKC group: hound

Family with young kids
◉◉◉◉◉◉◉◉◉◉

Owner with physical handicap
◉◉○○○○○○○○

Family with teenagers
◉◉◉◉◉◉◉◉◉◉

Allergy sufferers
◉◉◉◉◉◉◉○○○

Older single owner
◉◉◉◉◉◉○○○○

Trend-centric owner
◉◉◉◉◉◉◉◉○○

Older couple
◉◉◉◉◉◉○○○○

Individualist
◉◉◉◉◉◉◉○○○

Basset Hound and Boston Terrier

The **Basston** usually has shorter ears than a Basset Hound, combined with a broader, more compact face. The legs are longer, though, and the paws may often look disproportionately large.

Petit Basset Griffon Vendéen

Height	15 in (38 cm)
Weight	35 lb (16 kg)
Country of origin	France

Often simply referred to as the PBGV, this French breed, like other bassets, is a scaled-down version of a larger, longer-legged scent hound. The Petit Basset Griffon Vendéen has a lively, friendly personality, which, combined with its tousled appearance, adds to its appeal. The PBGV makes a great family companion, but don't forget that it has great stamina, requiring plenty of exercise—otherwise, it may become bored and destructive. The Petit Basset Griffon Vendéen's coat has a rough wiry texture, which protects the dog from injury in undergrowth. The coat does not need to be trimmed, but you will need to wash the long fur around the mouth.

Is this your perfect dog?

LIKES
* Exploring on walks
* Running off the leash
* Stealing food!

NEEDS
* Good recall training
* Discouragement from jumping up
* Careful feeding

Teen living with parents
●●●●●●●○○

Owner with physical handicap
●●○○○○○○○○

Young single owner
●●●●●●○○○○

Allergy sufferers
●●●●○○○○○○

Young couple
●●●●●●●○○

Trend-centric owner
●●●●●○○○○○

Family with young kids
●●●●●●●○○

Individualist
●●●●○○○○○○

Family with teenagers
●●●●●●●●●

Keen jogger
●●●●●●●○○

Older single owner
●●●○○○○○○

Enthusiastic hiker
●●●●●●●●●

Older couple
●●●●●●○○○

Countryside pursuits fan
●●●●●●●●●

City dweller
●●●○○○○○○

Beach lover
●●●●●○○○○○

Rural owner
●●●●●●●●●

Canine sports competitor
●●●●●●○○○

Hobby farmer
●●●●●●●●●

AKC group: hound

American Foxhound

Height 25 in (64 cm)
Weight 75 lb (34 kg)
Country of origin United States

Tall and long-legged, with an athletic build, the American Foxhound is descended largely from its English cousin, with its ancestors having reached North America as long ago as the 1650s. These pack hounds have a wonderful range of calls, which help them to keep in touch with each other when they are following a scent. Different packs have developed and are sometimes known under localized names, such as the Trigg American Foxhound. Foxhounds are lively and good-natured dogs, with great stamina. They are best-suited to living in groups in a rural environment, reflecting the type of landscape in which they were developed.

LIKES

* Forming a close bond
* Jumping fences
* Following scents

NEEDS

* Training not to chase cats
* Lots of exercise
* The chance to run free

Is this your perfect dog?

Teen living with parents
●●●●○○○○○○

Family with young kids
●●●●○○○○○○

City dweller
○○○○○○○○○○

Allergy sufferers
●●●●○○○○○○

Young single owner
●●●●●●○○○○

Family with teenagers
●●●●●●●●○○

Rural owner
●●●●●●●●●●

Trend-centric owner
●●○○○○○○○○

Young couple
●●●●●●○○○○

Older single owner
●●○○○○○○○○

Hobby farmer
●●●●●●●●●●

Individualist
●●○○○○○○○○

Older couple
●●○○○○○○○○

Owner with physical disability
●●○○○○○○○○

Keen jogger
●●●●●●●●●●

Enthusiastic hiker
●●●●●●●●●●

Countryside pursuits fan
●●●●●●●●●●

Beach lover
●●●●○○○○○○

Canine sports competitor
●●●●○○○○○○

AKC group: hound

American Foxhound and Great Dane

American Foxy Dane puppies will become large dogs, like their parents. The crossbreed has a muscular build, with a broad nose. The coloration is more variable than that of American Foxhounds.

Harrier

Height	22 in (56 cm)
Weight	60 lb (27 kg)
Country of origin	United Kingdom

Larger and less well known than the Beagle, the Harrier is a typical sight hound. Harriers can be prone to running off when out for a walk, particularly if they spot a rabbit or hare, which is their traditional quarry. The breed's parti-colored coat is typical of this type of dog, and it is often a combination of black, white, and tan. However, each Harrier's actual patterning is highly individual, enabling dogs in a pack to be distinguished easily. Although recognized for show purposes in the United States, it has yet to achieve this status in its homeland, the United Kingdom. As they were developed to hunt in packs, Harriers are usually quite happy in the company of other dogs.

Is this your perfect dog?

Teen living with parents	City dweller	Individualist	Beach lover
●●●●●●○○○○	●●○○○○○○○○	●●●●○○○○○○	●●●●●●●○○○

Young single owner	**Rural owner**	Keen jogger	Canine sports competitor
●●●●●○○○○○	●●●●●●●●●●	●●●●●●●●○○	●●●●●○○○○○

Young couple	**Hobby farmer**	**Enthusiastic hiker**	
●●●●●●●●○○	●●●●●●●●●●	●●●●●●●●●●	AKC group: hound

Family with young kids	Owner with physical disability	**Countryside pursuits fan**
●●●●●●○○○○	●●○○○○○○○○	●●●●●●●●●●

Family with teenagers	Allergy sufferers
●●●●●●●●●●	●●●●○○○○○○

Older single owner	Trend-centric owner
●●●●○○○○○○	●●○○○○○○○○

Older couple
●●●●○○○○○○

LIKES

* Exploring in fields
* Human company
* Other dogs

NEEDS

* Minimal grooming
* Effective recall training
* Plenty of exercise

Treeing Walker Coonhound

Height   27 in (69 cm)
Weight   70 lb (32 kg)
Country of origin   United States

These coonhounds were bred to drive raccoons up into trees, where they could be more easily shot by the accompanying huntsman. The "Walker" in their name refers to Thomas Walker, whose English Foxhounds reputedly played a key role in the development of the breed. Keen scenting skills combined with plenty of stamina are inherent characteristics, along with an affable nature. Treeing Walker Coonhounds are bred in combinations of either tan or black with white, as well as a tricolored form. They can run surprisingly fast, and will bark repeatedly both to intimidate their quarry and to alert the huntsman that they have successfully "treed" a raccoon.

LIKES

* Space to run
* Chasing
* Wooded areas

NEEDS

* Positive training
* Discouragement from barking
* Lots of exercise

Is this your perfect dog?

Teen living with parents
●●●●○○○○○○

Family with teenagers
●●●●●●●●●○

Rural owner
●●●●●●●●●○

Individualist
●●●●○○○○○○

Young single owner
●●●●●○○○○○

Older single owner
●●●●○○○○○○

Hobby farmer
●●●●●●●●●○

Keen jogger
●●●●●●○○○○

Young couple
●●●●●●○○○○

Older couple
●●●○○○○○○○

Owner with physical disability
●●○○○○○○○○

Enthusiastic hiker
●●●●●●●●●○

Family with young kids
●●●○○○○○○○

City dweller
○○○○○○○○○○

Allergy sufferers
●●●●○○○○○○

Countryside pursuits fan
●●●●●●●●●○

Trend-centric owner
●●●●○○○○○○

Beach lover
●●●●●○○○○○

Canine sports competitor
●●●●●●○○○○

AKC group: hound

Bluetick Coonhound

Height 27 in (69 cm)
Weight 80 lb (36 kg)
Country of origin United States

The navy blue coloration of the Bluetick Coonhound comes from a French hound ancestor, the Grand Bleu de Gascogne. This blueticking, unique among the coonhound breeds, results from the combination of black and white fur, rather than any actual blue coloration in the individual hairs. The calls of Bluetick Coonhounds are very loud and may seem intimidating, particularly in the case of male dogs, which are bigger than females. Their hunting instincts mean that sharing a home with a cat or other small pets can be problematic. In true hound fashion, Blueticks will steal any food or even wrappers left within reach, but they are also very charismatic dogs and form a strong bond with family members.

Is this your perfect dog?

LIKES
* Sniffing people
* Following trails
* Chasing cats

NEEDS
* Plenty of exercise
* Dedicated training
* Little grooming

Teen living with parents
●●●●○○○○○○

Owner with physical disability
●●○○○○○○○○

Young single owner
●●●●○○○○○○

Allergy sufferers
●●●○○○○○○○

Young couple
●●●●●●●○○○

Trend-centric owner
●●●●○○○○○○

Family with young kids
●●●●○○○○○○

Individualist
●●●●●●○○○○

Family with teenagers
●●●●●●●●●●

Keen jogger
●●●●●●●●●●

Older single owner
●●●●○○○○○○

Enthusiastic hiker
●●●●●●●●●●

Older couple
●●●●○○○○○○

Countryside pursuits fan
●●●●●●●●●●

City dweller
○○○○○○○○○○

Beach lover
●●●●●●○○○○

Rural owner
●●●●●●●●●●

Canine sports competitor
●●●●●●●●○○

Hobby farmer
●●●●●●●●●●

AKC group: hound

American English Coonhound

Height 27 in (69 cm)
Weight 65 lb (29.5 kg)
Country of origin United States

Descended from European Foxhounds brought to the United States about 300 years ago, the American English Coonhound is also known as the Redtick Coonhound, thanks to its coloration and ticked patterning. Developed to hunt raccoons, these hounds have only recently been kept as pets or for the show ring. They have an attractive range of melodious calls, but beware—they will tend to take off on their own if they discover an interesting scent. It is important to train these coonhounds effectively from puppyhood, so they will not be inclined to chase cats or small dogs. This breed can be prone to becoming overweight, as you can see in the picture on the right.

LIKES	NEEDS
✳ Spacious surroundings	✳ Patient training
✳ Rural environments	✳ Plenty of exercise
✳ Searching for scents	✳ Running off the leash

Is this your perfect dog?

Teen living with parents
●●●●○○○○○○

Owner with physical handicap
●●●●○○○○○○

Young single owner
●●●●●●○○○○

Allergy sufferers
●●●●○○○○○○

Young couple
●●●●●●○○○○

Trend-centric owner
●●●●○○○○○○

Family with young kids
●●●●○○○○○○

Individualist
●●●●●●○○○○

Family with teenagers
●●●●●●●●●○

Keen jogger
●●●●●●●●○○

Older single owner
●●●●○○○○○○

Enthusiastic hiker
●●●●●●●●●●

Older couple
●●●●●○○○○○

Countryside pursuits fan
●●●●●●●●●●

City dweller
●●○○○○○○○○

Beach lover
●●●●○○○○○○

Rural owner
●●●●●●●●●●

Canine sports competitor
●●●●●●○○○○

Hobby farmer
●●●●●●●●●

AKC group: hound

Black-and-Tan Coonhound

Height 27 in (69 cm)
Weight 75 lb (34 kg)
Country of origin United States

The Black-and-Tan Coonhound was the first member of the coonhound group, developed from bloodhounds crossed with English Foxhounds. The input of the Bloodhound (page 64) is still very evident in the breed today—as can be seen in its coloration—but the skin is free from the furrows that sometimes become a point of infection in Bloodhounds. Black-and-Tan Coonhounds have great stamina and excellent tracking skills. Patterning remains inconsistent, as some of the breed still show traces of their working ancestors in their coat coloring.

This is not a suitable breed for an apartment. These dogs are large, and need space to stretch out and laze around the home when they are not out playing in the backyard or being taken for a run.

LIKES

* Following scents
* Country walks
* Howling and barking

NEEDS

* Exercise in the countryside
* Little grooming
* Patient training

Is this your perfect dog?

Teen living with parents
●●●●○○○○○○

Young single owner
●●●●●●○○○○

Young couple
●●●●●●○○○○

Family with young kids
●●●●○○○○○○

Family with teenagers
●●●●●●●●●○

Older single owner
●●●●○○○○○○

Older couple
●●●●○○○○○○

City dweller
○○○○○○○○○○

Rural owner
●●●●●●●●●●

Hobby farmer
●●●●●●●●●●

Owner with physical disability
●●○○○○○○○○

Allergy sufferers
●●●●●●○○○○

Trend-centric owner
●●●●○○○○○○

Individualist
●●●●○○○○○○

Keen jogger
●●●●●●●●●○

Enthusiastic hiker
●●●●●●●●●●

Countryside pursuits fan
●●●●●●●●●●

Beach lover
●●●●○○○○○○

Canine sports competitor
●●●●●●○○○○

AKC group: hound

Bloodhound

Height	27 in (69 cm)
Weight	110 lb (50 kg)
Country of origin	Belgium

In spite of its name and often intimidating deep bark, the Bloodhound is not aggressive by nature, but is in fact very friendly and exuberant. It has always been used for tracking purposes, as reflected by its broad, long nostrils, which ensure that the scent-detecting ability of this ancient breed is unsurpassed. It is a direct descendant of the St. Hubert Hound, which existed in the 1700s. In some parts of the world, however, Bloodhound numbers have declined significantly in recent years for a variety of reasons—not least the fact that they are totally unsuited to the urban environment. It is also worth bearing in mind that health problems, including various cancers, mean that their life expectancy is less than seven years on average. In areas where there is plenty of space, these dogs remain popular companions.

LIKES

* Trail-hunting
* Being outdoors
* Running

NEEDS

* Country life
* Plenty of exercise
* Care near roads

Is this your perfect dog?

Teen living with parents
●●○○○○○○○○

Family with teenagers
●●●●●●●●●●

Older couple
●●●●●●○○○○

Allergy sufferers
●●●●○○○○○○

Young single owner
●●●●○○○○○○

Older single owner
●●●●○○○○○○

City dweller
○○○○○○○○○○

Trend-centric owner
●●●●●○○○○○

Young couple
●●●●●●○○○○

Rural owner
●●●●●●●●●○

Individualist
●●●●○○○○○○

Family with young kids
●●●●○○○○○○

Hobby farmer
●●●●●●●●○○

Keen jogger
●●●●●●●●●○

Owner with physical disability
●●○○○○○○○○

Enthusiastic hiker
●●●●●●●●●●

Countryside pursuits fan
●●●●●●●●●●

Beach lover
●●○○○○○○○○

Canine sports competitor
●●●●●●○○○○

AKC group: hound

Otterhound

Height	27 in (69 cm)
Weight	115 lb (53 kg)
Country of origin	United Kingdom

When otter hunting became illegal in the United Kingdom in 1978, packs of Otterhounds were put down, and the numbers of this ancient breed fell dramatically. Now, however, a welcome, though so far slight, revival is taking place, as more people are drawn to the attractive personality of these shaggy-coated dogs. Otterhounds are increasingly being seen in the show ring, as well as being kept as pets—although they are still relatively rare. When walking, Otterhounds display their unique shambling gait.

Active by nature, the Otterhound makes an excellent companion, forming a close bond with those in its immediate circle. Its unusually tousled coat is highly water-resistant and provides effective protection against the cold.

Is this your perfect dog?

Teen living with parents
● ● ○ ○ ○ ○ ○ ○ ○ ○

Rural owner
● ● ● ● ● ● ● ● ● ●

Allergy sufferers
● ● ○ ○ ○ ○ ○ ○ ○ ○

Keen jogger
● ● ● ● ● ● ● ● ● ●

Young single owner
● ● ● ● ○ ○ ○ ○ ○ ○

Hobby farmer
● ● ● ● ● ● ● ● ● ●

Trend-centric owner
● ● ● ● ● ○ ○ ○ ○ ○

Enthusiastic hiker
● ● ● ● ● ● ● ● ● ●

Young couple
● ● ● ● ● ● ○ ○ ○ ○

Owner with physical disability
● ● ○ ○ ○ ○ ○ ○ ○ ○

Individualist
● ● ● ● ○ ○ ○ ○ ○ ○

Countryside pursuits fan
● ● ● ● ● ● ● ● ○ ○

Family with young kids
● ● ● ● ○ ○ ○ ○ ○ ○

Beach lover
● ● ● ● ● ● ● ● ○ ○

Family with teenagers
● ● ● ● ● ● ● ● ● ●

Canine sports competitor
● ● ● ● ● ● ○ ○ ○ ○

Older single owner
● ● ● ● ○ ○ ○ ○ ○ ○

Older couple
● ● ● ● ○ ○ ○ ○ ○ ○

City dweller
○ ○ ○ ○ ○ ○ ○ ○ ○ ○

LIKES
* Outdoor life
* Exploring the countryside
* Plenty of exercise

NEEDS
* An active lifestyle
* Supervision near water
* Plenty of food

AKC group: hound

Pharaoh Hound

Height 25 in (64 cm)
Weight 55 lb (25 kg)
Country of origin Malta

The appearance of this Mediterranean breed is very similar to that of dogs portrayed on ancient Egyptian artifacts, although DNA studies now suggest that its origins are probably much more recent. The Pharaoh Hound is built for speed and stamina, traditionally bred for pursuing rabbits and other small game. As a companion, the Pharaoh Hound is energetic and enthusiastic. Watch out though—if it spots movement on the horizon, your pet is likely to give chase. This can make for stressful walks, particularly as Pharaoh Hounds may not always distinguish between their natural prey and small dogs or cats. If you are uncertain about your dog's behavior, it is sensible to obtain a muzzle.

Is this your perfect dog?

| Teen living with parents | Owner with physical disability | Canine sports competitor |
| ●●●●●●●○○○ | ●●○○○○○○○○ | ●●●●●●○○○○ |

| Young single owner | Allergy sufferers |
| ●●●●●●○○○○ | ●●●●○○○○○○ |

| Young couple | **Trend-centric owner** |
| ●●●●●●●●○○ | ●●●●●●●●●● |

| Family with young kids | Individualist |
| ●●●●●●○○○○ | ●●●●●●●●○○ |

| **Family with teenagers** | Keen jogger |
| ●●●●●●●●●● | ●●●●●●●●●○ |

| Older single owner | Enthusiastic hiker |
| ●●●●○○○○○○ | ●●●●●●●●○○ |

| Older couple | Countryside pursuits fan |
| ●●●●●○○○○○ | ●●●●●●●○○○ |

| City dweller | Beach lover |
| ●●○○○○○○○○ | ●●●●●●○○○○ |

| **Rural owner** |
| ●●●●●●●●●● |

| Hobby farmer |
| ●●●●●●●●○○ |

LIKES

* Chasing balls
* Lots of running
* Family life

NEEDS

* Plenty of exercise
* A winter coat
* Good training

AKC group: hound

Ibizan Hound

Height 28 in (71 cm)
Weight 55 lb (25 kg)
Country of origin Ibiza

Sleek and stylish, this sight hound is one of a number of similar breeds originating from around the Mediterranean. The Ibizan Hound's ancestors are thought to have been introduced to Ibiza by Phoenician traders nearly three millennia ago. It remained largely unknown up until the 1950s, when a Spanish dog breeder introduced it to a wider audience. These dogs are now very popular in the show ring.

The Ibizan Hound's lack of undercoat means that it can be susceptible to the cold, and may need to wear a coat in winter. It instinctively hunts rabbits, and is not an ideal choice if you keep them as pets. A puppy will also need training not to chase cats.

Is this your perfect dog?

Teen living with parents	Family with young kids	Older couple	Keen jogger
●●●●●●●○○○	●●●●●●●○○○	●●●●●●○○○○	●●●●●●●●○○
Young single owner	**Family with teenagers**	City dweller	Enthusiastic hiker
●●●●●●●○○○	●●●●●●●●●●	●●○○○○○○○○	●●●●●●●●●○
Young couple	Older single owner	**Rural owner**	Countryside pursuits fan
●●●●●●●●○○	●●●●○○○○○○	●●●●●●●●●●	●●●●○○○○○○
		Hobby farmer	Beach lover
		●●●●●●●○○○	●●●●●●●○○○
		Owner with physical disability	Canine sports competitor
		●●○○○○○○○○	●●●●●●○○○○
		Allergy sufferers	AKC group: hound
		●●●●○○○○○○	

Trend-centric owner
●●●●●●●●●●

Individualist
●●●●●●●●●●

LIKES
* Warm weather
* Country walks
* Running off

NEEDS
* Little grooming
* Training to stay
* Plenty of exercise

Saluki

Height   28 in (71 cm)
Weight   66 lb (30 kg)
Country of origin   Iran

Like other sight hounds, Salukis pursue their quarry at speed, and possess the typical profile: a deep chest and powerful hindquarters. In their traditional hunting grounds, they can even outpace gazelles, which rank among the most fleet-footed of antelopes, and were trained to hunt with falcons, which act as "spotters," allowing the Salukis to home in on their quarry. The breed is still used for hunting in the Middle East today. Salukis are intelligent and adaptable by nature, but they also have a strong independent streak. This can make training difficult, as they are liable to run off. Be prepared to comb the longer hair on their ears.

LIKES	NEEDS
* Running ahead	* Patient training
* An active lifestyle	* Countryside walks
* Being praised	* Good socialization

Is this your perfect dog?

Teen living with parents
●●●●○○○○○○

Owner with physical disability
●●○○○○○○○○

Young single owner
●●●●●●○○○○

Allergy sufferers
●●○○○○○○○○

Young couple
●●●●●●●●○○

Trend-centric owner
●●●●●●●●●○

Family with young kids
●●●●○○○○○○

Individualist
●●●●●●●●○○

Family with teenagers
●●●●●●●●●○

Keen jogger
●●●●●●●●●○

Older single owner
●●●●○○○○○○

Enthusiastic hiker
●●●●●●●●●○

Older couple
●●●●○○○○○○

Countryside pursuits fan
●●●●●●●●○○

City dweller
●●○○○○○○○○

Beach lover
●●●●●●●●○○

Rural owner
●●●●●●●●●○

Canine sports competitor
●●●●○○○○○○

Hobby farmer
●●●●●●●●○○

AKC group: hound

Afghan Hound

Height 29 in (74 cm)
Weight 60 lb (27 kg)
Country of origin Afghanistan

Stylish and elegant, the appearance of the Afghan Hound has changed since the 1920s when it was first brought to the West. Its coat has become longer, and the regional differences that exist between these hounds in their native country have disappeared. Because of their refined appearance, it is easy to overlook the fact that Afghan Hounds are hunting dogs, bred to work in very inhospitable countryside. In terms of temperament, they tend to be a little aloof and suspicious with strangers, and cannot be trusted with smaller pets. In recent years, Afghan racing has been introduced in some areas, with the dogs chasing a lure around a track.

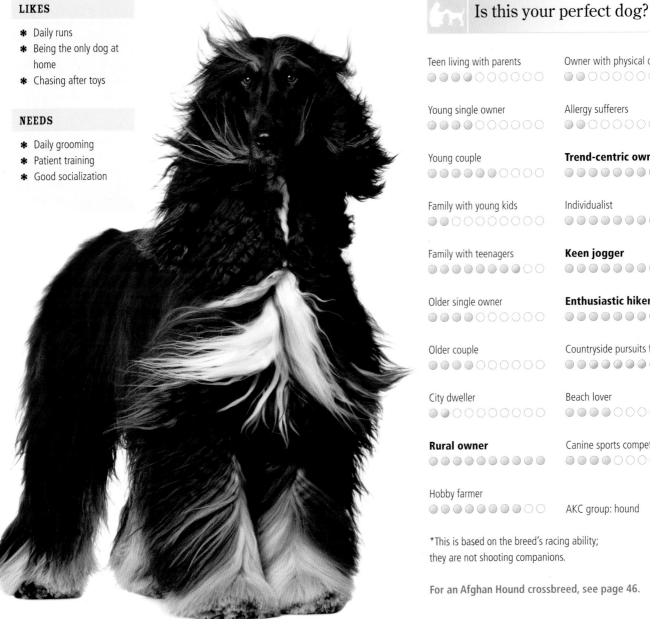

LIKES

* Daily runs
* Being the only dog at home
* Chasing after toys

NEEDS

* Daily grooming
* Patient training
* Good socialization

Is this your perfect dog?

Teen living with parents	Owner with physical disability
Young single owner	Allergy sufferers
Young couple	**Trend-centric owner**
Family with young kids	Individualist
Family with teenagers	**Keen jogger**
Older single owner	**Enthusiastic hiker**
Older couple	Countryside pursuits fan*
City dweller	Beach lover
Rural owner	Canine sports competitor
Hobby farmer	
	AKC group: hound

*This is based on the breed's racing ability; they are not shooting companions.

For an Afghan Hound crossbreed, see page 46.

Greyhound

Height	30 in (76 cm)
Weight	70 lb (32 kg)
Country of origin	United Kingdom

Being built for speed and well known for its racing prowess has counted against the Greyhound as a pet. Every year, many of these sensitive, gentle dogs find themselves in need of good homes, having failed to measure up on the racetrack. Contrary to popular belief, they do not require a lot of exercise, being happy with a fast run around the park. They are quiet by nature, and need very little grooming. Greyhounds are gentle, too, although their instinctive desire to chase means that these dogs in particular should be muzzled when running free off a leash, to ensure they cannot pursue small dogs or other animals: as they can reach speeds of over 40 mph (64 kph), Greyhounds are likely to be able to outpace them with ease.

LIKES

* Beanbags
* Calm environment
* Homes with yards

NEEDS

* A muzzle off the leash
* Daily runs
* A coat in cold weather

Is this your perfect dog?

Teen living with parents
●●●●●●●●○○

Owner with physical disability
●●●●○○○○○○

Young single owner
●●●●●●●○○○

Allergy sufferers
●●●●●●●●○○

Young couple
●●●●●●●●●○

Trend-centric owner
●●●○○○○○○○

Family with young kids
●●●●●●●○○○

Individualist
●●●●●●○○○○

Family with teenagers
●●●●●●●●○○

Keen jogger
●●●●●●●○○○

Older single owner
●●●●●○○○○○

Enthusiastic hiker
●●●●●●●●○○

Older couple
●●●●●●●●○○

Countryside pursuits fan*
●●●●●●●●●●

City dweller
●●●●●●●○○○

Beach lover
●●●●●●●●○○

Rural owner
●●●●●●●●●○

Canine sports competitor
●●●●●●●●●○

Hobby farmer
●●●●●●●○○○

AKC group: hound

*This is based on the breed's racing ability; Greyhounds are not shooting companions.

Borzoi

Height 31 in (79 cm)
Weight 105 lb (47.5 kg)
Country of origin Russia

Sometimes known as Russian Wolfhounds, these extremely elegant dogs were originally bred for pinning down wolves. They were popular with the nobility, who liked their aristocratic appearance. Borzois have more stamina than Greyhounds, and this must be reflected in their day-to-day care: unfortunately, these sight hounds are not suitable for an urban lifestyle. As befits a breed created in the far north, the Borzoi has a dense but relatively silky coat, which gives good protection against the cold, and grows thicker in winter. Traditionally they hunted in couples, and so they are quite social toward others of their kind. They are not overtly affectionate in comparison to some dogs, but they form a strong bond with those they know well.

LIKES	NEEDS
✳ A set routine	✳ Regular grooming
✳ Rural walks	✳ Running daily
✳ A tranquil home	✳ Care around small dogs

Is this your perfect dog?

Teen living with parents
●●●●●●●○○○

Owner with physical disability
●●○○○○○○○○

Young single owner
●●●●○○○○○○

Allergy sufferers
●●○○○○○○○○

Young couple
●●●●○○○○○○

Trend-centric owner
●●●●●●●●●●

Family with young kids
●●○○○○○○○○

Individualist
●●●●●●●●○○

Family with teenagers
●●●●●●○○○○

Keen jogger
●●●●●●●●○○

Older single owner
●●●●●●○○○○

Enthusiastic hiker
●●●●●●●●●●

Older couple
●●●●●●●○○○

Countryside pursuits fan
●●●●●●●○○○

City dweller
●●○○○○○○○○

Beach lover
●●●●●●○○○○

Rural owner
●●●●●●●●●●

Canine sports competitor
●●●●●●●○○○

Hobby farmer
●●●●●●●●○○

AKC group: hound

Scottish Deerhound

Height 30 in (76 cm)
Weight 100 lb (45 kg)
Country of origin United Kingdom

These large sight hounds were used to chase deer in the days before shooting became popular, and so Scottish Deerhounds were developed for both speed and strength. Closely associated with the nobility, when guns replaced dogs in the 1700s, these hounds faced an uncertain future. Luckily, the breed survived, and Scottish Deerhounds can usually be seen at shows, albeit only in small numbers. You need to have plenty of accessible outdoor space for exercise purposes if you choose this breed, as Deerhounds have high energy levels. They also have large appetites—matching their size—and this will be reflected in the cost of keeping them. Never feed your Deerhound before exercise, however, as this can cause the often fatal condition called bloat, as is the case with other similar breeds.

LIKES
* Resting indoors
* People
* Activity

NEEDS
* Good training
* Well-fenced surroundings
* Moderate grooming

 Is this your perfect dog?

Teen living with parents	Owner with physical disability
Young single owner	Allergy sufferers
Young couple	Trend-centric owner
Family with young kids	Individualist
Family with teenagers	Keen jogger
Older single owner	**Enthusiastic hiker**
Older couple	Countryside pursuits fan
City dweller	Beach lover
Rural owner	Canine sports competitor
Hobby farmer	AKC group: hound

Irish Wolfhound

Height 34 in (86 cm)
Weight 120 lb (54.5 kg)
Country of origin Ireland

A gentle giant of the dog world, fully-grown Irish Wolfhounds can be bigger than a small pony. This gives some idea of the space you need. You should also be aware of its powerful tail, which is capable of sweeping objects off a low table when your dog is in an exuberant mood. The size of these dogs means that it is particularly important to make sure the borders of your property are well maintained, to prevent your pet escaping. The breed's large appetite is also something to consider. Wolfhounds benefit from access to a small paddock, but take care not to over-exercise growing puppies, as this could affect their joint development. Sadly—in common with other large dogs—Irish Wolfhounds have a relatively short lifespan, which may be less than a decade, but in that time they will live life to the full.

Is this your perfect dog?

Teen living with parents
● ● ● ● ○ ○ ○ ○ ○ ○

Hobby farmer
● ● ● ● ● ● ● ● ● ●

Countryside pursuits fan
● ● ● ● ● ○ ○ ○ ○ ○

Young single owner
● ● ● ● ○ ○ ○ ○ ○ ○

Owner with physical disability
● ● ○ ○ ○ ○ ○ ○ ○ ○

Beach lover
● ● ● ● ● ● ○ ○ ○ ○

Young couple
● ● ● ● ● ● ○ ○ ○ ○

Allergy sufferers
● ● ○ ○ ○ ○ ○ ○ ○ ○

Canine sports competitor
● ● ● ● ○ ○ ○ ○ ○ ○

Family with young kids
● ● ○ ○ ○ ○ ○ ○ ○ ○

Trend-centric owner
● ● ● ● ● ○ ○ ○ ○ ○

Family with teenagers
● ● ● ● ● ● ● ● ● ●

Individualist
● ● ● ● ● ● ○ ○ ○ ○

Older single owner
● ● ● ● ○ ○ ○ ○ ○ ○

Keen jogger
● ● ● ● ● ● ● ○ ○ ○

Older couple
● ● ● ● ○ ○ ○ ○ ○ ○

Enthusiastic hiker
● ● ● ● ● ● ● ○ ○ ○

City dweller
● ● ○ ○ ○ ○ ○ ○ ○ ○

Rural owner
● ● ● ● ● ● ● ● ● ●

LIKES

* Running
* Playing
* Being friendly

NEEDS

* Moderate grooming
* Space to lie down
* Mobile, fit owners

Irish Wolfhound and Australian Cattle Dog

The combination of these two breeds has led to the **Australian Wolfhound**, which is significantly smaller in size than the Irish Wolfhound. Blue coloration is very evident in this crossbreed.

AKC group: hound

For another Irish Wolfhound crossbreed, see page 111.

Whippet

Height 20 in (51 cm)
Weight 28 lb (13 kg)
Country of origin United Kingdom

Although the Whippet looks like a scaled-down Greyhound, the breed differs in temperament. These sight hounds are more vocal and expressive than Greyhounds—although not noisy—and delight in chasing and retrieving toys, which is probably a reflection of the past terrier input into the Whippet's bloodline. They are built for speed rather than endurance running. Though normally outgoing, this breed can sometimes be nervous with strangers, and may not always get along well with other dogs. Socialization from early in life is important to minimize any potential problems. Whippets make very loyal companions. Be prepared to have to encourage your pet outside if it is raining or cold, as Whippets generally dislike this type of weather.

LIKES

* Sleeping on sofas
* Playing ball
* Being with people

NEEDS

* To wear a coat
* Opportunities to run
* Minimal grooming

Whippet and Italian Greyhound

The **Whippig** crossbreed reflects two breeds that are similar in appearance, both displaying characteristic sloping over the hindquarters. The resulting puppies tend to be intermediate in size between their parents.

Is this your perfect dog?

Teen living with parents
●●●●●●●●●●

Hobby farmer
●●●●●●●●○○

Young single owner
●●●●●●○○○○

Owner with physical disability
●●●●●○○○○○

Young couple
●●●●●●●○○○

Allergy sufferers
●●●●○○○○○○

Family with young kids
●●●●●●○○○○

Trend-centric owner
●●●●○○○○○○

Family with teenagers
●●●●●●●●●●

Individualist
●●●●●●○○○○

Older single owner
●●●●●●●●○○

Keen jogger
●●●●●●●●○○

Older couple
●●●●●●●●●○

Enthusiastic hiker
●●●●●●●●○○

City dweller
●●●●●●○○○○

Countryside pursuits fan
●●●●●●○○○○

Rural owner
●●●●●●●●●●

Beach lover
●●●●●●●●○○

Canine sports competitor
●●●●●●●●●●

AKC group: hound

Plott Hound

Height 27 in (69 cm)
Weight 60 lb (27 kg)
Country of origin United States

Named after a German immigrant who settled with his hounds in the Smoky Mountain region of North Carolina around 1800, the Plott Hound remained localized for many years, rarely being seen outside its homeland until the mid-1900s. In the Great Smoky Mountains, Plott Hounds became treeing dogs, driving their quarry up into the trees and developing into a type of coonhound—although their ancestors originally pursued wild boar. These hounds have plenty of stamina, and are dedicated to their task. Plott Hounds are vocal, and can be heard over a wide area, helping huntsmen to track their positions when they may be hidden from view.

 ## Is this your perfect dog?

Teen living with parents
Young single owner
Young couple
Family with young kids
Family with teenagers
Older single owner
Older couple
City dweller
Rural owner
Hobby farmer
Owner with physical disability

Allergy sufferers

Trend-centric owner
Individualist
Keen jogger
Enthusiastic hiker

Countryside pursuits fan
Beach lover

Canine sports competitor

AKC group: hound

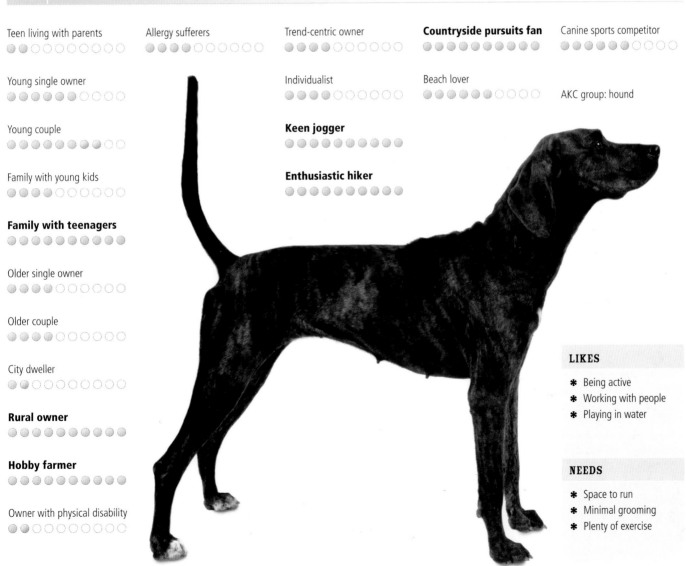

LIKES

* Being active
* Working with people
* Playing in water

NEEDS

* Space to run
* Minimal grooming
* Plenty of exercise

Norwegian Elkhound

Height 21 in (53 cm)
Weight 55 lb (25 kg)
Country of origin Norway

A hunting breed originally from the far north, the Norwegian Elkhound has proved adept as a tracking dog, either on or off the leash. It works closely with its owner, and, as a result, these dogs make excellent companions, as well as being alert to the approach of strangers. The Elkhound is from a different lineage than other hounds, being a member of the Spitz group—as shown by its pricked ears and tightly curled tail. The breed's appearance changes throughout the year—its coat becomes naturally more profuse in colder months, creating a ruff of longer hair around the neck. This longer hair is shed again in the spring, with more grooming being required at that time.

Is this your perfect dog?

LIKES	NEEDS
✳ Outdoor life	✳ Daily exercise
✳ Being active	✳ Regular grooming
✳ Family life	✳ Determined training

Teen living with parents
●●●●○○○○○○

Owner with physical disability
●●○○○○○○○○

Young single owner
●●●●●●○○○○

Allergy sufferers
●●○○○○○○○○

Young couple
●●●●●●●●○○

Trend-centric owner
●●●●○○○○○○

Family with young kids
●●●●○○○○○○

Individualist
●●●●○○○○○○

Family with teenagers
●●●●●●●●●●

Keen jogger
●●●●●●●●○○

Older single owner
●●●●●●○○○○

Enthusiastic hiker
●●●●●●●●●●

Older couple
●●●●●●○○○○

Countryside pursuits fan
●●●●●●●●●●

City dweller
●●○○○○○○○○

Beach lover
●●●●●●○○○○

Rural owner
●●●●●●●●●●

Canine sports competitor
●●●●●●○○○○

Hobby farmer
●●●●●●●●●●

AKC group: hound

Rhodesian Ridgeback

Height 27 in (69 cm)
Weight 80 lb (36 kg)
Country of origin Zimbabwe

One of the relatively few breeds from Africa, the Rhodesian Ridgeback was created by European settlers to hunt lions. The distinctive characteristic of the breed—the ridge of hair running down its back—came from crossings involving the now-extinct Hottentot Dog, kept by the native Khoikhoi people. As might be expected, the Rhodesian Ridgeback is a bold, powerful breed, and is always a wheaten shade. It is instinctively wary of strangers, and very protective toward members of its immediate family. The breed possesses a very distinctive, intimidating growl. Rhodesian Ridgebacks are loyal rather than protective.

Is this your perfect dog?

Teen living with parents
◐●○○○○○○○○

Young single owner
●●●●●●○○○○

Young couple
●●●●●●○○○○

Allergy sufferers
◐●○○○○○○○○

Family with young kids
●●○○○○○○○○

Trend-centric owner
●●●●●○○○○○

Family with teenagers
●●●●●●●●●●

Individualist
●●●●●●○○○○

Older single owner
●●●●○○○○○○

Keen jogger
●●●●●●●●●○

Older couple
●●●●●●○○○○

Enthusiastic hiker
●●●●●●●●●●

City dweller
●●○○○○○○○○

Countryside pursuits fan
●●●●●●○○○○

Rural owner
●●●●●●●●●○

Beach lover
●●●●●○○○○○

Hobby farmer
●●●●●●●●●○

Canine sports competitor
●●●●○○○○○○

Owner with physical disability
◐●○○○○○○○○

AKC group: hound

LIKES

* Warm climates
* A single-dog household
* Positive leadership

NEEDS

* Plenty of exercise
* Reward-based training
* Checking by a veterinarian for dermoid sinus

West Highland White Terrier

Height 10 in (25 cm)
Weight 22 lb (10 kg)
Country of origin United Kingdom

Often known today simply as the Westie, the West Highland White Terrier's origins are founded in tragedy. In the late 1800s, Colonel Edward Malcolm mistook one of his favorite brown terriers for a fox and shot it. Wracked by grief, he decided to establish a strain of white terriers that could never be confused with a fox. These white terriers were originally named Poltalloch Terriers, after his estate in Argyll, Scotland.

Westies have become one of the most popular of all terriers. Unfortunately, inherited skin problems are common in this breed, though the risk is lower in bitches. Westies are jaunty, hardy dogs that thrive in human company, but they can prove to be stubborn, so will require careful training.

West Highland White Terrier and Poodle

Westiepoos are one of the most popular designer dogs, with either Toy or Miniature Poodles contributing to such crosses. Puppies are usually white in color, like their terrier parent.

LIKES

* An active lifestyle
* Meeting other dogs
* Being out in all weathers

NEEDS

* Plenty of exercise
* Training not to be possessive
* Playing games

Is this your perfect dog?

Teen living with parents
●●●●●●●●○○

Owner with physical handicap
●●●●●●●○○○

Young single owner
●●●●●●●●○○

Allergy sufferers
●●○○○○○○○○

Young couple
●●●●●●●●○○

Trend-centric owner
●●●●●●●●○○

Family with young kids
●●○○○○○○○○

Individualist
●●●●●○○○○○

Family with teenagers
●●●●●●●●○○

Keen jogger
●●○○○○○○○○

Older single owner
●●●●●●●●●○

Enthusiastic hiker
●●○○○○○○○○

Older couple
●●●●●●●●○○

Countryside pursuits fan
●●○○○○○○○○

City dweller
●●●●●●●○○○

Beach lover
●●●●●●○○○○

Rural owner
●●●●●●●○○○

Canine sports competitor
●●●●●●●●○○

Hobby farmer
●●●●●●●○○○

AKC group: terrier

For other West Highland White Terrier crossbreeds, see pages 105 and 124.

Cairn Terrier

Height 10 in (25 cm)
Weight 14 lb (6.5 kg)
Country of origin United Kingdom

The Cairn Terrier is named after piles of rocks—called cairns—in its native Scotland, where its ancestors were used to hunt vermin. Cairn Terriers have a tendency to dig, and this behavior is hard to curb. They are also eager to chase cats and other small creatures such as squirrels, so firm training from an early age is essential. Even then, be prepared for lapses on occasion—they can be stubborn! Hand-stripping of the coat is recommended during the summer months to remove dead hair; this needs to be carried out by a professional groomer, familiar with the breed. Cutting the coat of these lively terriers yourself is not recommended. Despite these considerations, Cairn Terriers make lively and engaging companions.

LIKES

* City life
* Playing with toys
* Daily walks

NEEDS

* Patient training
* Careful grooming
* Socialization

Is this your perfect dog?

Teen living with parents	Family with young kids	**Older couple**	Hobby farmer
●●●●●●●●○○	●●○○○○○○○○	●●●●●●●●●●	●●●●●●●●○○

Young single owner	Family with teenagers	City dweller	Owner with physical disability
●●●●●●●●○○	●●●●●●●●○○	●●●●●●●●○○	●●●○○○○○○○

Young couple	**Older single owner**	Rural owner	Allergy sufferers
●●●●●●●●○○	●●●●●●●●●●	●●●●●●●●○○	●●●●●●○○○○

Trend-centric owner
●●○○○○○○○○

Individualist
●●●●●○○○○○

Keen jogger
●●○○○○○○○○

Enthusiastic hiker
●●○○○○○○○○

Countryside pursuits fan
●●○○○○○○○○

Beach lover
●●●●●●○○○○

Canine sports competitor
●●●●●●●●○○

AKC group: terrier

Cairn Terrier and Scottish Terrier

The contribution of the Scottie parent is usually very apparent in this cross. Some **Bushland Terrier** puppies in a litter may have broader, less tapered heads, reflecting the Cairn Terrier's influence.

Scottish Terrier

Height 11 in (28 cm)
Weight 23 lb (10.5 kg)
Country of origin United Kingdom

The long, relatively broad shape of the Scottish Terrier's head, combined with its bushy eyebrows and beard, creates an appealing and very distinctive appearance. The Scottie, as this breed is affectionately called, is very determined by nature and also quite reserved. Unfortunately, these terriers can occasionally suffer from an inherited—though treatable—condition known as "Scottie cramp," which causes them to have difficulty walking and may cause them to fall over unexpectedly. The breed has attracted its share of famous owners, including Britain's Queen Victoria and presidents George W. Bush and F. D. Roosevelt. A Scottie is even featured as one of the tokens of the board game Monopoly.

LIKES

* Its own territory
* Playing
* Exploring

NEEDS

* Socialization as a puppy
* Regular coat trimming
* Good training

Scottish Terrier and Silky Terrier

Skilky Terriers are similar in size to the parent breeds, but their coat type and coloration are more variable.

Is this your perfect dog?

Teen living with parents
●●●●●●●●○○

Young single owner
●●●●●●●●○○

Young couple
●●●●●●●○○○

Family with young kids
●●○○○○○○○○

Family with teenagers
●●●●●●○○○○

Older single owner
●●●●●●●●○○

Older couple
●●●●●●●●○○

City dweller
●●●●●●●○○○

Rural owner
●●●●●●●●●●

Hobby farmer
●●●●●●●●●●

Owner with physical disability
●●○○○○○○○○

Allergy sufferers
●●○○○○○○○○

Trend-centric owner
●●●●●●○○○○

Individualist
●●●●●○○○○○

Keen jogger
●●○○○○○○○○

Enthusiastic hiker
●●○○○○○○○○

Countryside pursuits fan
●●○○○○○○○○

Beach lover
●●●●●●○○○○

Canine sports competitor
●●●●●●●●○○

AKC group: terrier

For another Scottish Terrier crossbreed, see page 79.

Skye Terrier

Height 10 in (25 cm)
Weight 25 lb (11.5 kg)
Country of origin United Kingdom

Named after the Isle of Skye—one of the Inner Hebrides, Scotland—the appearance of this rare breed has changed significantly over time. Skye Terriers are now larger, with longer bodies, and selective breeding has led to their large, batlike ears increasing in size. Perhaps more significantly, the coat is soft and less wiry, making it less weather-resistant. The loyalty of the Skye Terrier is legendary, as demonstrated by the popular story of Scotland's Greyfriars Bobby. Following his owner's death, this terrier returned every day for 14 years to Greyfriars Kirkyard Cemetery to be near his master's grave. A memorial commemorating Greyfriars Bobby was paid for out of public donations.

Skye Terrier and Poodle

Both Miniature and Toy Poodles may be used in this cross. **Skypoos** with a Miniature Poodle ancestry are slightly larger in size than those bred from Toy Poodle crosses.

LIKES

* Exploring outdoors
* Bonding with one person
* Being a watchdog

NEEDS

* Discouragement from jumping up
* A medium walk
* Twice-weekly combing

 ## Is this your perfect dog?

Teen living with parents ●●●●●●●●○○	**Older couple** ●●●●●●●●●●	Trend-centric owner ●●●●○○○○○○
Young single owner ●●●●●●●●○○	City dweller ●●●●●●●●○○	Individualist ●●●●●○○○○○
Young couple ●●●●●●●●○○	Rural owner ●●●●●●●●○○	Keen jogger ●●○○○○○○○○
Family with young kids ●●●●○○○○○○	Hobby farmer ●●●●●●●●○○	Enthusiastic hiker ●●○○○○○○○○
Family with teenagers ●●●●●○○○○○	Owner with physical disability ●●●●○○○○○○	Countryside pursuits fan ●●○○○○○○○○
Older single owner ●●●●●●●●●●	Allergy sufferers ●●●●●●○○○○	Beach lover ●●●●○○○○○○
		Canine sports competitor ●●●●○○○○○○

AKC group: terrier

Dandie Dinmont Terrier

Height 11 in (28 cm)
Weight 24 lb (11 kg)
Country of origin United Kingdom

The Dandie Dinmont is the only dog breed named after a fictional character. A novel written by Sir Walter Scott in 1814, *Guy Mannering*, featured a farmer from the Borders region between England and Scotland, who kept terriers. Reputedly based on a local man known as James Davidson, the character was called "Dandie Dinmont," and this name was soon adopted for Davidson's own terriers. The Dandie Dinmont is a highly distinctive breed, thanks to its silky top-knot. It is short-legged and long-bodied, with large, pendulous ears and a loud bark. Like other long-bodied terriers, these dogs can be prone to back problems. Dandie Dinmonts are today quite scarce.

LIKES

* Playing with toys
* Digging
* Being a household guardian

NEEDS

* Discouragement from jumping up
* Socialization in puppyhood
* Screening for glaucoma

 Is this your perfect dog?

Teen living with parents
●●●●●●●●○○

Older couple
●●●●●●●●●●

Trend-centric owner
●●●●○○○○○○

Young single owner
●●●●●●●●○○

City dweller
●●●●●●●●○○

Individualist
●●●●●●●○○○

Young couple
●●●●●●●●○○

Rural owner
●●●●●●●●○○

Keen jogger
●●○○○○○○○○

Family with young kids
●●●●○○○○○○

Hobby farmer
●●●●●●●○○○

Enthusiastic hiker
●●○○○○○○○○

Family with teenagers
●●●●○○○○○○

Owner with physical disability
●●●●○○○○○○

Countryside pursuits fan
●●○○○○○○○○

Older single owner
●●●●●●●●●○

Allergy sufferers
●●○○○○○○○○

Beach lover
●●●●●●○○○○

Canine sports competitor
●●●●○○○○○○

AKC group: terrier

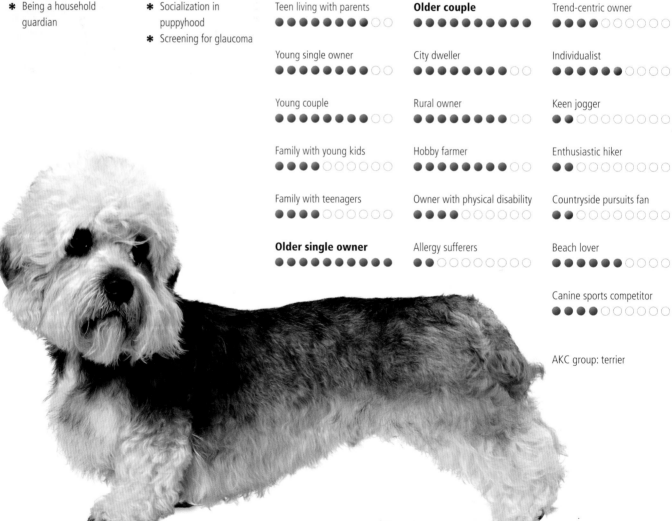

Bedlington Terrier

Height 17 in (43 cm)
Weight 23 lb (10.5 kg)
Country of origin United Kingdom

There is no mistaking the Bedlington Terrier, which looks like a lamb. Bred in the north of England, it is one of the most athletic of the terriers in terms of its racing abilities. Crosses involving Whippets are thought to have contributed to the Bedlington's speed.

Known until 1825 as Rothbury Terriers—named after a village near Bedlington where the breed originated—Bedlingtons are lively characters. Unfortunately, the breed has been blighted by the genetic condition of copper toxicosis, which causes copper to accumulate in the liver. However, as long as you acquire a puppy from breeding stock that has been screened for this illness, you should have a very healthy companion.

LIKES	NEEDS
* Swimming and running	* Good socialization
* Being active	* Clipping of its coat
* Chasing toys	* Discouragement from barking

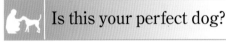

Is this your perfect dog?

Teen living with parents
●●●●●●●●●○

Owner with physical disability
●●●●○○○○○○

Young single owner
●●●●●●●○○

Allergy sufferers
●●●●●●●●○○

Young couple
●●●●●●●○○

Trend-centric owner
●●●●●●●●○○

Family with young kids
●●●●○○○○○○

Individualist
●●●●●●○○○○

Family with teenagers
●●●●●●●●●●

Keen jogger
●●●●●●●○○○

Older single owner
●●●●●●●●●●

Enthusiastic hiker
●●●●●●○○○○

Older couple
●●●●●●●●●●

Countryside pursuits fan
●●●●●●●○○○

City dweller
●●●●●●●●○○

Beach lover
●●●●●●●○○○

Rural owner
●●●●●●●○○

Canine sports competitor
●●●●●●●●○○

Hobby farmer
●●●●●●●○○

AKC group: terrier

Toy Fox Terrier

Height 10 in (25 cm)
Weight 7 lb (3 kg)
Country of origin United States

There has been a tendency toward miniaturization in the case of some breeds over the past century, in order to increase their appeal as companion dogs. The Toy Fox Terrier is a scaled-down version of the Smooth Fox Terrier, but its shorter muzzle and more rounded head shape reveal the Chihuahua's contribution to its ancestry. This has also added to the vocal performance of the breed, and may explain its less active nature compared to true terriers. These small dogs are also described as American Toy Terriers, or Amertoys, and are not difficult to train. Toy Fox Terriers can suit apartment living, but should not be left alone for long periods and are better kept in a home with a yard.

LIKES

* Attention
* Chasing balls
* Seeking rodents

NEEDS

* Little grooming
* Good dental hygiene
* A coat in colder months

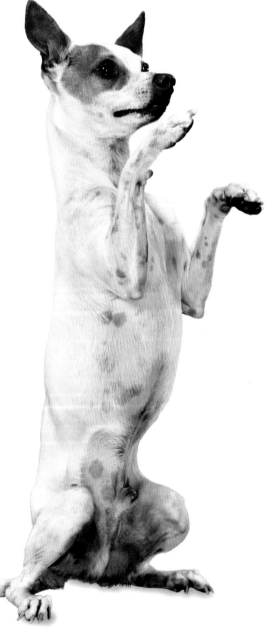

Toy Fox Terrier and Pug

The Pug is quite widely used in the creation of designer dogs. **Toy Poxer** puppies resulting from this cross are undeniably cute—they are small and have an alert, friendly disposition.

Is this your perfect dog?

Teen living with parents
●●●●●●●●●●

Owner with physical disability
●●●●●●●●○○

Young single owner
●●●●●●●●○○

Allergy sufferers
●●●●○○○○○○

Young couple
●●●●●●●○○

Trend-centric owner
●●●●○○○○○○

Family with young kids
●●●●●●○○○○

Individualist
●●●●○○○○○○

Family with teenagers
●●●●●●●●○○

Keen jogger
●●○○○○○○○○

Older single owner
●●●●●●●●●●

Enthusiastic hiker
●●●●○○○○○○

Older couple
●●●●●●●●●●

Countryside pursuits fan
●●●●○○○○○○

City dweller
●●●●●●●●○○

Beach lover
●●●●●●○○○○

Rural owner
●●●●●●●●○○

Canine sports competitor
●●●●●●●●●○

Hobby farmer
●●●●●●●●●●

AKC group: toy

Fox Terrier

Height	11 in (28 cm)
Weight	22 lb (10 kg)
Country of origin	United Kingdom

During the first half of the twentieth century, Fox Terriers were highly regarded as pets, but their popularity has declined dramatically, largely because of their temperament. Fox Terriers are dedicated hunting dogs, and this means they can be quite stubborn. These terriers, like many others, are also not very patient, which can result in them snapping unexpectedly. The Wire Fox Terrier is more frequently seen than its smooth-coated relative—although they share a common ancestry, the two forms are not interbred today and are generally recognized as separate breeds. White often predominates in the Fox Terrier's striking appearance, clearly distinguishing the breed from the foxes they were bred to flush from their underground lairs.

LIKES

* Digging
* An energetic lifestyle
* The countryside

NEEDS

* Plenty of exercise
* Dedicated training
* More grooming if wire-coated

Is this your perfect dog?

Teen living with parents
●●●●●●○○○○

Owner with physical disability
●●○○○○○○○○

Young single owner
●●●●●●○○○○

Allergy sufferers
●●○○○○○○○○

Young couple
●●●●●●○○○○

Trend-centric owner
●●○○○○○○○○

Family with young kids
●●○○○○○○○○

Individualist
●●○○○○○○○○

Family with teenagers
●●●●●●●●○○

Keen jogger
●●●●○○○○○○

Older single owner
●●●●●●○○○○

Enthusiastic hiker
●●●●●●●●○○

Older couple
●●●●●●○○○○

Countryside pursuits fan
●●●●●●●○○○

City dweller
●●○○○○○○○○

Beach lover
●●●●●●○○○○

Rural owner
●●●●●●●●●●

Canine sports competitor
●●●●●●○○○○

Hobby farmer
●●●●●●●●●●

AKC group: terrier

Glen of Imaal Terrier

Height 14 in (36 cm)
Weight 35 lb (16 kg)
Country of origin Ireland

The Glen of Imaal Terrier is one of the oldest of Ireland's native terriers, and now one of the rarest. It has changed little down the centuries. Developed as a bold hunting breed, it was also frequently employed in dogfighting contests. As a result, although very amenable toward people, the Glen of Imaal Terrier is often not particularly well-disposed to other dogs. The Glen of Imaal Terrier may not rank as the most attractive breed in terms of looks, but it makes an unusual, personable companion. These dogs are quieter and less excitable than most terriers, though they do have a surprisingly loud bark.

LIKES

* The countryside
* Its immediate family
* Good walks

NEEDS

* Good training
* Careful introductions to cats
* Hand-stripping

 Is this your perfect dog?

Teen living with parents
●●●●●●●●○○

Older single owner
●●●●●●●●●●

Rural owner
●●●●●●●●●●

Owner with physical disability
●●●●○○○○○○

Young single owner
●●●●●●●●○○

Older couple
●●●●●●●●●●

Hobby farmer
●●●●●●●●●●

Allergy sufferers
●●●●●●●○○○

Young couple
●●●●●●●●○○

City dweller
●●●●●●○○○○

Trend-centric owner
●●○○○○○○○○

Family with young kids
●●●●●●○○○○

Individualist
●●●●●○○○○○

Family with teenagers
●●●●●●●●○○

Keen jogger
●●○○○○○○○○

Enthusiastic hiker
●●●●●●●●○○

Countryside pursuits fan
●●●●●●●○○○

Beach lover
●●●●●●○○○○

Canine sports competitor
●●●●●●●●○○

AKC group: terrier

Irish Terrier

Height   18 in (46 cm)
Weight   26 lb (12 kg)
Country of origin   Ireland

Thanks to its appearance, this breed is often described unofficially as the Irish Red Terrier. Its coloration tends to be a dark shade of red—a characteristic linked with the hardness of the wiry coat, which was highly valued in these working dogs, affording them good protection. The rectangular shape of their torso is unique among terriers. Irish Terriers were kept both to hunt vermin and act as guardians. The breed has a loud bark and is often quite quarrelsome toward other dogs, especially terriers. Irish Terriers are loyal companions, but are highly energetic and often noisy. They can run surprisingly fast if necessary.

Is this your perfect dog?

Teen living with parents
●●●●○○○○○○

Allergy sufferers
●●●●○○○○○○

Young single owner
●●●●●●○○○○

Trend-centric owner
●●●●●●○○○○

Young couple
●●●●●●●○○○

Individualist
●●○○○○○○○○

Family with young kids
●●●●○○○○○○

Keen jogger
●●●●●●●●○○

Family with teenagers
●●●●●●●○○○

Enthusiastic hiker
●●●●●●●●●●

Older single owner
●●●●●●○○○○

Countryside pursuits fan
●●●●●●●●○○

Older couple
●●●●●●●○○○

Beach lover
●●●●●●○○○○

City dweller
●●●●○○○○○○

Canine sports competitor
●●●●●●●●●●

Rural owner
●●●●●●●●●●

AKC group: terrier

Hobby farmer
●●●●●●●●●●

Owner with physical disability
●●○○○○○○○○

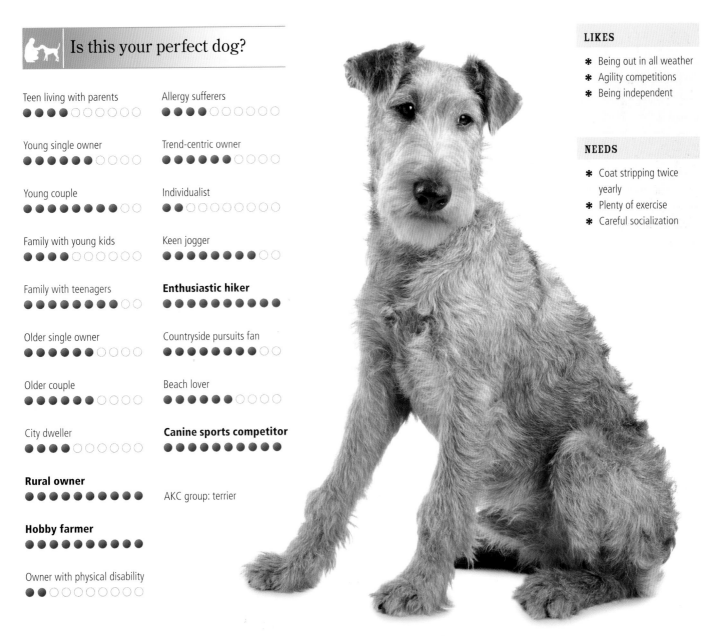

Soft-coated Wheaten Terrier

Height 19 in (48 cm)
Weight 40 lb (18 kg)
Country of origin Ireland

In contrast to most other terriers, this breed has a very different coat texture, with a soft feel to it. The Soft-coated Wheaten Terrier's coloration, as reflected in its name, should resemble that of ripening wheat. Puppies tend to be a coppery-red shade at birth, but they lighten in color as they mature. Although described as a terrier, this breed was developed as a general-purpose farm dog, hunting vermin and working with stock as well. As a result, these dogs tend to have a more laid-back nature than many terriers. Their single-layered coat does not shed, so Soft-coated Wheaten Terriers are ideal for those who dislike housework; however, the coat will definitely need trimming.

LIKES	NEEDS
* Exercise outdoors	* Daily grooming
* Family life	* Positive training
* Jumping up	* Socialization with cats

Soft-coated Wheaten Terrier and Poodle

Bred using Poodles of any size or color, the **Whoodle**'s appearance can be quite varied, although the faces of puppies are usually more rounded compared to their terrier ancestors.

Is this your perfect dog?

Teen living with parents
●●●●●●●●○○

Owner with physical disability
●●●●○○○○○○

Young single owner
●●●●●●○○○○

Allergy sufferers
●●●●●●●●○○

Young couple
●●●●●●●●○○

Trend-centric owner
●●●●●●○○○○

Family with young kids
●●●●●○○○○○

Individualist
●●●●●●○○○○

Family with teenagers
●●●●●●●●●●

Keen jogger
●●●●●●●●○○

Older single owner
●●●●●●○○○○

Enthusiastic hiker
●●●●●●●●●●

Older couple
●●●●●●○○○○

Countryside pursuits fan
●●●●●●○○○○

City dweller
●●●●○○○○○○

Beach lover
●●●●●●○○○○

Rural owner
●●●●●●●●●●

Canine sports competitor
●●●●●●●●●●

Hobby farmer
●●●●●●●●●●

AKC group: terrier

Kerry Blue Terrier

Height 19 in (48 cm)
Weight 40 lb (18 kg)
Country of origin Ireland

Don't be surprised, when looking at a litter of Kerry Blue Terrier puppies, to discover that they are black. It can take up to two years for these terriers to acquire their distinctive blue coloration, although—as with other breeds—this will appear to be grayish. The Kerry Blue's coat has a silky, woolly feel, with no undercoat. Grooming is a very important aspect of the breed's care, and should be carried out several times a week to prevent matting. The hair is not shed, so it will require clipping every six to eight weeks. Kerry Blues are generally friendly, but they do seem to have an instinctive dislike of cats, so you may need to take this into consideration.

Is this your perfect dog?

Teen living with parents	City dweller	Trend-centric owner	Countryside pursuits fan
●●●●●●○○○○	●●●●●○○○○○	●●●●●●○○○○	●●●●●●○○○○

Young single owner	**Rural owner**	Individualist	Beach lover
●●●●●●○○○○	●●●●●●●●○○	●●●●○○○○○○	●●●●●●○○○○

Young couple	**Hobby farmer**	Keen jogger	Canine sports competitor
●●●●●●●●○○	●●●●●●●●○○	●●●●●●●●○○	●●●●●●●●○○

Family with young kids	Owner with physical disability	**Enthusiastic hiker**	
●●●●●●○○○○	●●●●○○○○○○	●●●●●●●●●●	AKC group: terrier

Family with teenagers	Allergy sufferers
●●●●●●●●●●	●●●●●●●●○○

Older single owner
●●●●●●○○○○

Older couple
●●●●●●○○○○

LIKES
* Announcing visitors
* Farm work
* Being active

NEEDS
* Good socialization
* Daily exercise
* Obedience training

Manchester Terrier

Height   16 in (41 cm)
Weight   22 lb (10 kg)
Country of origin   United Kingdom

Both a standard and a smaller toy variety of this breed exist in the United States, where the Manchester Terrier (named after the city in northwest England) was one of the first breeds to be officially recognized for show purposes. Its characteristic black-and-tan coloration has been a feature of British terriers for centuries—the tan areas tend to be confined to the extremities of the body. Manchester Terriers were crossed with Whippets in the mid-1800s to increase their speed, so they could be used to chase down rabbits as well as hunting rats. Like other terriers, they have a very determined nature, in spite of their small size.

LIKES	NEEDS
* Investigating undergrowth	* Socialization when young
* Chasing toys	* Occasional brushing
* City life	* Lots of exercise

Is this your perfect dog?

Teen living with parents
●●●●●●●●○○

Hobby farmer
●●●●●●●●●●

Young single owner
●●●●●●○○○○

Owner with physical disability
●●●●○○○○○○

Young couple
●●●●●●●○○

Allergy sufferers
●●●●●○○○○○

Family with young kids
●●●○○○○○○○

Trend-centric owner
●●●●○○○○○○

Family with teenagers
●●●●●●●●○○

Individualist
●●●●○○○○○○

Older single owner
●●●●●●●●●●

Keen jogger
●●●●○○○○○○

Older couple
●●●●●●●●●●

Enthusiastic hiker
●●●●●●●○○○

City dweller
●●●●●●●●●●

Countryside pursuits fan
●●●●○○○○○○

Rural owner
●●●●●●●●○○

Beach lover
●●●●●●●○○○

Canine sports competitor
●●●●●●●●○○

AKC group: terrier

Border Terrier

Height 16 in (41 cm)
Weight 15.5 lb (7 kg)
Country of origin United Kingdom

Border Terriers originated in the area between England and Scotland—which explains their name—and were used underground to drive foxes from their lairs. These lively, friendly terriers are typically taller than most similar breeds, as they were expected to keep up with the hounds when out hunting, rather than being carried on horseback. This meant that they needed to be able to run quite fast, and is also the reason that they can jump well. Their coat is weather-resistant, comprised of a soft undercoat with a longer, wiry top coat. Hand stripping will be needed every six months on average, in order to remove the dead hair from the coat, and this can be carried out at a grooming parlor.

LIKES

* Being with people
* Exploring on walks
* Earthdog trials

NEEDS

* Training to live with cats
* Secure backyard fencing
* To be kept away from small pets

Is this your perfect dog?

Teen living with parents
●●●●●●●○○

Owner with physical disability
●●●●●●○○○○

Young single owner
●●●●●●●○○

Allergy sufferers
●●●●○○○○○○

Young couple
●●●●●●●●●

Trend-centric owner
●●●●○○○○○○

Family with young kids
●●●●●●○○○○

Individualist
●●●●●●○○○○

Family with teenagers
●●●●●●●●●

Keen jogger
●●●●●●○○○○

Older single owner
●●●●●●●○○

Enthusiastic hiker
●●●●●●●●○○

Older couple
●●●●●●●○○

Countryside pursuits fan
●●●●●●●○○○

City dweller
●●●●●●○○○○

Beach lover
●●●●●○○○○○

Rural owner
●●●●●●●●●

Canine sports competitor
●●●●●●●●●

Hobby farmer
●●●●●●●●○○

AKC group: terrier

Norfolk Terrier

Height 10 in (25 cm)
Weight 12 lb (5.5 kg)
Country of origin United Kingdom

The Norfolk Terrier is one of a pair of very similar breeds developed in eastern England: the Norfolk Terrier and the Norwich Terrier. Both exist in a similar range of colors—notably gold or gray, as well as red and tan or black and tan—but the Norfolk has drop ears, folded over at their tips. Among the smallest of working terriers, neither breed was used on hunts, but they were kept around farms for hunting vermin, and barking to highlight the arrival of visitors. Unusually for terriers, groups of these dogs worked together in small packs. The Norfolk Terrier is therefore more social by nature than many other terrier breeds.

LIKES

* Exploring around sheds
* Human company
* Investigating holes underground

NEEDS

* Yard access
* Grooming by hand-stripping
* Hip dysplasia certification

Is this your perfect dog?

Teen living with parents
●●●●●●●●●●

Young single owner
●●●●●●●●○○

Older single owner
●●●●●●●●●●

Older couple
●●●●●●●●●●

City dweller
●●●●●●●●●●

Rural owner
●●●●●●●●○○

Hobby farmer
●●●●●●●●●●

Young couple
●●●●●●●●●●

Family with young kids
●●●●●●●○○○

Family with teenagers
●●●●●●●●○○

Older single owner
●●●●●●●●●●

Owner with physical disability
●●○○○○○○○○

Allergy sufferers
●●●●●●●●○○

Trend-centric owner
●●●●○○○○○○

Individualist
●●○○○○○○○○

Keen jogger
●●○○○○○○○○

Enthusiastic hiker
●●●●●●○○○○

Countryside pursuits fan
●●○○○○○○○○

Beach lover
●●●●●●●●○○

Canine sports competitor
●●●●●●●●○○

AKC group: terrier

Norwich Terrier

Height 10 in (25 cm)
Weight 12 lb (5.5 kg)
Country of origin United Kingdom

Just as the Norfolk Terrier is named after the English county, the Norwich Terrier is named after the English city where it was originally developed. These small dogs were popularized in the late 1800s as pets kept by students at Cambridge University. In 1914, the first Norwich Terrier was taken to the United States. Because it was bred by a horse-breaker called Roughrider Jones, the breed was initially known in the States as the Jones Terrier, before it took on its current name. Norwich Terriers, unlike Norfolks, always have pricked ears. They have a soft undercoat beneath their wiry topcoat. They have a friendly disposition and are quite calm.

LIKES

* Being active
* Overeating
* Being assertive

NEEDS

* Consistent daily exercise
* Grooming by hand-stripping
* Hip dysplasia certification

Is this your perfect dog?

Teen living with parents
●●●●●●●●●●

Owner with physical disability
●●○○○○○○○○

Young single owner
●●●●●●●○○

Allergy sufferers
●●●●●●●●○○

Young couple
●●●●●●●●●●

Trend-centric owner
●●●●○○○○○○

Family with young kids
●●●●●●○○○○

Individualist
●●○○○○○○○○

Family with teenagers
●●●●●●●●○○

Keen jogger
●●○○○○○○○○

Older single owner
●●●●●●●●●●

Enthusiastic hiker
●●●●●●○○○○

Older couple
●●●●●●●●●●

Countryside pursuits fan
●●○○○○○○○○

City dweller
●●●●●●●●●●

Beach lover
●●●●●●●●○○

Rural owner
●●●●●●●●○○

Canine sports competitor
●●●●●●●●○○

Hobby farmer
●●●●●●●●●●

AKC group: terrier

Parson Jack Russell Terrier

Height 15 in (38 cm)
Weight 18 lb (8 kg)
Country of origin United Kingdom

For many years, there was opposition to any attempts to standardize Jack Russells, but in the end a taller version of this popular terrier—the Parson Jack Russell Terrier—was given a show standard. Sometimes known as the Parson Russell, these dogs reflect the original form of the breed, created by a parson living in southwest England. Parson John "Jack" Russell was an avid foxhunter and wanted to create distinctive terriers that could run alongside the foxhounds, but were also small and brave enough to venture underground and drive a fox from its lair.

The coat is mostly white, with smaller colored patches, typically on the head and around the tail. The wire-haired (or "broken") coat type is traditional, but smooth-coated examples are acceptable too.

LIKES

* Exploring the countryside
* Chasing a ball
* Plenty of exercise

NEEDS

* Little grooming
* Careful feeding
* Discouragement from barking

Norfolk Terrier and Jack Russell Terrier

When a Parson Jack Russell is used in this cross, this tends to result in a **Norjack**, which is taller than a Norfolk Terrier. Norjacks are alert, typically wire-haired, and make great companions.

Is this your perfect dog?

Teen living with parents
●●●●●●●●○○

Owner with physical disability
●●●●○○○○○○

Young single owner
●●●●●●○○○○

Allergy sufferers
●●●●○○○○○○

Young couple
●●●●●●●●○○

Trend-centric owner
●●●●○○○○○○

Family with young kids
●●○○○○○○○○

Individualist
●●○○○○○○○○

Family with teenagers
●●●●●●●●○○

Keen jogger
●●●●●●●●○○

Older single owner
●●●●●●●●○○

Enthusiastic hiker
●●●●●●●●●●

Older couple
●●●●●●●●○○

Countryside pursuits fan
●●●●●●●●○○

City dweller
●●●●●○○○○○

Beach lover
●●●●●●○○○○

Rural owner
●●●●●●●●●●

Canine sports competitor
●●●●●●●●●●

Hobby farmer
●●●●●●●●●●

AKC group: terrier

Jack Russell Terriers

Height 12 in (30 cm)
Weight 15 lb (7 kg)
Country of origin United Kingdom

Aside from the standardized Parson form, there exists a wide range of recognizable Jack Russell Terriers. Traditionally valued for their working ability rather than their appearance, Jack Russells were not standardized as a show breed until 1989 in the United Kingdom. Today's shorter-legged forms of the breed were traditionally kept in urban areas for hunting rats, although now they are more likely to be chosen simply as companions. These small terriers require daily exercise and careful feeding—otherwise, your dog will soon start to show signs of obesity. The Jack Russell's patterning is highly individual, but the coat is mostly white, with black, tan, and lemon areas. There is now a standardized form recognized by the AKC, known as the Russell Terrier.

LIKES

* An active lifestyle
* Venturing underground
* Exploring off the leash

NEEDS

* Minimal grooming
* Plenty of exercise
* Good socialization

Is this your perfect dog?

Teen living with parents
●●●●●●●●○○

Owner with physical disability
●●●●○○○○○○

Young single owner
●●●●●●○○○○

Allergy sufferers
●●●●○○○○○○

Young couple
●●●●●●●●●○

Trend-centric owner
●●●●○○○○○○

Family with young kids
●●○○○○○○○○

Individualist
●●●●●●○○●○

Family with teenagers
●●●●●●●●○○

Keen jogger
●●●●●●●●○○

Older single owner
●●●●●●●●○○

Enthusiastic hiker
●●●●●●●●●●

Older couple
●●●●●●●●○○

Countryside pursuits fan
●●●●●●●●○○

City dweller
●●●●○○○○○○

Beach lover
●●●●●●●○○○

Rural owner
●●●●●●●●●●

Canine sports competitor
●●●●●●●●●●

Hobby farmer
●●●●●●●●●●

AKC group: terrier

For another Jack Russell crossbreed, see page 164.

Sealyham Terrier

Height 11 in (28 cm)
Weight 25 lb (11.5 kg)
Country of origin United Kingdom

No one knows the exact ancestry of these predominantly white Welsh Terriers, as their creator—an army captain called John Edwards—left no records. It is believed that Edwards used a number of other terrier breeds, and probably Welsh Corgis, too, to develop the Sealyham Terrier in the mid-1800s. He wanted a brave terrier to flush otters out of their holts (dens), working alongside Otterhounds (see page 65). During the twentieth century, Sealyham Terriers started to enter the show ring and became very popular as pets, before fashion moved on and they fell out of favor. Although now rare, these dogs are adaptable and attractive. Their coat care can be quite demanding, though, particularly for show purposes.

LIKES

* Country walks
* Urban life
* Getting muddy

NEEDS

* Hand-stripping
* Consistent training
* Plenty of play

Is this your perfect dog?

Teen living with parents
●●●●●●●●○○

Older single owner
●●●●●●●●○○

Owner with physical disability
●●●●○○○○○○

Young single owner
●●●●●○○○○

Older couple
●●●●●●●●○○

Allergy sufferers
●●●●●●●○○

Young couple
●●●●●●●○○

City dweller
●●●●●●●●●●

Trend-centric owner
●●●●●●○○○○

Family with young kids
●●●○○○○○○

Rural owner
●●●●●●●●●●

Individualist
●●●●○○○○○

Family with teenagers
●●●●●●●●●●

Hobby farmer
●●●●●●●●●●

Keen jogger
●●○○○○○○○

Enthusiastic hiker
●●●●●●○○○

Countryside pursuits fan
●●●●●●○○○

Beach lover
●●●●●●●●○○

Canine sports competitor
●●●●●●●●○○

AKC group: terrier

Boston Terrier

Height	17 in (43 cm)
Weight	25 lb (11.5 kg)
Country of origin	United States

The friendly and playful nature of the modern Boston Terrier belies its ancestry as a breed developed for dogfighting. The Boston Terrier was created in New England in the 1870s, and entered the show ring some 20 years later. It has remained popular ever since. The breed's ears are large and batlike, while its tail is naturally short. These dogs may sometimes snuffle—like all short-nosed breeds—and snore when sleeping, particularly with age. Boston Terriers are also vulnerable to heatstroke if exercised in hot weather. They are not noisy dogs, unlike many terriers (in fact, the American Kennel Club does not even group the breed as a terrier).

LIKES

* Interacting with people
* Playing with toys
* Training sessions

NEEDS

* Little grooming
* Diet to avoid flatulence
* Care under anesthesia

Boston Terrier and Pekingese

This cross usually results in really cute **Bostinese** puppies, which are taller than the Pekingese and have shorter hair. In many cases, their longer hair is restricted mainly to the ears and tail.

Is this your perfect dog?

Teen living with parents
●●●●●●●●●●

Owner with physical disability
●●●○○○○○○○

Young single owner
●●●●●●●●○○

Allergy sufferers
●●●●○○○○○○

Young couple
●●●●●●●●●●

Trend-centric owner
●●●●●●○○○○

Family with young kids
●●●●●●○○○○

Individualist
●●●●○○○○○○

Family with teenagers
●●●●●●●●●●

Keen jogger
●●○○○○○○○○

Older single owner
●●●●●●●●●●

Enthusiastic hiker
●●●●○○○○○○

Older couple
●●●●●●●●●●

Countryside pursuits fan
●●○○○○○○○○

City dweller
●●●●●●●●●●

Beach lover
●●●●●●●●○○

Rural owner
●●●●●●●●○○

Canine sports competitor
●●●●●●●○○○

Hobby farmer
●●●●○○○○○○

AKC group: non-sporting

For another Boston Terrier crossbreed, see page 56.

German Pinscher

Height 20 in (51 cm)
Weight 35 lb (16 kg)
Country of origin Germany

The description of "pinscher" probably comes from a German word, translating as "biter." Although this should not be taken too literally, it reflects a typical terrierlike trait of this particular group of dogs. The German Pinscher—better known in its homeland as the Deutscher Pinscher—is of medium size, and was developed in the early 1800s. German Pinschers remain eager hunters, dispatching rodents instinctively. They tend to be always alert, so they do not make the most relaxing companions, compared with some breeds. However, these dogs are intelligent and learn quickly, reacting well to training. The German Pinscher is a relatively recent arrival in the United States, but its sleek good looks have seen its popularity in the show ring rise rapidly.

LIKES

* An active lifestyle
* A varied training routine
* Chasing toys

NEEDS

* Plenty of exercise
* Socialization
* Little grooming

Is this your perfect dog?

Teen living with parents
●●●●●●●○○○

Hobby farmer
●●●●●●●●●●

Young single owner
●●●●●●○○○○

Owner with physical disability
●●○○○○○○○○

Young couple
●●●●●●●●○○

Allergy sufferers
●●●●○○○○○○

Family with young kids
●●○○○○○○○○

Trend-centric owner
●●●●●●○○○○

Family with teenagers
●●●●●●●●○○

Individualist
●●●●●●●○○○

Older single owner
●●●○○○○○○○

Keen jogger
●●●●●●●○○○

Older couple
●●●○○○○○○○

Enthusiastic hiker
●●●●●●●●●●

City dweller
●●●●●●○○○○

Countryside pursuits fan
●●●●○○○○○○

Rural owner
●●●●●●●●●●

Beach lover
●●●●●●○○○○

Canine sports competitor
●●●●●●●●●●

AKC group: working

American Staffordshire Terrier

Height 19 in (48 cm)
Weight 50 lb (23 kg)
Country of origin United States

Strong and determined, the American Staffie, or AmStaff, is a more powerfully built breed than its English cousin (page 100), and is much more akin to the American Pit Bull Terrier, with its popular reputation for aggression. All these breeds have been used for dogfighting in the past, and even today they are not kindly disposed to other dogs—particularly other bull terriers. However, good socialization with other dogs in puppyhood can help to curb displays of aggression. American Staffordshire Terriers are usually very friendly and loyal toward people they know well. They love playing with tug toys and chews, and have a generally positive outlook on life. When out for a walk with your dog, remember that American Staffies often pull hard on the leash.

LIKES

* Playing
* Solo living
* Plenty of exercise

NEEDS

* Consistent training
* Neutering to curb aggression
* Minimal grooming

American Staffordshire Terrier and Mastiff

A formidable cross, **Amstiff** puppies tend to grow up to be large, determined, and very powerful. Typically smooth-coated, they come in a range of colors. Amstiffs require firm training to ensure they are under control at all times. Potentially aggressive, this cross should not be considered by inexperienced owners.

Is this your perfect dog?

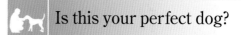

Teen living with parents
●●●●○○○○○○

Owner with physical disability
●●○○○○○○○○

Young single owner
●●●●●●○○○○

Allergy sufferers
●●●●○○○○○○

Young couple
●●●●●●○○○○

Trend-centric owner
●●○○○○○○○○

Family with young kids
●●○○○○○○○○

Individualist
●●●●●●○○○○

Family with teenagers
●●●●●●○○○○

Keen jogger
●●●●●●○○○○

Older single owner
●●●●●●○○○○

Enthusiastic hiker
●●●●●●●●○○

Older couple
●●●●●●○○○○

Countryside pursuits fan
●●○○○○○○○○

City dweller
●●●●○○○○○○

Beach lover
●●●●○○○○○○

Rural owner
●●●●●●●●●●

Canine sports competitor
●●●●●●○○○○

Hobby farmer
●●●●●●●●●●

AKC group: terrier

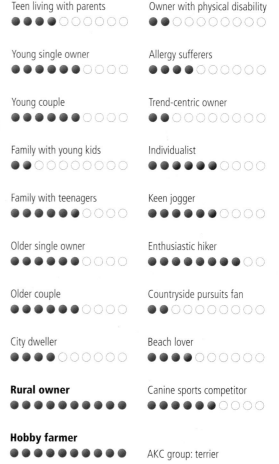

Staffordshire Bull Terrier

Height 16 in (41 cm)
Weight 38 lb (17.5 kg)
Country of origin United Kingdom

The Staffordshire Bull Terrier is named after the English county where it was first bred. Created to take part in dogfighting, these terriers are still likely to be aggressive toward other dogs—particularly those of its own kind—so should always be muzzled when allowed off the leash in areas where encounters with other dogs are likely. As household pets, Staffies make very friendly and loyal companions, but this is not a breed for someone who is unenthusiastic about investing considerable time in training a dog, starting with puppy socialization classes. As a typical fighting breed, the Staffie has a short, broad, powerful jaw, with relatively small, close-lying ears set back on the head.

LIKES	NEEDS
* Playing with toys	* Good training
* Solo living	* Careful supervision
* A large yard	* Veterinary care if suffering skin irritation

Is this your perfect dog?

Teen living with parents
●●●●○○○○○○

Owner with physical disability
●●○○○○○○○○

Young single owner
●●●●○○○○○○

Allergy sufferers
●●●●○○○○○○

Young couple
●●●●●●○○○○

Trend-centric owner
●●○○○○○○○○

Family with young kids
●●○○○○○○○○

Individualist
●●●●○○○○○○

Family with teenagers
●●●●●●○○○○

Keen jogger
●●●●●●●○○○

Older single owner
●●●●●●●●○○

Enthusiastic hiker
●●●●●●●●●●

Older couple
●●●●●●○○○○

Countryside pursuits fan
●●○○○○○○○○

City dweller
●●●●○○○○○○

Beach lover
●●●●●○○○○○

Rural owner
●●●●●●●●●●

Canine sports competitor
●●●●●●○○○○

Hobby farmer
●●●●●●●●●●

AKC group: terrier

Bull Terrier

Height 22 in (56 cm)
Weight 62 lb (28 kg)
Country of origin United Kingdom

There is no mistaking the Bull Terrier, thanks to its broad, convex Roman nose. These solidly built dogs are surprisingly powerful, and are not suitable for children, older people, or anyone unable to take them out for exercise. They are very determined, with an independent mindset, but equally, these traits enhance their character. Bull Terriers enjoy interacting with people. Many are white or predominantly white, reflecting the role played in their development by the now-extinct English White Terrier. Bull Terriers need to be kept out of the sun as much as possible, as they can develop skin cancers, particularly on the tips of their ears; however, special canine sunblock can help prevent this.

LIKES
* Tug toys
* Plenty of exercise
* Solo living

NEEDS
* Little grooming
* Care around other dogs
* Good leash control

Bull Terrier and Chihuahua

The ears are a very prominent feature of the **Bullhuahua**—large, broad, and upright—and enhance its appeal. These dogs are significantly smaller than Bull Terriers.

Is this your perfect dog?

Teen living with parents
●●●●○○○○○○

Owner with physical disability
●●○○○○○○○○

Young single owner
●●●●●●●●○○

Allergy sufferers
●●●●○○○○○○

Young couple
●●●●●●●●●●

Trend-centric owner
●●●●●●○○○○

Family with young kids
●●●●○○○○○○

Individualist
●●●●●●○○○○

Family with teenagers
●●●●●●●●●●

Keen jogger
●●●●●●●○○○

Older single owner
●●●●○○○○○○

Enthusiastic hiker
●●●●●●●●●●

Older couple
●●●●○○○○○○

Countryside pursuits fan
●●○○○○○○○○

City dweller
●●●●●●○○○○

Beach lover
●●●●●●○○○○

Rural owner
●●●●●●●●○○

Canine sports competitor
●●●●●●●○○○

Hobby farmer
●●●●●●○○○○

AKC group: terrier

Miniature Bull Terrier

Height 14 in (36 cm)
Weight 35 lb (16 kg)
Country of origin United Kingdom

This breed is basically identical in appearance to the Bull Terrier, but is smaller in size. It has all the attributes of its cousin (see page 101), including straightforward grooming needs, but is easier to accommodate and control. They make great companions, although they do have a stubborn streak. Training from an early age combined with good socialization is very important, because Miniature Bull Terriers are not instinctively friendly toward other dogs. They are very playful, especially as puppies, but choose toys carefully as these terriers are destructive. The Miniature Bull Terrier (unlike its larger relative) suffers from a condition known as primary lens luxation (PLL), typically from the age of three years onwards. There is now a DNA test for this condition, to ensure breeding stock will not pass it on to puppies.

LIKES

* Playing
* Being the only dog at home
* Plenty of exercise

NEEDS

* Careful feeding
* A yard
* Protection from sunburn

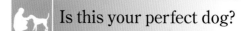

Is this your perfect dog?

Teen living with parents
●●●●●●○○○○

Owner with physical disability
●●○○○○○○○○

Young single owner
●●●●●●●●○○

Allergy sufferers
●●●●○○○○○○

Young couple
●●●●●●●●●○

Trend-centric owner
●●●●○○○○○○

Family with young kids
●●●●○○○○○○

Individualist
●●●●●●●○○○

Family with teenagers
●●●●●●●●●○

Keen jogger
●●●●●●●○○○

Older single owner
●●●●○○○○○○

Enthusiastic hiker
●●●●●●●●●●

Older couple
●●●●●●○○○○

Countryside pursuits fan
●●○○○○○○○○

City dweller
●●●●●●○○○○

Beach lover
●●●●●●●○○○

Rural owner
●●●●●●●●●●

Canine sports competitor
●●●●●●●○○○

Hobby farmer
●●●●●●○○○○

AKC group: terrier

Yorkshire Terrier

Height 9 in (23 cm)
Weight 7 lb (3 kg)
Country of origin United Kingdom

Do not be fooled by the coddled appearance of the Yorkshire Terrier, often portrayed with a bow in its hair. Yorkies still retain strong terrier instincts. There has been a tendency in the past toward miniaturization of this breed, which has contributed to some health issues, such as luxating patellas (slipped kneecaps). This condition hinders the dog's ability to move freely, and may require surgical correction. Named after its native county in England, the Yorkshire Terrier was created from a mixture of breeds, including the English Black-and-Tan Terrier. All Yorkies are black and tan at birth, and it can take three years for their coats to develop fully.

Is this your perfect dog?

LIKES
* Training sessions
* Urban life
* Exploring when walking

NEEDS
* Considerable grooming
* Discouragement from barking
* Dental health checks

Teen living with parents
●●●●●●●●○○

Hobby farmer
●●●●●●○○○○

Keen jogger
●●○○○○○○○○

Beach lover
●●●●○○○○○○

Young single owner
●●●●●●●●○○

Owner with physical disability
●●●●●●●○○○

Enthusiastic hiker
●●○○○○○○○○

Canine sports competitor
●●●●●●●○○○

Young couple
●●●●●●●●○○

Allergy sufferers
●●●●●●●●●○

Countryside pursuits fan
●●○○○○○○○○

AKC group: toy

Family with young kids
●●●●○○○○○○

Trend-centric owner
●●●●○○○○○○

Family with teenagers
●●●●●●○○○○

Individualist
●●○○○○○○○○

Older single owner
●●●●●●●●●●

Older couple
●●●●●●●●●●

City dweller
●●●●●●●●●●

Rural owner
●●●●●●●●○○

Yorkshire Terrier and Pomeranian

The **Yoranian**'s coat may be long, but it is not as tidy as the Yorkie's. Expect a much wider range of colors than with Yorkshire Terriers, and a generally more docile nature.

Australian Terrier

Height 10 in (25 cm)
Weight 14 lb (6.5 kg)
Country of origin Australia

There are two different types of Australian Terrier to choose from—the Australian Terrier and the Silky Terrier (opposite). The Australian Terrier is the earlier breed, created from crosses involving various terriers, including both the Skye and Yorkshire breeds. Further crossbreeding has since led to the development of the Australian Silky Terrier. In terms of temperament, Australian Terriers are typical of their kind, being alert, inquisitive, and ready to tackle rats or mice if given the chance. Extrovert by nature, this terrier has a big personality in a relatively small body. This may be reflected in a dislike for other dogs—sometimes even much larger individuals—when out for a walk, so close supervision is recommended.

LIKES

* Familiar people
* Acting as a watchdog
* Investigating burrows

NEEDS

* Barking deterrents
* Regular grooming
* A choice of toys

Australian Terrier and Australian Shepherd

Small in stature and friendly by nature, **Australian Shepterrier** puppies are likely to have rough coats and "blue" coloration (in reality, usually gray).

Is this your perfect dog?

Teen living with parents
●●●●●●●●○○

Hobby farmer
●●●●●●●●○○

Young single owner
●●●●●●●●○○

Owner with physical disability
●●●●●●●○○○○

Young couple
●●●●●●●●○○

Allergy sufferers
●●●●●●○○○○

Family with young kids
●●●●○○○○○○

Trend-centric owner
●●●○○○○○○○

Family with teenagers
●●●●●●○○○○

Individualist
●●○○○○○○○○

Older single owner
●●●●●●●●●●

Keen jogger
●●○○○○○○○○

Older couple
●●●●●●●●●●

Enthusiastic hiker
●●○○○○○○○○

City dweller
●●●●●●●●○○

Countryside pursuits fan
●●○○○○○○○○

Rural owner
●●●●●●●●○○

Beach lover
●●●●●○○○○○

Canine sports competitor
●●●●●●○○○○

AKC group: terrier

Silky Terrier

Height 10 in (25 cm)
Weight 10 lb (4.5 kg)
Country of origin Australia

Known by a wide variety of names—including the Australian Silky, the Sydney Silky, and the Silky Toy Terrier—crosses between the Australian Terrier and the Yorkshire Terrier gave rise to this popular, smaller companion breed. The Silky Terrier has a strong following in Australia, but is less common elsewhere—sometimes overlooked as a result of the popularity of dogs like the Yorkshire Terrier (page 103). As its name suggests, one of the breed's distinctive features is its coat, which has a silky texture and is not shed, making it hypoallergenic. Silky Terriers are lively, make alert watchdogs in spite of their small size, and can settle well in an apartment.

Is this your perfect dog?

LIKES	NEEDS
✷ Plenty of attention	✷ Considerable coat care
✷ Urban living	✷ Its teeth brushed
✷ Playing ball	✷ Lots of activities

Teen living with parents
●●●●●●●●○○

Owner with physical disability
●●●●●●○○○○

Beach lover
●●●●○○○○○○

Young single owner
●●●●●●●○○○

Allergy sufferers
●●●●●●●●●●

Canine sports competitor
●●●●●●●○○○

Young couple
●●●●●●●○○○

Trend-centric owner
●●●●○○○○○○

AKC group: toy

Family with young kids
●●●●○○○○○○

Individualist
●●○○○○○○○○

Family with teenagers
●●●●●●○○○○

Keen jogger
●●○○○○○○○○

Older single owner
●●●●●●●●●○

Enthusiastic hiker
●●○○○○○○○○

Older couple
●●●●●●●●●●

Countryside pursuits fan
●●○○○○○○○○

City dweller
●●●●●●●●○○

Rural owner
●●●●●●●○○○

Hobby farmer
●●●●●●●●○○

Silky Terrier and West Highland White Terrier

This cross between two terrier breeds results in very cute puppies of similar sizes. **Silklands** are great characters, and are often pale in color, but not pure white.

For another Silky Terrier crossbreed, see page 80.

Welsh Terrier

Height 15 in (38 cm)
Weight 20 lb (9 kg)
Country of origin United Kingdom

This traditional form of British terrier has tan coloring on the legs and face, offset against its predominantly black body. The Welsh Terrier is rough coated—traditionally described as "broken." Sometimes confused with the Airedale (page 110), the Welsh Terrier is in fact decidedly smaller in size. The breed's height meant that it was able to accompany hounds on foot—rather than being carried on horseback—venturing underground to flush out quarry, such as foxes. Welsh Terriers must be socialized, as they can be aggressive toward other dogs. Although wary of strangers, they will strike up a close bond with all people in their immediate family.

Welsh Terrier and Dachshund

An unusual but appealing cross, the appearance of the puppies depends on the size and coat type of their Dachshund parent. **Welshunds** will, however, be smaller than Welsh Terriers.

LIKES
* Digging
* Exploring countryside
* Plenty of praise

NEEDS
* Hand-stripping
* Patient training
* Lots of exercise

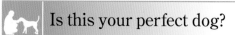

Is this your perfect dog?

Teen living with parents ●●●●●●○○○○	Owner with physical disability ●●●●○○○○○○
Young single owner ●●●●●●●○○○	Allergy sufferers ●●●●●●●●○○
Young couple ●●●●●●○○○○	Trend-centric owner ●●●●○○○○○○
Family with young kids ●●●●○○○○○○	Individualist ●●●●○○○○○○
Family with teenagers ●●●●●●●●●●	Keen jogger ●●●●●●●○○○
Older single owner ●●●●●●○○○○	**Enthusiastic hiker** ●●●●●●●●●●
Older couple ●●●●●●○○○○	Countryside pursuits fan ●●○○○○○○○○
City dweller ●●●●●●●●○○	Beach lover ●●●●●●●●○○
Rural owner ●●●●●●●●●●	**Canine sports competitor** ●●●●●●●●●●
Hobby farmer ●●●●●●●●●●	AKC group: terrier

Lakeland Terrier

Height 18 in (46 cm)
Weight 17 lb (7.5 kg)
Country of origin United Kingdom

The Lakeland Terrier evolved in England's Lake District as a working terrier, and was used to hunt a variety of quarry. Like other breeds, it appears to share its ancestry with the extinct Black-and-Tan Terrier. Its coat is suitably weatherproof, as it comes from one of the wettest areas in the United Kingdom. In typical terrier fashion, the coat consists of a dense, insulating undercoat and a wiry, weather-resistant topcoat. The hair is not generally shed, so stripping and trimming are required. The Lakeland can be hard to find, but it will prove a good pet and an alert guard dog.

LIKES

* Plenty of exercise
* Playing with toys
* Digging holes

NEEDS

* Time outside
* Secure fencing
* Recall training

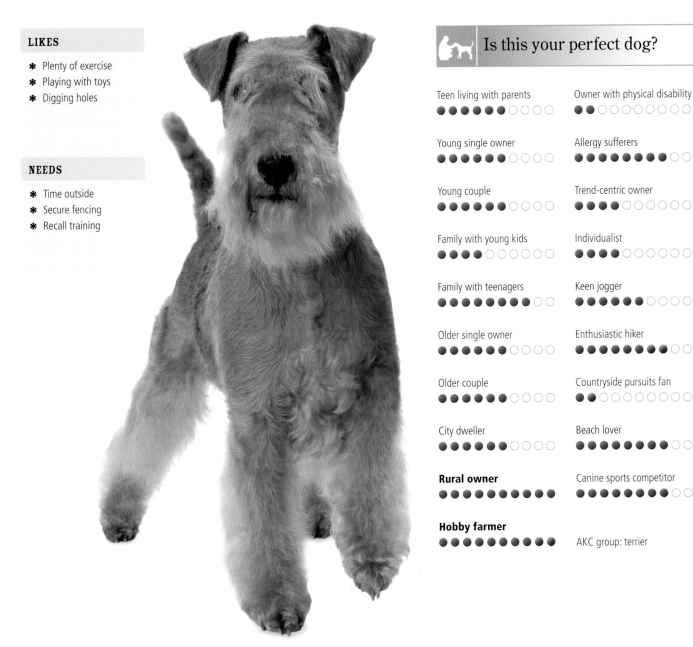

Is this your perfect dog?

Teen living with parents
●●●●●●○○○○

Owner with physical disability
●●○○○○○○○○

Young single owner
●●●●●●○○○○

Allergy sufferers
●●●●●●●●○○

Young couple
●●●●●●○○○○

Trend-centric owner
●●●●○○○○○○

Family with young kids
●●●●○○○○○○

Individualist
●●●●○○○○○○

Family with teenagers
●●●●●●●●○○

Keen jogger
●●●●●●●○○○

Older single owner
●●●●●●○○○○

Enthusiastic hiker
●●●●●●●●○○

Older couple
●●●●●●○○○○

Countryside pursuits fan
●●○○○○○○○○

City dweller
●●●●●●○○○○

Beach lover
●●●●●●●●○○

Rural owner
●●●●●●●●●●

Canine sports competitor
●●●●●●●●○○

Hobby farmer
●●●●●●●●●●

AKC group: terrier

Cesky Terrier

Height 14 in (36 cm)
Weight 18 lb (8 kg)
Country of origin Czech Republic

The Cesky Terrier (pronounced *ses-ki*)—also called the Bohemian Terrier—is a relative newcomer on the terrier scene, created in the mid 1900s by a Czech geneticist called Dr. František Horák. Horák's aim was to develop a type of short-legged terrier that was suited to working underground. He used various British terriers for this purpose, particularly the Sealyham, which the Cesky now resembles. There was no attempt made to dilute the feisty terrier temperament. These terriers are real personalities. The use of the Scottish Terrier (page 80) in the development of this breed has resulted in the transference of the gene for Scottie cramp.

LIKES

* Vanishing underground
* Exploring countryside
* Playing with toys

NEEDS

* Coat clipping
* Careful feeding
* Good training

Is this your perfect dog?

Teen living with parents
●●●●●●○○○○

Young single owner
●●●●●●●●○○

Young couple
●●●●●●●○○

Family with young kids
●●○○○○○○○○

Family with teenagers
●●●●●●●●○○

Older single owner
●●●●●●●●●○

Older couple
●●●●●●●●○○

City dweller
●●●●○○○○○○

Rural owner
●●●●●●●●●●

Hobby farmer
●●●●●●●●●●

Owner with physical disability
●●○○○○○○○○

Allergy sufferers
●●●●●●○○○○

Trend-centric owner
●●●○○○○○○○

Individualist
●●●●○○○○○○

Keen jogger
●●○○○○○○○○

Enthusiastic hiker
●●●●●●○○○○

Countryside pursuits fan
●●●●●●●●○○

Beach lover
●●●●●●○○○○

Canine sports competitor
●●●●●●○○○○

AKC group: terrier

Miniature Schnauzer

Height 14 in (36 cm)
Weight 20 lb (9 kg)
Country of origin Germany

A scaled-down version of the Standard Schnauzer, the Miniature Schnauzer's reduced size is thought to have been achieved by crossings using the Affenpinscher (page 113). Other breeds, including Pomeranians (page 133) and Miniature Poodles (page 126), may have also played a part in the development of this breed. As a result, the Miniature Schnauzer is more suited to being a companion than a working terrier, although it will still catch vermin, given the chance. These dogs also make good guardians.

The Miniature Schnauzer's wiry coat is typical of a Schnauzer, as is its coloration— you can choose from the traditional black, black and white patterning, a distinctive "salt-and-pepper" color, or a white variant, though this form is not commonly seen in the show ring.

Is this your perfect dog?

Teen living with parents	Allergy sufferers	Countryside pursuits fan
●●●●●●●●○○	●●●●●●●●○○	●●●●○○○○○○
Young single owner	Trend-centric owner	Beach lover
●●●●●●●●○○	●●●●●○○○○○	●●●●●●●●○○
Young couple	Individualist	**Canine sports competitor**
●●●●●●●●●●	●●●●○○○○○○	●●●●●●●●●●
Family with young kids	Keen jogger	
●●●●○○○○○○	●●○○○○○○○○	
Family with teenagers	Enthusiastic hiker	
●●●●●●●●●●	●●●●●●○○○○	
Older single owner		
●●●●●●●●○○	AKC group: terrier	
Older couple		
●●●●●●●●○○		
City dweller		
●●●●●●●●○○		
Rural owner		
●●●●●●●●●●		
Hobby farmer		
●●●●●●●●●●		
Owner with physical disability		
●●●●○○○○○○		

LIKES
* Being playful
* Careful grooming
* Chasing cats

NEEDS
* Checking for hip dysplasia
* No sweet foods
* No high-fat foods

Miniature Schnauzer and Brussels Griffon

Sniffons make lively companions. They are wire coated—as may be anticipated from their parents—but the hair is not as profuse as the Brussels Griffon.

Airedale Terrier

Height 23 in (58 cm)
Weight 44 lb (20 kg)
Country of origin United Kingdom

The distinctive Airedale is the largest of the British terriers, and originates from the region of the River Aire in Yorkshire, England. First used to hunt badgers in the 1800s, Airedales were used as messengers in the First World War, confirming their bravery. Unfortunately, Airedales tend to be less social than many breeds. They are not afraid to show dislike for other dogs, so close supervision when out for walks is important. Coat care is quite demanding, too. They are all black and tan, reflecting their ancestral link to the now-extinct English Terrier.

LIKES

* The outdoor life
* Exploring its environment
* Being the only dog at home

NEEDS

* Sound training
* Plenty of socialization
* Lots of exercise

Airedale Terrier and Poodle

Good-looking dogs, with long legs and curly coats, **Airedoodles** tend to be more social than Airedales. If a Standard Poodle is involved, the resulting puppies will grow to a similar size.

Is this your perfect dog?

Teen living with parents
●●●●○○○○○○

Young single owner
●●●●○○○○○○

Young couple
●●●●○○○○○○

Family with young kids
●●○○○○○○○○

Family with teenagers
●●●●●●○○○○

Older single owner
●●●●●●●●○○

Older couple
●●●●●●●●○○

City dweller
●●○○○○○○○○

Rural owner
●●●●●●●●●○

Hobby farmer
●●●●●●●●●●

Owner with physical disability
●●○○○○○○○○

Allergy sufferers
●●●●●●○○○○

Trend-centric owner
●●●●●○○○○○

Individualist
●●●●○○○○○○

Keen jogger
●●●●●●○○○○

Enthusiastic hiker
●●●●●●●●●●

Countryside pursuits fan
●●○○○○○○○○

Beach lover
●●●●○○○○○○

Canine sports competitor
●●●●●●●●○○

AKC group: terrier

Black Russian Terrier

Height 30 in (76 cm)
Weight 144 lb (65 kg)
Country of origin Russia

Although popularly described as a terrier, this breed is effectively a working dog, bred by the Russian military after the Second World War. The Airedale Terrier and German Schnauzer contributed to the breed's development, along with many other dogs including the Rottweiler (page 194), Borzoi (page 71), Great Dane (page 174), and Moscow Retriever. No fewer than 17 different crosses were used to create the Black Russian Terrier of today. This helps explain why these dogs can be quite variable in size, although standardization is now well advanced, with the breed being seen in the show ring. The Black Russian Terrier's long coat protects against the bitterly cold Russian winters, and its black coloration was required for stealth.

LIKES

* Being outdoors
* Family members
* Being protective

NEEDS

* Sensible training
* Regular grooming
* Good socialization

Is this your perfect dog?

Teen living with parents	Young couple	Older single owner	Hobby farmer
●●●●●○○○○○	●●●●●●●○○○	●●●●○○○○○○	●●●●●●●●○○

Young single owner	Family with young kids	Older couple	Owner with physical disability
●●●●○○○○○○	●●○○○○○○○○	●●●●○○○○○○	●●○○○○○○○○

Family with teenagers	City dweller	Allergy sufferers
●●●●●●●●●○	●●○○○○○○○○	●●●●●●○○○○

Rural owner	Trend-centric owner
●●●●●●●●●●	●●●●○○○○○○

Individualist
●●●●○○○○○○

Keen jogger
●●●●●●●●○○

Enthusiastic hiker
●●●●●●●●●●

Countryside pursuits fan
●●○○○○○○○○

Beach lover
●●●●●●○○○○

Canine sports competitor
●●●●●●●●○○

AKC group: working

Black Russian Terrier and Irish Wolfhound

The input of the Irish Wolfhound means that **Wolf Terriers** will grow into large dogs, as hinted at in early life by their large feet. Dogs of this crossbreed have a relatively laid-back personality.

Brussels Griffon

Height 8 in (20 cm)
Weight 11 lb (5 kg)
Country of origin Belgium

Named after the Belgian capital, where it originated, the Brussels Griffon is known in its homeland as the Griffon Bruxellois. Traditionally, it is black, but there is also a reddish-brown variant, the Griffon Belge (Belgian Griffon). The "griffon" description refers to the rough, tousled coat, but there is also a smooth-coated dog in the Brussels Griffon group called a Petit Brabançon, developed by crossing griffons with Pugs (page 125). All dogs in the griffon group are lively, with a terrier-type personality, as a result of their origins as rodent catchers. They enjoy investigating holes. Bold by nature, they make alert guardians and are not especially social with other dogs.

LIKES

* Time to be curious
* Being a one-person dog
* Playing games

NEEDS

* Careful socialization
* Opportunities to run
* Plenty of attention

Brussels Griffon and Pug

The coat of the **Brug** is relatively short and tousled, and its face is quite compact and rounded, creating an attractive appearance. Fawn-colored puppies retain the Pug's black mask.

Is this your perfect dog?

Teen living with parents
●●●●●●●●○○

Owner with physical disability
●●●●●●●○○○

Young single owner
●●●●●●●●○○

Allergy sufferers
●●○○○○○○○○

Young couple
●●●●●●○○○○

Trend-centric owner
●●●●○○○○○○

Family with young kids
●●●○○○○○○○

Individualist
●●●●●●○○○○

Family with teenagers
●●●●●○○○○○

Keen jogger
●●○○○○○○○○

Older single owner
●●●●●●●●●●

Enthusiastic hiker
●●○○○○○○○○

Older couple
●●●●●●●●●●

Countryside pursuits fan
●●○○○○○○○○

City dweller
●●●●●●●●●●

Beach lover
●●●●●●○○○○

Rural owner
●●●●●●●●○○

Canine sports competitor
●●●●●●○○○○

Hobby farmer
●●●●●●●●○○

AKC group: toy

For other Brussels Griffon crossbreeds, see pages 109 and 118.

Affenpinscher

Height 10 in (25 cm)
Weight 8 lb (4 kg)
Country of origin Germany

Part of the Affenpinscher's appeal stems from its cheeky, monkeylike face, which reflects its mischievous nature—particularly when the head is tilted to the side, looking up at you. This has led the breed to be fondly referred to as the monkey dog.

Affenpinschers were originally bred as rat-catching dogs several centuries ago, and today this translates to an instinctive curiosity. Black individuals are most commonly seen, but there are other colors, too, including bicolors such as red and tan. They have a very determined side to their character, and are not easily intimidated, which makes them excellent guardians. These terrierlike dogs have strong personalities, but are usually friendly with other dogs and even cats.

Affenpinscher and Chihuahua

Although quite variable in appearance, the **Affenhuahua**'s ears are large in most cases, and may be relatively widely spaced. Black coloration inherited from the Affenpinscher parent is often seen.

LIKES
* Exploring on walks
* Chasing toys
* Being a companion

NEEDS
* Tearstaining wiped away
* Efficient house-training
* Activity to prevent boredom

 ## Is this your perfect dog?

Teen living with parents
●●●●●●●●○○

Owner with physical disability
●●●●●●○○○○

Young single owner
●●●●●○○○○○

Allergy sufferers
●●○○○○○○○○

Young couple
●●●●●●○○○○

Trend-centric owner
●●○○○○○○○○

Family with young kids
●●●●○○○○○○

Individualist
●●●●○○○○○○

Family with teenagers
●●●●●●●○○○

Keen jogger
●●○○○○○○○○

Older single owner
●●●●●●●●●●

Enthusiastic hiker
●●○○○○○○○○

Older couple
●●●●●●●●●○

Countryside pursuits fan
●●○○○○○○○○

City dweller
●●●●●●●●●●

Beach lover
●●●●●●●○○○

Rural owner
●●●●●●●●○○

Canine sports competitor
●●●●●●●○○○

Hobby farmer
●●●●●●●●○○

AKC group: toy

Shih Tzu

Height 11 in (28 cm)
Weight 16 lb (7 kg)
Country of origin Tibet

This ancient Chinese breed was unknown in Europe until the early twentieth century. Like some of the other small companion breeds, the Shih Tzu—whose name is pronounced *sheet-soo* and translates as "lion dog"—is bold by nature. Although generally quiet, it is capable of barking loudly if disturbed. Puppies are born with relatively short coats, but they soon grow the magnificent long, trailing hair that typifies the breed. This luxurious coat gives protection against the cold in the Shih Tzu's homeland; the undercoat has a dense and woolly texture. Coloration is variable. They are sometimes called chrysanthemum dogs, because of the resemblance of the hair to the flower.

LIKES

* Children and other dogs
* Playing games
* Family life

NEEDS

* Dedicated grooming
* Discouragement from jumping up
* Walks in parks

Shih Tzu and Bichon Frisé

These particular designer dogs have a very cute appearance. **Zuchons** tend to be light in color, with dark areas on the face and ears, sometimes extending down the back.

 ## Is this your perfect dog?

Teen living with parents
●●●●●●○○○○

Older single owner
●●●●●●●●○○

Owner with physical disability
●●●●●●○○○○

Young single owner
●●●●●●○○○○

Older couple
●●●●●●●●○○

Allergy sufferers
●●○○○○○○○○

Young couple
●●●●●●●○○○

City dweller
●●●●●●●●○○

Trend-centric owner
●●●●○○○○○○

Family with young kids
●●●●●●●○○○

Rural owner
●●●●●●○○○○

Individualist
●●●●●○○○○○

Family with teenagers
●●●●●●○○○○

Hobby farmer
●●●●○○○○○○

Keen jogger
●●○○○○○○○○

Enthusiastic hiker
●●○○○○○○○○

Countryside pursuits fan
●●○○○○○○○○

Beach lover
●●●●●●○○○○

Canine sports competitor
●●●●○○○○○○

AKC group: toy

For another Shih Tzu crossbreed, see page 131.

Bichon Frisé

Height   12 in (30 cm)
Weight   16 lb (7 kg)
Country of origin   Tenerife, Canary Islands

The Bichon Frisé—pronounced *bee-shon free-zay*—is a popular, playful breed. It is typically white in color, with large, dark eyes. The Bichon Frisé shares a common ancestry with the Poodle, tracing its roots back to the French water retriever known as the Barbet. For this reason, it is often regarded as a hypoallergenic breed; however, dander from the coat can be released into the air, and may cause a reaction if you are very sensitive. The Bichon Frisé is an ideal companion breed, well-suited to urban living. These little dogs respond well to training and thrive on positive encouragement, as they are very sensitive by nature.

Bichon Frisé and Miniature Schnauzer

Likely to have a more assertive character than a Bichon Frisé, the **Chonzer** is an alert and inquisitive companion. Its coloring is normally quite pale.

LIKES

* Playing games
* Lots of attention
* Family life

NEEDS

* Daily brushing
* Regular coat trimming
* Early training

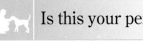

Is this your perfect dog?

Teen living with parents
●●●●●●●●○○

Owner with physical disability
●●●●●●●●○○

Young single owner
●●●●●●●●○○

Allergy sufferers
●●●●●●●●●●

Young couple
●●●●●●●●○○

Trend-centric owner
●●●●●●●●●○○

Family with young kids
●●●●●●●●○○

Individualist
●●●●○○○○○○

Family with teenagers
●●●●●●●●○○

Keen jogger
●●○○○○○○○○

Older single owner
●●●●●●●●●●

Enthusiastic hiker
●●○○○○○○○○

Older couple
●●●●●●●●●●

Countryside pursuits fan
●●○○○○○○○○

City dweller
●●●●●●●●●●

Beach lover
●●●●●●○○○○

Rural owner
●●●●●●○○○○

Canine sports competitor
●●●●●●●●○○

Hobby farmer
●●●●○○○○○○

AKC group: non-sporting

For another Bichon Frisé crossbreed, see page 114.

Maltese

Height 10 in (25 cm)
Weight 13 lb (6 kg)
Country of origin Malta

Like many ancient breeds, the Maltese has altered in appearance down the centuries, with its coat today being longer, flatter, and seemingly silkier than that of its ancestors. This gives the breed a more elegant appearance, but also means that grooming is very important. These dogs have no undercoat, and are considered relatively hypoallergenic. Being white in color, the coat can get very muddy on country walks. Tearstaining from the large eyes can be a problem, so be prepared to wipe these deposits away as necessary. Despite its appearance, the Maltese is a relatively tough, hardy breed, and, like other small dogs, can be quite noisy.

LIKES

* Being with people
* Urban living
* Playing games

NEEDS

* Daily coat care
* Training not to bark
* Plenty of exercise

Maltese and Cavalier King Charles Spaniel

A broad head and expressive eyes are typical features of this cross between two attractive companion breeds. The **Cav-a-malt**'s coat often has a tousled appearance, and is usually bi- or tricolored.

Is this your perfect dog?

Teen living with parents	Owner with physical disability
●●●●●●○○○○	●●●●●●●●○○
Young single owner	**Allergy sufferers**
●●●●●●○○○○	●●●●●●●●●●
Young couple	Trend-centric owner
●●●●●●●●○○	●●●●●●○○○○
Family with young kids	Individualist
●●●●●●●○○○	●●●●○○○○○○
Family with teenagers	Keen jogger
●●●●●●●●○○	●●○○○○○○○○
Older single owner	Enthusiastic hiker
●●●●●●●●●●	●●○○○○○○○○
Older couple	Countryside pursuits fan
●●●●●●●●●●	●●○○○○○○○○
City dweller	Beach lover
●●●●●●●●●●	●●●●●●○○○○
Rural owner	Canine sports competitor
●●●●○○○○○○	●●●●●●●○○○
Hobby farmer	
●●●●●○○○○○	AKC group: toy

Havanese

Height 14 in (36 cm)
Weight 13 lb (6 kg)
Country of origin Cuba

Believed to have close links to the bichon breeds, which were developed around the Mediterranean, the Havanese was actually developed thousands of miles away on the Caribbean island of Cuba. The Havanese's coat is lightweight, meaning that in spite of their long hair, these little dogs can feel the cold. One obvious point of difference from the bichon breeds is the Havanese's more lively gait. Like other members of the group, it has been developed as a companion breed, and enjoys human company. Havanese will start to show signs of stress if left alone for long periods on a regular basis. They are likely to develop symptoms of separation anxiety, such as barking repeatedly and becoming destructive. However, they are usually quiet by nature.

LIKES	NEEDS
✽ Being with people	✽ Lots of affection
✽ Playing games	✽ Daily coat care
✽ Plenty of activity	✽ Early house-training

Is this your perfect dog?

Teen living with parents	Owner with physical disability
●●●●●●●●○○	●●●●●●●●○○
Young single owner	**Allergy sufferers**
●●●●●●○○○○	●●●●●●●●●●
Young couple	Trend-centric owner
●●●●●●●●○○	●●●●●●○○○○
Family with young kids	Individualist
●●●●●●○○○○	●●●●●○○○○
Family with teenagers	Keen jogger
●●●●●●●●○○	●●○○○○○○○○
Older single owner	Enthusiastic hiker
●●●●●●●●●●	●●○○○○○○○○
Older couple	Countryside pursuits fan
●●●●●●●●●●	●●○○○○○○○○
City dweller	Beach lover
●●●●●●●●●●	●●●●●●○○○○
Rural owner	Canine sports competitor
●●●●○○○○○○	●●●●●●●○○○
Hobby farmer	
●●●●○○○○○○	AKC group: toy

For a Havanese crossbreed, see page 119.

English Toy Spaniel

Height 12 in (30 cm)
Weight 18 lb (8 kg)
Country of origin United Kingdom

The English Toy Spaniel became popular at the court of the English King Charles II in the late 1600s, and so it is also known as the King Charles Spaniel. The traditional color is black and tan, although in the past there were other variants. These were ultimately grouped together as English Toy Spaniels, having previously been separate breeds. The breed now includes the ruby (solid red), Blenheim (red and white), and the tricolored Prince Charles. English Toy Spaniels are excellent pets, particularly for homes with young children, although they have been usurped in popularity by the Cavalier King Charles Spaniel (opposite). Puppies should receive a thorough health check from your veterinarian in order to identify any potential problems that this breed might be susceptible to.

English Toy Spaniel and Brussels Griffon

A compact face is a common feature of the **English Toy Griffon**, a characteristic shared by both parent breeds. The crossbreed's coloration and coat type is far more variable.

Is this your perfect dog?

Teen living with parents
●●●●●●●●○○

Owner with physical disability
●●●●●●○○○○

Young single owner
●●●●●●○○○○

Allergy sufferers
●●○○○○○○○○

Young couple
●●●●●●●●○○

Trend-centric owner
●●●●○○○○○○

Family with young kids
●●●●●●●●●●

Individualist
●●●●●○○○○○

Family with teenagers
●●●●●●●●○○

Keen jogger
●●○○○○○○○○

Older single owner
●●●●●●●●●●

Enthusiastic hiker
●●○○○○○○○○

Older couple
●●●●●●●●●○

Countryside pursuits fan
●●○○○○○○○○

City dweller
●●●●●●●●●●

Beach lover
●●●●●○○○○○

Rural owner
●●●●●●○○○○

Canine sports competitor
●●●●●●○○○○

Hobby farmer
●●●●○○○○○○

AKC group: toy

LIKES

* Human company
* Urban living
* Limited exercise

NEEDS

* Daily grooming
* Patient house-training
* Regular ear checks

Cavalier King Charles Spaniel

Height 12 in (30 cm)
Weight 18 lb (8 kg)
Country of origin United Kingdom

The appearance of the English Toy Spaniel, or King Charles Spaniel, has radically changed over time, to the extent that, by the early twentieth century, it was very different in appearance from dogs portrayed in contemporary paintings of King Charles II's court. Perhaps most significantly, the facial shape of these dogs has become more compact, resulting in a stubby nose. One wealthy American enthusiast was eager to revert to the original type of toy spaniel, and put up a large prize in the 1920s at Britain's Crufts dog show to entice breeders to produce the classic form again. The emerging breed type became known as the Cavalier King Charles Spaniel. It has since become very popular, and is far more common today than its relative. A thorough health check when you first acquire your pet is essential.

Is this your perfect dog?

LIKES

* Playing
* Family life
* Lots of attention

NEEDS

* Regular health checks
* Strict feeding
* Moderate exercise

AKC group: toy

Teen living with parents	City dweller	Keen jogger
●●●●●●●●○○	●●●●●●●●●●	●●○○○○○○○○

Young single owner	Rural owner	Enthusiastic hiker
●●●●●●○○○○	●●●●●●○○○○	●●○○○○○○○○

Young couple	Hobby farmer	Countryside pursuits fan
●●●●●●●○○○	●●●●○○○○○○	●●○○○○○○○○

Family with young kids	Owner with physical disability	Beach lover
●●●●●●●●●●	●●●●●●○○○○	●●●●●●○○○○

Family with teenagers	Allergy sufferers	Canine sports competitor
●●●●●●●●○○	●●●●○○○○○○	●●●●●●○○○○

Older single owner	Trend-centric owner
●●●●●●●●●○	●●●●●●○○○○

Older couple	Individualist
●●●●●●●●●●	●●●●○○○○○○

Cavalier King Charles Spaniel and Havanese

This cross tends to result in puppies with straighter, less tousled coats than some similar crosses. A **Cavanese** should be a good choice for allergy sufferers, as these dogs don't tend to shed.

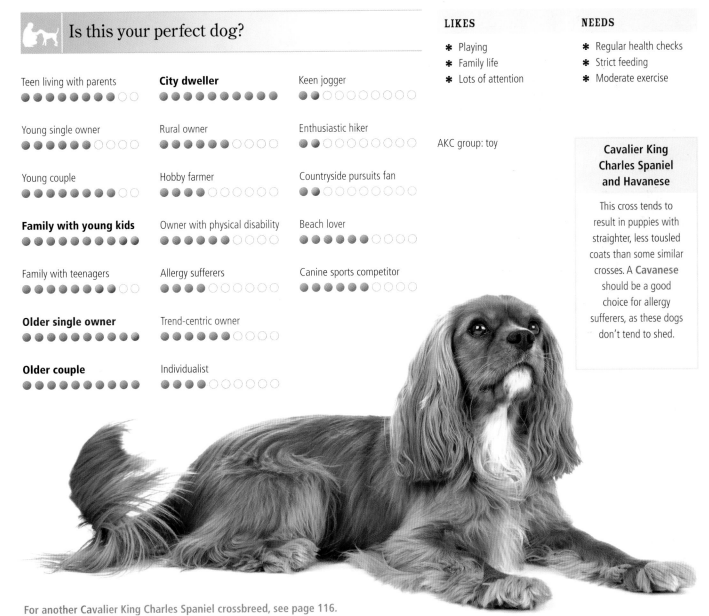

For another Cavalier King Charles Spaniel crossbreed, see page 116.

Löwchen

Height 13 in (33 cm)
Weight 18 lb (8 kg)
Country of origin France

In the early 1970s, the Löwchen was regarded as the rarest breed in the world, and even today it is scarce. The breed has a very long history, dating back to the 1400s, and deserves to be more popular, being instinctively friendly by nature and patient with children. Its name—pronounced *lerv-chun*—literally means "little lion dog," and this describes the way in which its coat is traditionally trimmed. This trimming style may have been adopted because these dogs were originally used as bed-warmers in the homes of their wealthy owners. Löwchens' coats are various solid (single) colors, and some individuals are stockier than others. The Löwchen is a member of the bichon group, which is more obvious in its untrimmed state.

LIKES

* Regular exercise
* Being a family pet
* Playing

NEEDS

* Good training
* Some trimming
* Lots of attention

Is this your perfect dog?

Teen living with parents
● ● ● ● ● ● ● ○ ○

Owner with physical disability
● ● ● ● ● ● ● ○ ○

Young single owner
● ● ● ● ● ○ ○ ○ ○

Allergy sufferers
● ● ● ● ● ● ● ● ○

Young couple
● ● ● ● ● ● ● ○ ○

Trend-centric owner
● ● ● ● ○ ○ ○ ○ ○

Family with young kids
● ● ● ● ● ● ● ○ ○

Individualist
● ● ● ● ● ● ● ○ ○

Family with teenagers
● ● ● ● ● ● ● ● ●

Keen jogger
● ● ○ ○ ○ ○ ○ ○ ○

Older single owner
● ● ● ● ● ● ● ● ●

Enthusiastic hiker
● ● ○ ○ ○ ○ ○ ○ ○

Older couple
● ● ● ● ● ● ● ● ●

Countryside pursuits fan
● ● ○ ○ ○ ○ ○ ○ ○

City dweller
● ● ● ● ● ● ● ● ●

Beach lover
● ● ● ● ● ● ○ ○ ○

Rural owner
● ● ● ● ● ● ○ ○ ○

Canine sports competitor
● ● ● ● ● ● ○ ○ ○

Hobby farmer
● ● ● ● ○ ○ ○ ○ ○

AKC group: non-sporting

Italian Greyhound

Height 15 in (38 cm)
Weight 15 lb (7 kg)
Country of origin Italy

While some companion breeds were developed independently, the Italian Greyhound was created by scaling down larger Greyhounds through selective breeding. This miniaturization process led to the small breed becoming vulnerable to mobility problems for a period at the end of the 1800s, but careful breeding since then has overcome this. One characteristic of this breed is its high-stepping gait, which means the Italian Greyhound is much more inclined to prance than its larger relative. These small greyhounds can be nervous with strangers, but otherwise make excellent companions. Italian Greyhounds are often used for lure coursing and thrive on short runs, in terms of exercise. The Italian Greyhound's sleek coat needs very little grooming, but the dog has no undercoat and is vulnerable to the cold.

Is this your perfect dog?

Italian Greyhound and Jack Russell Terrier

This cross combines the best traits of both parents, lessening the instinctive nervousness of the Italian Greyhound and the readiness of the Jack Russell to venture underground. **Italjacks** dislike the cold.

Teen living with parents
●●●●●●●●○○

Allergy sufferers
●●●●●●●●○○

Countryside pursuits fan
●●●●●●○○○○

Young single owner
●●●●●●●●○○

Trend-centric owner
●●●●●●○○○○

Beach lover
●●●●●●○○○○

Young couple
●●●●●●●●●●

Individualist
●●●●○○○○○○

Canine sports competitor
●●●●●●○○○○

AKC group: toy

Family with young kids
●●○○○○○○○○

Keen jogger
●●●●○○○○○○

Family with teenagers
●●●●○○○○○○

Enthusiastic hiker
●●●●○○○○○○

Older single owner
●●●●●●●●●●

Older couple
●●●●●●●●●●

City dweller
●●●●●●●●●●

Rural owner
●●●●●●●●○○

Hobby farmer
●●●●●○○○○○

Owner with physical disability
●●●●●●○○○○

LIKES

* A quiet life
* Careful handling
* Stretching out

NEEDS

* A coat for cold or wet days
* Good socialization
* A daily run

Chihuahua

Height 9 in (23 cm)
Weight 6 lb (2.5 kg)
Country of origin Mexico

The Chihuahua has become very popular in recent years, thanks to a range of celebrity owners and film and television appearances. Chihuahuas are the smallest breed in the world, and this has also enhanced their appeal, ensuring their status as the ultimate "handbag dog," well suited to city living. There are both smooth- and long-coated forms, and, in contrast to many breeds, no restrictions on either their coloration or patterning apply in the show ring. The Chihuahua—named after a Mexican state—first became popular in the United States in the 1850s. Its origins are unknown, but it may be a relic breed, descended from dogs kept by the indigenous people of Central America in the pre-Columbian era. As they are not particularly robust dogs, Chihuahuas are less suited to homes with young children.

LIKES

* Other Chihuahuas
* Being quite noisy
* Lots of attention

NEEDS

* Careful handling
* A varied diet
* Sensible training

Chihuahua and Dachshunds

Their large, low-set ears give **Chiweenies** a very distinctive appearance. Coat type is influenced by individual parents, but smooth-coated crosses seem to be the most popular.

Is this your perfect dog?

Teen living with parents	●●●●●●○○○○
Young single owner	●●●●○○○○○○
Young couple	●●●●●●○○○○
Family with young kids	●●○○○○○○○○
Family with teenagers	●●●●○○○○○○
Older single owner	●●●●●●●●●○
Older couple	●●●●●●●●●○
City dweller	●●●●●●●●●●
Rural owner	●●●●●●○○○○
Hobby farmer	●●●●○○○○○○
Owner with physical disability	●●●●●●●●○○
Allergy sufferers	●●●●●●○○○○
Trend-centric owner	●●●●●●●●●●
Individualist	●●●●●●●●○○
Keen jogger	●●○○○○○○○○
Enthusiastic hiker	●●○○○○○○○○
Countryside pursuits fan	●●○○○○○○○○
Beach lover	●●●●●●○○○○
Canine sports competitor	●●●●●●●●○○
AKC group: toy	

For another Chihuahua crossbreed, see page 101.

Chinese Crested

Height	13 in (33 cm)
Weight	10 lb (4.5 kg)
Country of origin	China

The Chinese Crested is an unusual breed, occurring in two forms: those with normal coats—known as powderpuffs—which play an important part in the breeding program, and the better-known, hairless form. In breeding, one of each coat type is always paired together to ensure these dogs are kept healthy, and both coat types may be expected in a litter. Be sure to check the mouth of the hairless form of the breed to make sure your dog has a good set of teeth, as hairlessness can affect the number of teeth. In hairless Chinese Crested dogs, there will still be hair present on the extremities of the body, and variable skin patterning. The hair on the head forms the crest, while that on the tail creates a plume. The hair around the feet is described as the breed's socks.

LIKES

* Indoor life
* Exploring when walking
* Sleeping with a blanket

NEEDS

* Protection from cold and sunburn
* Good socialization
* Occasional wiping of skin

Is this your perfect dog?

Teen living with parents	Owner with physical disability
●●●●●●●○○○	●●●●○○○○○○
Young single owner	Allergy sufferers
●●●●●●●●○○	●●●●●●○○○○
Young couple	Trend-centric owner
●●●●●●●●○○	●●●●●●●●○○
Family with young kids	**Individualist**
●●●●○○○○○○	●●●●●●●●●●
Family with teenagers	Keen jogger
●●●●●○○○○○	●●○○○○○○○○
Older single owner	Enthusiastic hiker
●●●●●●●●●●	●●●●○○○○○○
Older couple	Countryside pursuits fan
●●●●●●●●●●	●●○○○○○○○○
City dweller	Beach lover
●●●●●●●●●●	●●●●○○○○○○
Rural owner	Canine sports competitor
●●●●●●○○○○	●●●●●●●○○○
Hobby farmer	
●●●●○○○○○○	AKC group: toy

Chinese Crested and Bichon Frisé

The **Chinese Frisé** is a relatively uncommon cross. When the powderpuff form is used, the resulting puppies will have a shorter coat than their Chinese Crested parent. White coats often predominate in the hairless cross, leaving these dogs vulnerable to sunburn.

Pekingese

Height 9 in (23 cm)
Weight 12 lb (5.5 kg)
Country of origin China

Pekingese were highly popular at the Chinese imperial court, but remained unknown in the West until the 1860s. Affectionately known as Pekes, these small toy dogs were originally called "sleeve dogs," as they could be carried in the sleeves of a courtier's garment. Today, these dogs retain characteristics of their aristocratic breeding, such as hair covering their paws, which allows them to move silently, and bowed legs, which prevents them from wandering too far. Pekes are very alert dogs, and make excellent guardians. Unfortunately, the breed is vulnerable to intervertebral disk problems, and must not be encouraged to jump on furniture or run up stairs. When exercising a Pekingese, a harness and leash combination, rather than a collar, is recommended, to lessen the risk of injury.

LIKES

* Being obstinate
* A lapdog lifestyle
* Apartment living

NEEDS

* Tearstaining wiped away
* To avoid exercise in hot weather
* Regular grooming

AKC group: toy

 ## Is this your perfect dog?

Teen living with parents ●●●●●●○○○○	Family with teenagers ●●●●○○○○○○	Allergy sufferers ●●○○○○○○○○
Young single owner ●●●●●●○○○○	**Older single owner** ●●●●●●●●○○	Trend-centric owner ●●●●○○○○○○
Young couple ●●●●●●○○○○	**Older couple** ●●●●●●●●●○	Individualist ●●●●○○○○○○
Family with young kids ●●●●○○○○○○	**City dweller** ●●●●●●●●●○	Keen jogger ●●○○○○○○○○
	Rural owner ●●●●○○○○○○	Enthusiastic hiker ●●○○○○○○○○
	Hobby farmer ●●○○○○○○○○	Countryside pursuits fan ●●○○○○○○○○
	Owner with physical disability ●●●●●●●●●○	Beach lover ●●○○○○○○○○
		Canine sports competitor ●●○○○○○○○○

Pekingese and West Highland White Terrier

The West Highland White's influence is more likely to be apparent in the conformation (build) of these dogs than their coloration. **Peke-a-wests** usually have longer, straighter legs compared to pure Pekingese.

For another Pekingese crossbreed, see page 97.

Pug

Height 11 in (28 cm)
Weight 18 lb (8 kg)
Country of origin China

Pugs are assertive little dogs, and are very popular. Their appearance has changed over time, with their faces becoming flatter, and the noses more compact. This has made them more inclined to snore loudly when sleeping, particularly as they grow older. Pugs' wrinkled faces may suggest that they are frowning, but these mini-mastiffs are lively and friendly dogs by nature. They have been around for 2,000 years, and the breed is closely associated with the Dutch House of Orange. The breed was thought to have been brought to Europe originally by Dutch merchants. A Pug also once saved the life of Prince William of Orange, barking to alert him to an assassin, which is especially unusual—Pugs are normally quiet by nature.

LIKES

* Being greedy
* Playing
* Family life

NEEDS

* Little grooming
* Moderate exercise
* Good training

 ## Is this your perfect dog?

Teen living with parents
●●●●●●●●●●

Family with teenagers
●●●●●●●●○○

Rural owner
●●●●●●○○○○

Keen jogger
●●○○○○○○○○

Young single owner
●●●●●●●●○○

Older single owner
●●●●●●●●●●

Hobby farmer
●●●●○○○○○○

Enthusiastic hiker
●●○○○○○○○○

Young couple
●●●●●●●●○○

Older couple
●●●●●●●●●●

Owner with physical disability
●●●●●●●●○○

Countryside pursuits fan
●●○○○○○○○○

Family with young kids
●●●●●●○○○○

City dweller
●●●●●●●●●●

Allergy sufferers
●●●●●○○○○○

Beach lover
●●●●●●●○○○

Trend-centric owner
●●●●●●●●○○

Canine sports competitor
●●●●●●○○○○

Individualist
●●●●●●○○○○

AKC group: toy

Pug and Beagle

One of the most popular designer dogs, the **Puggle** represents a combination of two extrovert, attractive breeds. Puggles need less exercise than Beagles, and are also less inclined to run off after scents.

For other Pug crossbreeds, see pages 112 and 157.

Miniature and Toy Poodles

Height 9–15 in (23–38 cm)
Weight 4–18 lb (2–8 kg)
Country of origin France

Scaled down from the larger standard variety (page 46), with a view to creating companion breeds, the Toy and Miniature Poodles are identical, except in terms of their size. Sometimes when breeds are reduced in size, there can be health issues. However, a veterinary check during the puppy's vaccinations should highlight any potential concerns. The Miniature was intended to be the only smaller variant, but in time the Toy was created, and was even smaller. Both forms are bred in a typical range of Poodle coat colors, and require similar grooming care. The most straightforward coat styling is the lamb or puppy clip—perfect if you just want your Poodle as a companion and pet.

LIKES

✱ Showing off
✱ Learning tricks
✱ Agility competitions

NEEDS

✱ Good dental care
✱ Regular coat trimming
✱ Plenty of toys

Is this your perfect dog?

Teen living with parents
●●●●●●●●○○

Owner with physical disability
●●●●●●●●○○

Young single owner
●●●●●●●●○○

Allergy sufferers
●●●●●●●●●●

Young couple
●●●●●●●●○○

Trend-centric owner
●●●●●●●●○○

Family with young kids
●●●●●●●○○○

Individualist
●●●●●●○○○○

Family with teenagers
●●●●●○○○○○

Keen jogger
●●○○○○○○○○

Older single owner
●●●●●●●●●○

Enthusiastic hiker
●●○○○○○○○○

Older couple
●●●●●●●●●●

Countryside pursuits fan
●●○○○○○○○○

City dweller
●●●●●●●○○○

Beach lover
●●●●●●●●○○

Rural owner
●●●●●●○○○○

Canine sports competitor
●●●●●●●●●●

Hobby farmer
●●●●○○○○○○

AKC group: Miniature Poodles, non-sporting; Toy Poodles, toy.

For other Toy and Miniature Poodle crossbreeds, see pages 30, 78, 81, and 88.

Miniature Pinscher

Height 16 in (41 cm)
Weight 22 lb (10 kg)
Country of origin Germany

Another scaled-down version of a larger dog, the Min Pin, as it is often known, was bred from the old German Pinscher breed. In spite of its looks, the Miniature Pinscher is not a miniature Doberman, as is sometimes suggested. In fact, it is an old breed, developed originally as a working terrier, and has since become a very lively type of companion dog. Min Pins also make alert watchdogs. Miniature Pinschers look very athletic and have an attractive prancing gait. They have a sleek, two-toned coat, which can be either red and tan or black and tan in color. Individuals can be assertive, and may even challenge larger dogs if not well trained. These small dogs have relatively high energy levels.

LIKES

* Digging
* Chasing balls
* Exploring undergrowth

NEEDS

* Little grooming
* Good socialization
* A coat during cold weather

Is this your perfect dog?

Teen living with parents
●●●●●●●●○○

Owner with physical disability
●●●●○○○○○○

Young single owner
●●●●●●●●○○

Allergy sufferers
●●●●●●○○○○

Young couple
●●●●●●●●●●

Trend-centric owner
●●●●○○○○○○

Family with young kids
●●●●○○○○○○

Individualist
●●●●○○○○○○

Family with teenagers
●●●●●●●●●○

Keen jogger
●●○○○○○○○○

Older single owner
●●●●●●●●●●

Enthusiastic hiker
●●●●○○○○○○

Older couple
●●●●●●●●●●

Countryside pursuits fan
●●○○○○○○○○

City dweller
●●●●●●●●○○

Beach lover
●●●●●●○○○○

Rural owner
●●●●●●●●○○

Canine sports competitor
●●●●●●●●○○

Hobby farmer
●●●●●●●○○

AKC group: toy

Lhasa Apso

Height 11 in (28 cm)
Weight 15 lb (7 kg)
Country of origin Tibet

These small dogs were originally kept in Tibetan monasteries, where an interesting belief emerged. Lhasa Apsos were regarded as the repositories for the souls of dead monks, and as such they were very precious to these communities, and not given to foreigners. It was only about a century ago that they started to become known in the West, and the breed did not become fully established until the 1960s. Virtually all Lhasa Apsos are long-coated, although very occasionally a smooth-coated individual crops up in a litter. The coat is very thick, to give these small dogs good protection against what can be bitterly cold conditions in their native country. They are often long-lived, with a typical life expectancy approaching 15 years.

LIKES	NEEDS
* Being a watchdog	* Daily grooming
* Family life	* Good training
* Being independent	* Early socialization

Is this your perfect dog?

Teen living with parents
●●●●●●●●○○

Owner with physical disability
●●●●○○○○○○

Young single owner
●●●●●●○○○○

Allergy sufferers
●●●●○○○○○○

Young couple
●●●●●●○○○○

Trend-centric owner
●●●●●●○○○○

Family with young kids
●●●●○○○○○○

Individualist
●●●●○○○○○○

Family with teenagers
●●●●●●○○○○

Keen jogger
●●○○○○○○○○

Older single owner
●●●●●●●●●●

Enthusiastic hiker
●●○○○○○○○○

Older couple
●●●●●●●●●●

Countryside pursuits fan
●●○○○○○○○○

City dweller
●●●●●●●●●●

Beach lover
●●●●●●○○○○

Rural owner
●●●●●●○○○○

Canine sports competitor
●●●●○○○○○○

Hobby farmer
●●●●○○○○○○

AKC group: non-sporting

Tibetan Spaniel

Height 10 in (25 cm)
Weight 15 lb (7 kg)
Country of origin Tibet

Like the Lhasa Apso (opposite), this breed was created and developed by Tibetan monks. Tibetan Spaniels served primarily as watchdogs, warning of the approach of strangers. They will still instinctively perform this task, and so may prove to be quite noisy—early training will help to curb their urge to bark unnecessarily. Tibetan Spaniels traditionally played an active role at the monastery, performing the role of "prayer dogs," turning the larger prayer wheels that the monks used. This helps to explain why they are such lively dogs, with relatively high energy levels, and need more exercise than most small breeds. They are not true spaniels, having never been used for hunting purposes, though they look very similar to English Toy Spaniels.

LIKES

* Family life
* Sitting up high
* Being groomed

NEEDS

* Good daily walks
* Discouragement from barking
* Socialization with people

Is this your perfect dog?

Teen living with parents	Family with young kids	**Older couple**	Trend-centric owner
●●●●●●●●○○	●●●●○○○○○○	●●●●●●●●●●	●●●●○○○○○○
Young single owner	Family with teenagers	**City dweller**	Individualist
●●●●●●○○○○	●●●●●●●○○○	●●●●●●●●●●	●●●●○○○○○○
Young couple	**Older single owner**	Rural owner	Keen jogger
●●●●●●○○○○	●●●●●●●●●●	●●●●●●●○○○	●●○○○○○○○○
		Hobby farmer	Enthusiastic hiker
		●●●●○○○○○○	●●○○○○○○○○
		Owner with physical disability	Countryside pursuits fan
		●●●●○○○○○○	●●○○○○○○○○
		Allergy sufferers	Beach lover
		●●●●○○○○○○	●●●●●○○○○○
			Canine sports competitor
			●●●●○○○○○○

AKC group: non-sporting

Tibetan Spaniel and Shar-pei

This cross between these breeds of Asian origin is unusual. **Tibetanpei** puppies look almost like a scaled-down version of their Shar-pei parent (page 184), with fewer wrinkles.

Tibetan Terrier

Height 16 in (41 cm)
Weight 30 lb (13.5 kg)
Country of origin Tibet

In spite of its name, the Tibetan Terrier is not a true terrier, but more of a farm dog. The Tibetan Terrier is among the oldest dog breeds, originating in Tibet's Tsang province. The first Western explorers to encounter these dogs assumed they were terriers based on their appearance. In reality, the breed has been used in its native country—over the course of millennia—for herding livestock, guarding temples, and acting as companion dogs, too. They are therefore very adaptable and make good household companions, although they can bark quite loudly at any perceived hint of danger. Tibetan Terriers have a distinctive, double-layered coat, with a dense undercoat developed to protect them against the cold in the mountainous surroundings of their homeland.

LIKES

* Solo living
* Encouragement
* Agility activities

NEEDS

* Plenty of exercise
* Regular grooming
* Occasional trimming

Is this your perfect dog?

Teen living with parents
●●●●●●●●○○

Owner with physical disability
●●●●○○○○○○

Young single owner
●●●●●●●●○○

Allergy sufferers
●●○○○○○○○○

Young couple
●●●●●●●○○○

Trend-centric owner
●●●●●●○○○○

Family with young kids
●●●●●○○○○○

Individualist
●●●●●●○○○○

Family with teenagers
●●●●●●●●●●

Keen jogger
●●●●○○○○○○

Older single owner
●●●●●●●●○○

Enthusiastic hiker
●●●●●●●●●●

Older couple
●●●●●●●●○○

Countryside pursuits fan
●●○○○○○○○○

City dweller
●●●●●●○○○○

Beach lover
●●●●●●●●○○

Rural owner
●●●●●●●●○○

Canine sports competitor
●●●●●●●●●●

Hobby farmer
●●●●●●●●●●

AKC group: non-sporting

Papillon

Height	11 in (28 cm)
Weight	10 lb (4.5 kg)
Country of origin	France

The graceful appearance of the Papillon—or butterfly dog—is emphasized by its raised ears. Along with its drop-eared cousin, the Phalène (right), these continental toy spaniels were originally popular with the aristocracy, and a frequent sight at royal courts around Europe. They have always been companion dogs, and this is reflected in their personalities—Papillons are very affectionate and loyal by nature. This loyalty may sometimes spill over into possessiveness, though, and socialization with other dogs is important from an early age to prevent any problems developing. The coat is not very thick, so Papillons can feel the cold, but do not require a lot of grooming.

LIKES
* Being active
* Learning tricks
* Agility competitions

NEEDS
* Plenty of attention
* Daily exercise
* Gentle handling

Papillon and Shih Tzu

The ears of **Papastzus** tend to hint at their Papillon ancestry, but the coat is both longer and denser, overall. Sometimes though, the ears may resemble their Shih Tzu parent.

Is this your perfect dog?

Teen living with parents
●●●●●●●●○○

Owner with physical disability
●●●●●●○○○○

Young single owner
●●●●●●○○○○

Allergy sufferers
●●●●○○○○○○

Young couple
●●●●●●●●○○

Trend-centric owner
●●●●●●●●○○

Family with young kids
●●●●●●○○○○

Individualist
●●●●●●○○○○

Family with teenagers
●●●●●●●○○○

Keen jogger
●●●●○○○○○○

Older single owner
●●●●●●●●●○

Enthusiastic hiker
●●●●○○○○○○

Older couple
●●●●●●●●○

Countryside pursuits fan
●●○○○○○○○○

City dweller
●●●●●●●●●●

Beach lover
●●●●●●○○○○

Rural owner
●●●●●●○○○○

Canine sports competitor
●●●●●●●●○○

Hobby farmer
●●●●○○○○○○

AKC group: toy

For another Papillon crossbreed, see page 135.

Japanese Chin

Height 14 in (36 cm)
Weight 7 lb (3 kg)
Country of origin Japan

It may be that the Japanese Chin and Pekingese (page 124) share a common ancestry, given their similarity in appearance and determined personalities. The coat of the Japanese Chin is not as profuse as that of the Pekingese, though, and differs in color, being either black and white or brown and white. In terms of behavior, these small dogs have been likened to cats due to their overall agility, and the way in which they wash their faces with their paws. They can climb well, and have a decidedly playful side to their personalities—sometimes spinning around with excitement. Japanese Chins are well suited to urban living, and make excellent companions, being disinclined to bark. Their responsive nature means training is usually quite straightforward.

LIKES

* Family life
* Playing games
* Meeting people

NEEDS

* Regular grooming
* Tearstaining wiped away
* A daily walk

Japanese Chin and Pomeranian

The coloration of the **Chineranian** tends to mirror that of the Japanese Chin, rather than the Pomeranian, and its snout is longer and broader overall, making for a less extreme appearance.

 ## Is this your perfect dog?

Teen living with parents
●●●●●●●●○○

Young single owner
●●●●●●○○○○

Young couple
●●●●●●●●○○

Family with young kids
●●●●○○○○○○

Family with teenagers
●●●●●●○○○○

Older single owner
●●●●●●●●●●

Older couple
●●●●●●●●●●

City dweller
●●●●●●●●●●

Rural owner
●●●●●●●○○○

Hobby farmer
●●●●○○○○○○

Owner with physical disability
●●●●●●●●●●

Allergy sufferers
●●●●●○○○○○

Trend-centric owner
●●●●○○○○○○

Individualist
●●●●○○○○○○

Keen jogger
●●○○○○○○○○

Enthusiastic hiker
●●○○○○○○○○

Countryside pursuits fan
●●○○○○○○○○

Beach lover
●●●●○○○○○○

Canine sports competitor
●●●●○○○○○○

AKC group: toy

Pomeranian

Height 11 in (28 cm)
Weight 7 lb (3 kg)
Country of origin Germany

The pricked ears and tail that folds forward over the back indicate that the Pomeranian is the smallest of the spitz breeds, which originate from the far north—from Alaska and Canada to Russia. However, the Pomeranian has been bred purely as a companion breed rather than for pulling sleds. Its devotees included Queen Victoria, who helped to popularize the breed in the United Kingdom in the late 1800s. The Pomeranian makes an ideal companion, being lively, responsive to training, and full of personality. Its coat tends to be thicker in the colder months, and it develops a more profuse bib of longer hair at this time. Their thick coats mean these dogs can become uncomfortable in hot weather. Care needs to be taken with food as, like many small dogs, the Pomeranian can be quite greedy.

LIKES

* Plenty of attention
* Family life
* Playing games

NEEDS

* Daily brushing
* Care when around larger dogs
* Patient house-training

Pomeranian and Siberian Husky

Pomsky puppies have a really cute appearance, with shorter but denser coats than the Pomeranian, and may end up looking surprisingly like miniature Siberian Huskies. They are full of energy.

Is this your perfect dog?

Teen living with parents
●●●●●●●●○○

Owner with physical disability
●●●●●●○○○○

Young single owner
●●●●●●●●○○

Allergy sufferers
●●○○○○○○○○

Young couple
●●●●●●●●●●

Trend-centric owner
●●●●●●●●○○

Family with young kids
●●●●●●○○○○

Individualist
●●●●●●○○○○

Family with teenagers
●●●●●●●●●○

Keen jogger
●●○○○○○○○○

Older single owner
●●●●●●●●●●

Enthusiastic hiker
●●○○○○○○○○

Older couple
●●●●●●●●●●

Countryside pursuits fan
●●○○○○○○○○

City dweller
●●●●●●●●●●

Beach lover
●●●●●●●○○○

Rural owner
●●●●●●○○○○

Canine sports competitor
●●●●●●○○○○

Hobby farmer
●●●●○○○○○○

AKC group: toy

For other Pomeranian crossbreeds, see pages 103 and 132.

English Bulldog

Height 14 in (36 cm)
Weight 55 lb (25 kg)
Country of origin United Kingdom

Although now bred purely as a companion, the English Bulldog was originally used for bull-baiting purposes. Any signs of aggression have disappeared from the breed today, however, and it has a lovely personality as a pet. Even so, its physical appearance is less than ideal, and it can suffer from a range of congenital problems. A thorough veterinary examination is always advisable when acquiring any puppy, and is especially true for this breed. Be aware, too, that as they grow older, these bulldogs may have a tendency to snore. The English Bulldog's compact facial shape means that you should be careful when exercising the breed in hot weather, as there is an increased risk of heatstroke.

LIKES	NEEDS
✱ Food	✱ Moderate exercise
✱ Urban parks	✱ Good veterinary care
✱ People	✱ Possible cesarean births

Is this your perfect dog?

Teen living with parents
●●●●●●●●○○

Owner with physical disability
●●●●○○○○○○

Young single owner
●●●●●●●●○○

Allergy sufferers
●●●●○○○○○○

Young couple
●●●●●●●●○○

Trend-centric owner
●●●●●●●○○○

Family with young kids
●●●●●●○○○○

Individualist
●●●●●●●○○○

Family with teenagers
●●●●●●○○○○

Keen jogger
●●○○○○○○○○

Older single owner
●●●●●●●●●○

Enthusiastic hiker
●●○○○○○○○○

Older couple
●●●●●●●●●●

Countryside pursuits fan
●●○○○○○○○○

City dweller
●●●●●●●●●●

Beach lover
●●●●○○○○○○

Rural owner
●●●●●●●●○○

Canine sports competitor
●●○○○○○○○○

Hobby farmer
●●●●○○○○○○

AKC group: non-sporting

French Bulldog

Height 12 in (30 cm)
Weight 28 lb (13 kg)
Country of origin France

The original ancestor of the French Bulldog was a strain of Toy Bulldog from the English county of Nottinghamshire. When some of the region's lace-makers emigrated to France in the early 1800s, they took their dogs with them, and crossings with France's terriers transformed the strain into today's highly distinctive French Bulldog. The most distinctive feature of the breed is the raised, batlike ears that give it a very alert appearance. Their easy-going personality means Bulldogs make excellent companions. However, they can suffer quite badly from flatulence, particularly if their diet is changed. Garlic tablets may help, if there is no underlying medical problem.

LIKES

* Short daily walks
* Playing games
* Being affectionate

NEEDS

* Cool surroundings in hot weather
* Careful feeding
* Possible cesarean births

French Bulldog and Papillon

This is a rare cross, which can introduce another dimension to the sleek coat of the French Bulldog and bring further emphasis to its large, upright ears. However, **French Bullions** can prove quite variable in appearance.

Is this your perfect dog?

Teen living with parents
●●●●●●●○○

Allergy sufferers
●●●●○○○○○

Keen jogger
●●○○○○○○○

Countryside pursuits fan
●●○○○○○○○

Young single owner
●●●●●●○○

Trend-centric owner
●●●●●○○○

Enthusiastic hiker
●●○○○○○○○

Beach lover
●●●●○○○○○

Young couple
●●●●●●●○○

Individualist
●●●●●●○○○

Canine sports competitor
●●○○○○○○○

Family with young kids
●●●○○○○○

AKC group: non-sporting

Family with teenagers
●●●●●●○○○

Older single owner
●●●●●●●●

Older couple
●●●●●●●●

City dweller
●●●●●●●●

Rural owner
●●●●●●●○○

Hobby farmer
●●●●○○○○○

Owner with physical disability
●●●●●●●○○

Australian Cattle Dog

Height	20 in (51 cm)
Weight	44 lb (20 kg)
Country of origin	Australia

Developed from collies and other breeds taken to Australia during the early days of European settlement, the Australian Cattle Dog reputedly has a dash of dingo in its genes to improve stamina. An Australian Cattle Dog called Bluey holds the record for the longest-lived dog: born in 1910, he lived for 29½ years. New studies have confirmed that this breed has an above-average life expectancy. In recent years, Australian Cattle Dogs have proved their versatility as working companions, assisting the police by sniffing out drugs, and even tracking endangered animals for conservation field workers by locating the animal's droppings. When training an Australian Cattle Dog puppy, the program needs to cater to the breed's intelligent nature, in order to get the best results.

LIKES
* Being active
* Canine sports
* Working with people

NEEDS
* Good socialization
* Activities to prevent boredom
* Little coat care

Is this your perfect dog?

Teen living with parents ●●●●○○○○○○
Owner with physical disability ●●○○○○○○○○
Young single owner ●●●●●●○○○○
Allergy sufferers ●●●●○○○○○○
Young couple ●●●●●●○○○○
Trend-centric owner ●●●●○○○○○○
Family with young kids ●●●●○○○○○○
Individualist ●●●●●●○○○○
Family with teenagers ●●●●●●●○○○
Keen jogger ●●●●●●●●○○
Older single owner ●●●●○○○○○○
Enthusiastic hiker ●●●●●●●●●●
Older couple ●●●●●○○○○○
Countryside pursuits fan ●●○○○○○○○○
City dweller ●●●●○○○○○○
Beach lover ●●●●●●○○○○
Rural owner ●●●●●●●●●●
Canine sports competitor ●●●●●●●●●●
Hobby farmer ●●●●●●●●●○
AKC group: herding

Australian Cattle Dog and Siberian Husky

As in all first-generation crosses, puppies will vary in appearance, but **Auskys** with blue eyes clearly reveal their Siberian Husky ancestry. Pricked ears are common, being a feature of both ancestral breeds.

For another Australian Cattle Dog crossbreed, see page 73.

Australian Shepherd

Height 23 in (58 cm)
Weight 70 lb (32 kg)
Country of origin United States

A notable exception to the rule that a geographic reference in a dog's name indicates country of origin, the Australian Shepherd is actually an American breed, created in California. Its ancestors include dogs brought to the United States from Australia and New Zealand, as well as Spain, during the 1800s. As with some other herding breeds, many Australian Shepherd puppies are born with bobtails, and these dogs should not be paired together for genetic reasons. Aussie Shepherds learn quickly, and will soon master a wide range of tricks and tasks. They thrive in the canine sports arena, and excel in agility competitions, as well as in the show ring. Recently, breeders have been creating a smaller, scaled-down version of the Australian Shepherd, designed for urban living.

LIKES

* Working with people
* Family life
* An active lifestyle

NEEDS

* Space for exercise
* To meet people
* Regular brushing

Australian Shepherd and Poodle

Aussiedoodles have now been bred for several generations, and subsequent pairings between first generation crossbreed puppies and Poodles make it much more likely that puppies will be hypoallergenic.

Is this your perfect dog?

Teen living with parents
●●●●●●○○○○

Owner with physical disability
●●●●○○○○○○

Young single owner
●●●●●●○○○○

Allergy sufferers
●●○○○○○○○○

Young couple
●●●●●●●●○○

Trend-centric owner
●●●●●●●○○○

Family with young kids
●●●●●●○○○○

Individualist
●●●●●●○○○○

Family with teenagers
●●●●●●●●●●

Keen jogger
●●●●●●●●○○

Older single owner
●●●○○○○○○○

Enthusiastic hiker
●●●●●●●●○○

Older couple
●●●●●●○○○○

Countryside pursuits fan
●●○○○○○○○○

City dweller
●●●○○○○○○○

Beach lover
●●●●●●○○○○

Rural owner
●●●●●●●●●●

Canine sports competitor
●●●●●●●●●●

Hobby farmer
●●●●●●●●●●

AKC group: herding

For another Australian Shepherd crossbreed, see page 104.

Cardigan Welsh Corgi

Height 13 in (33 cm)
Weight 26 lb (12 kg)
Country of origin United Kingdom

The two breeds of Welsh Corgi—Cardigan and Pembroke (opposite)—are similar in appearance, having evolved from common ancestral stock. They were paired together indiscriminately in the United Kingdom until 1934, when they were recognized as distinct breeds. The two corgi forms are named after different areas of Wales, and were originally used for driving cattle to and from local markets. Their small size meant they could move easily through a herd, with minimal risk of being kicked as they did so, and were able to dodge out of the way easily. The Cardigan Welsh Corgi is the larger of the pair, and is also distinguished by its bigger ears. Its nose is broader and blunter than that of its Pembroke counterpart.

Cardigan Welsh Corgi and Border Collie

The typical **Bordigan** is black and white in color, with a relatively long coat, reflecting its Border Collie ancestry. Its large, upright ears are typical of the Welsh Corgi parent.

LIKES

* Plenty of exercise
* Playing games
* A watchdog role

NEEDS

* Training not to be snappy
* Little grooming
* Good socialization

Is this your perfect dog?

Teen living with parents
●●●●○○○○○○

Young single owner
●●●●○○○○○○

Young couple
●●●●●●○○○○

Family with young kids
●●○○○○○○○○

Family with teenagers
●●●●●●●○○○

Older single owner
●●●●●●●●○○

Older couple
●●●●●●●●○○

City dweller
●●●●●●○○○○

Rural owner
●●●●●●●●●●

Hobby farmer
●●●●●●●●●●

Owner with physical disability
●●○○○○○○○○

Allergy sufferers
●●●●○○○○○○

Trend-centric owner
●●●●●●●○○○

Individualist
●●●●○○○○○○

Keen jogger
●●●○○○○○○○

Enthusiastic hiker
●●●●●●○○○○

Countryside pursuits fan
●●●○○○○○○○

Beach lover
●●●●○○○○○○

Canine sports competitor
●●●●●●●●○○

AKC group: herding

Pembroke Welsh Corgi

Height 12 in (30 cm)
Weight 25 lb (11.5 kg)
Country of origin United Kingdom

The Pembroke Corgi's origins are unclear, but similar dogs have existed in Wales for over a millennium. The more popular of the two Welsh Corgi breeds, the Pembroke is commonly seen in the company of Queen Elizabeth II. Even the Queen and her immediate circle have not been exempt from being nipped occasionally by these dogs, though. This instinct—the nipping of heels—was the means by which this cattle-herding breed persuaded reluctant cows to move, and young corgis may do this occasionally to their owners. This trait means that Pembroke Corgis are less suitable than other breeds for homes with young children. They are nevertheless friendly and eager to follow their owners around, proving quite obedient in other respects.

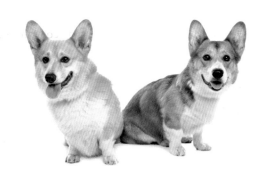

LIKES

* Herding stock
* Agility and flyball
* Being affectionate

NEEDS

* Sensible training
* Good walks
* Effective socialization

Pembroke Welsh Corgi, Basenji, and Border Collie

Not all designer dogs result from crossbreeding between two purebreds. In this case, after a mating between a Corgi and a Basenji, the puppies are then crossed with a Border Collie.

Is this your perfect dog?

Teen living with parents
●●●●○○○○○○

Owner with physical disability
●●○○○○○○○○

Young single owner
●●●●○○○○○○

Allergy sufferers
●●●●○○○○○○

Young couple
●●●●●●○○○○

Trend-centric owner
●●●●●●●●○○

Family with young kids
●●○○○○○○○○

Individualist
●●●●○○○○○○

Family with teenagers
●●●●●●○○○○

Keen jogger
●●○○○○○○○○

Older single owner
●●●●●●●●○○

Enthusiastic hiker
●●●●●●●○○○

Older couple
●●●●●●●○○○

Countryside pursuits fan
●●○○○○○○○○

City dweller
●●●●●●○○○○

Beach lover
●●●●●○○○○○

Rural owner
●●●●●●●●●●

Canine sports competitor
●●●●●●●●○○

Hobby farmer
●●●●●●●●●●

AKC group: herding

For another Pembroke Welsh Corgi crossbreed, see page 52.

Bearded Collie

Height 22 in (56 cm)
Weight 66 lb (30 kg)
Country of origin United Kingdom

Affectionately known as the Beardie, this breed started out as a herding dog, working on farms in Scotland. Its long, dense, trailing coat provides good protection against the elements, reflecting the fact that Beardies had to work outside in all weather. Today it is seen in the show ring, and is also kept as a pet. The breed is very lively, and these dogs have a distinctive bouncing gait. This characteristic, coupled with its wagging tail, reflects its friendly personality. Bearded Collies like people in general, and so do not make good watchdogs. It is very important that pet Beardies are kept away from livestock when out walking, to keep them from bothering the animals.

Bearded Collie and Beagle

Tending to be smooth-coated, with ears that extend slightly farther down the sides of the face than those of the Beagle, the **Beacol** is a lively, medium-sized dog.

LIKES

* Playing outdoors
* Human companionship
* Agility events

NEEDS

* Lots of company
* Plenty of exercise
* Regular eye checks

 ## Is this your perfect dog?

Teen living with parents
●●●●●●○○○○

Owner with physical disability
●●●●○○○○○○

Young single owner
●●●●○○○○○○

Allergy sufferers
●●○○○○○○○○

Young couple
●●●●●●○○○○

Trend-centric owner
●●●●●●●●○○

Family with young kids
●●●●●●○○○○

Individualist
●●●●●●○○○○

Family with teenagers
●●●●●●●●●●

Keen jogger
●●●●●●●●○○

Older single owner
●●●●○○○○○○

Enthusiastic hiker
●●●●●●●●●●

Older couple
●●●●●●○○○○

Countryside pursuits fan
●●○○○○○○○○

City dweller
●●●●○○○○○○

Beach lover
●●●●●●○○○○

Rural owner
●●●●●●●●●●

Canine sports competitor
●●●●●●●●●●

Hobby farmer
●●●●●●●●●●

AKC group: herding

Old English Sheepdog

Height	24 in (61 cm)
Weight	66 lb (30 kg)
Country of origin	United Kingdom

The Old English Sheepdog was not actually developed to work with sheep, nor was it intended to herd them. Confusingly, the breed was used as a herding dog, moving cattle from one area to another in northern England. It has a very distinctive and appealing rolling gait, and its profuse coat naturally covers its entire face, including its eyes. Dogs of this breed used to be shorn each year—like sheep—and the wool they produced was often turned into yarn, and ultimately made into garments. The breed is often tailless, accounting for its alternative name, Bobtail, or, more formally, the Bobtailed Sheepdog.

LIKES	NEEDS
* "Herding" people	* Lots of exercise
* Being a guard dog	* Dedicated grooming
* Canine competitions	* Human company

Old English Sheepdog and Poodle

Often black and white in color, with a much shorter coat than the Old English Sheepdog, the **Sheepadoodle** is a very playful designer dog that is likely to be hypoallergenic.

Is this your perfect dog?

Teen living with parents
●●●●●●○○○○

Young single owner
●●●●○○○○○○

Young couple
●●●●●●○○○○

Family with young kids
●●●●○○○○○○

Family with teenagers
●●●●●●●●●●

Older single owner
●●●●○○○○○○

Older couple
●●●●●○○○○○

City dweller
●●●●○○○○○○

Rural owner
●●●●●●●●●●

Hobby farmer
●●●●●●●●●●

Owner with physical disability
●●○○○○○○○○

Allergy sufferers
●●○○○○○○○○

Trend-centric owner
●●●●●●●●○○

Individualist
●●●●●●○○○○

Keen jogger
●●●●●●●●○○

Enthusiastic hiker
●●●●●●●●●●

Countryside pursuits fan
●●●○○○○○○○

Beach lover
●●●●●●●○○○

Canine sports competitor
●●●●●●●●●●

AKC group: herding

Border Collie

Height	21 in (53 cm)
Weight	49 lb (22 kg)
Country of origin	United Kingdom

Seeing these dogs in action, working closely with their handler to control sheep, or taking part in canine sports, might give the impression that the Border Collie is one of the best choices as a pet. However, don't be misled—the high-energy lifestyle of these collies must be a serious consideration for any potential pet owner. Most of them are still kept as farm dogs, working mainly with sheep, and they are not suitable for indoor environments, where they will rapidly become bored and then destructive. The Border Collie typically has a black-and-white coat of variable length, but other colors are recognized. Smooth-haired examples are rare, as this type of coat affords less protection in bad weather. Like the Bearded Collie (page 140), these dogs can develop eye ailments.

LIKES	NEEDS
* Responding to commands	* Plenty of exercise
* Agility and similar events	* Intelligent challenges
* Learning hand signals	* Good training

Border Collie and Dalmatian

These dogs are usually a combination of black or chocolate and white, reflecting their Dalmatian ancestry. **Bodacions** have spots and larger dark patches, and their coat length is variable. They are better suited to home life than Border Collies.

Is this your perfect dog?

Teen living with parents
● ● ● ● ○ ○ ○ ○ ○ ○

Owner with physical disability
● ● ● ● ○ ○ ○ ○ ○ ○

Young single owner
● ● ● ● ○ ○ ○ ○ ○ ○

Allergy sufferers
● ● ○ ○ ○ ○ ○ ○ ○ ○

Young couple
● ● ● ● ● ● ○ ○ ○ ○

Trend-centric owner
● ● ● ● ○ ○ ○ ○ ○ ○

Family with young kids
● ● ○ ○ ○ ○ ○ ○ ○ ○

Individualist
● ● ● ○ ○ ○ ○ ○ ○ ○

Family with teenagers
● ● ● ● ● ● ● ● ● ●

Keen jogger
● ● ● ● ● ● ● ○ ○ ○

Older single owner
● ● ● ● ○ ○ ○ ○ ○ ○

Enthusiastic hiker
● ● ● ● ● ● ● ● ○ ○

Older couple
● ● ● ● ● ○ ○ ○ ○ ○

Countryside pursuits fan
● ● ○ ○ ○ ○ ○ ○ ○ ○

City dweller
● ● ○ ○ ○ ○ ○ ○ ○ ○

Beach lover
● ● ● ● ● ● ○ ○ ○ ○

Rural owner
● ● ● ● ● ● ● ● ● ●

Canine sports competitor
● ● ● ● ● ● ● ● ● ●

Hobby farmer
● ● ● ● ● ● ● ● ● ●

AKC group: herding

For other Border Collie crossbreeds, see pages 138, 139, and 151.

Polish Lowland Sheepdog

Height	20 in (51 cm)
Weight	35 lb (16 kg)
Country of origin	Poland

The Polish Lowland Sheepdog has become much better known internationally in recent years, with its friendly nature contributing to its popularity. Its full Polish name is Polski Owczarek Nizinny, leading to its nickname of Nizzy and, in the United States, PON. There is a key point of difference in the way that the Polish Lowland Sheepdog works, compared to similar breeds, which makes it more suitable as a pet. Rather than running back and forth steering the sheep, this dog is particularly effective at guiding the flock using its "sheepdog eye." The sheep are largely controlled by the dog staring at them intently, and by the dog's body language. This calm approach means these sheepdogs make relaxed household pets. Be prepared for lengthy grooming sessions, though.

LIKES

* Playing games
* Human interaction
* Canine sports

NEEDS

* Regular grooming
* Temperate surroundings
* Plenty of exercise

 ## Is this your perfect dog?

Teen living with parents
●●●●●●○○○○

Owner with physical disability
●●○○○○○○○○

Young single owner
●●●●●●○○○○

Allergy sufferers
●●○○○○○○○○

Young couple
●●●●●●●●○○

Trend-centric owner
●●●●●●○○○○

Family with young kids
●●●●●●○○○○

Individualist
●●●●○○○○○○

Family with teenagers
●●●●●●●○○○

Keen jogger
●●●●●●●●○○

Older single owner
●●●●●●○○○○

Enthusiastic hiker
●●●●●●●●○○

Older couple
●●●●●●○○○○

Countryside pursuits fan
●●○○○○○○○○

City dweller
●●●●○○○○○○

Beach lover
●●●●○○○○○○

Rural owner
●●●●●●●●●●

Canine sports competitor
●●●●●●●●●●

Hobby farmer
●●●●●●●●●●

AKC group: herding

Rough Collie

Height	24 in (61 cm)
Weight	66 lb (30 kg)
Country of origin	United Kingdom

Immortalized in the *Lassie* films and stories of the 1940s and 1950s, the Rough Collie first became fashionable during the 1860s, as one of Queen Victoria's favorite breeds. Its elegant appearance is thought to be the result of crossbreeding involving the Borzoi (page 71). Unfortunately, some bloodlines can be afflicted by serious eye disorders, but you can avoid this worry by checking breeding stock. Rough Collies have become less popular in recent years. These dogs tend to be quite impatient by nature, and can nip, meaning they are less suitable for a home with young children than other breeds. In the right surroundings, though, Rough Collies make superb companions, as they are very responsive and intelligent by nature.

Is this your perfect dog?

Teen living with parents
●●●●●●○○○○

Young single owner
●●●●●●○○○○

Young couple
●●●●●●●●○○

Family with young kids
●●○○○○○○○○

Family with teenagers
●●●●●●●●○○

Older single owner
●●●●●●○○○○

Older couple
●●●●●●○○○○

City dweller
●●●●○○○○○○

Rural owner
●●●●●●●●●●

Hobby farmer
●●●●●●●●●●

Owner with physical disability
●●○○○○○○○○

Allergy sufferers
●●○○○○○○○○

Trend-centric owner
●●●●●●●●○○

Individualist
●●●●●○○○○○

Keen jogger
●●●●●●○○○○

Enthusiastic hiker
●●●●●●●●●●

Countryside pursuits fan
●●○○○○○○○○

Beach lover
●●●●●●○○○○

Canine sports competitor
●●●●●●●●○○

AKC group: herding

LIKES

* Space to run
* Working with people
* Being outdoors

NEEDS

* Daily grooming
* Plenty of exercise
* Regular health checks

Collie and Standard Poodle

The **Cadoodle**'s coat length is influenced by whether a Rough or Smooth Collie contributes to this cross. Some display merle coloration from the Collie parent as well, while others more closely resemble Poodles.

Smooth Collie

Height 24 in (61 cm)
Weight 66 lb (30 kg)
Country of origin United Kingdom

The classification of the Rough and Smooth Collies varies. In the United States, they are regarded as varieties of a single breed, distinguished on the basis of coat length, whereas in the United Kingdom they are classed separately. The Smooth Collie is today very similar to its rough relative, although originally it had a slightly less elegant appearance. Crosses with Greyhounds changed the Smooth Collie's profile, and further crosses with Rough Collies brought the two breeds much closer together in appearance, so now they are largely indistinguishable apart from coat length. Despite the two breeds' similarities, the Smooth Collie has become much scarcer, perhaps because it lacks the attractive flowing coat of its close relative—yet if you do not have the time to devote to grooming, it will be a better choice of pet.

Is this your perfect dog?

Teen living with parents
●●●●●●○○○○

City dweller
●●●●○○○○○○

Owner with physical disability
●●○○○○○○○○

Enthusiastic hiker
●●●●●●●●●●

Young single owner
●●●●●●○○○○

Rural owner
●●●●●●●●●●

Allergy sufferers
●●○○○○○○○○

Countryside pursuits fan
●●○○○○○○○○

Young couple
●●●●●●●●○○

Hobby farmer
●●●●●●●●●●

Trend-centric owner
●●●●●●○○○○

Beach lover
●●●●●●○○○○

Family with young kids
●●○○○○○○○○

Individualist
●●●●○○○○○○

Canine sports competitor
●●●●●●●●○○

Family with teenagers
●●●●●●●●○○

Keen jogger
●●●●●●○○○○

AKC group: herding

Older single owner
●●●●●●○○○○

Older couple
●●●●●●○○○○

LIKES

❋ Working with people
❋ Training sessions
❋ An adult environment

NEEDS

❋ Eye checks
❋ Plenty of exercise
❋ Minimal grooming

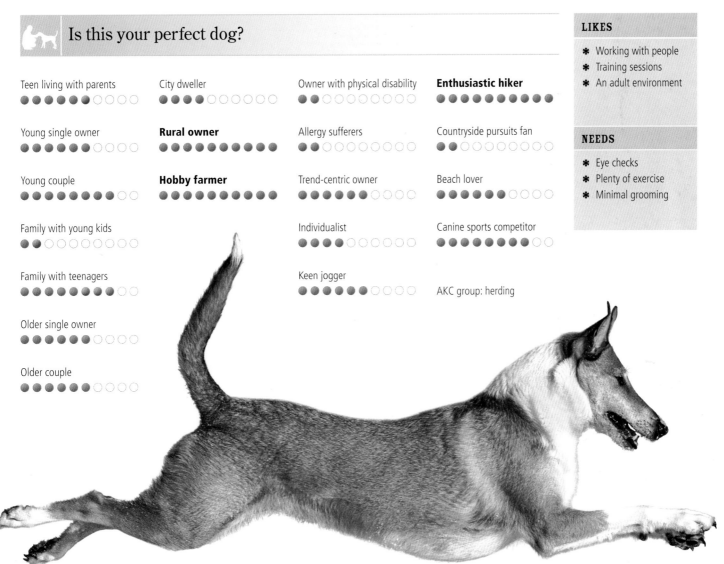

Shetland Sheepdog

Height 15 in (38 cm)
Weight 15 lb (7 kg)
Country of origin United Kingdom

Looking like a scaled-down version of the Rough Collie, the Shetland Sheepdog is named after the remote Scottish islands where its ancestors lived over 300 years ago. It is bred in various colors, usually broken by white areas on the chest that extend down to the forelegs. Its small size and attractive personality have led to this breed—often described as the Sheltie—being widely kept both as a companion and a show dog. It is quite patient with children, and fits in well as part of a family, just as its ancestors did on their small Scottish farms. Shelties will not be happy in cramped, urban surroundings, especially if left alone for long periods every day, but otherwise they are versatile, adaptable dogs.

Is this your perfect dog?

Teen living with parents
●●●●●●●●●●

Owner with physical disability
●●●●○○○○○○

Young single owner
●●●●●●○○○○

Allergy sufferers
●●○○○○○○○○

Young couple
●●●●●●●●○○

Trend-centric owner
●●●●●●●●○○

Family with young kids
●●●●●●○○○○

Individualist
●●●●○○○○○○

Family with teenagers
●●●●●●●●○○

Keen jogger
●●●●●●●○○○

Older single owner
●●●●●●●●●●

Enthusiastic hiker
●●●●●●●●○○

Older couple
●●●●●●●●●●

Countryside pursuits fan
●●○○○○○○○○

City dweller
●●●●○○○○○○

Beach lover
●●●●●●●○○○

Rural owner
●●●●●●●●●●

Canine sports competitor
●●●●●●●●●●

Hobby farmer
●●●●●●●●●●

AKC group: herding

LIKES

* Being active
* Training
* Canine sports

NEEDS

* Eye checks
* Regular grooming
* Walks off the leash

Shetland Sheepdog, Beagle, and Black-and-Tan Coonhound

This is a complex cross, and the predominant hound input to the breeding program means that **Shelbea Hound** puppies are more likely to resemble a hound, with a short coat, rather than a Sheltie.

Puli

Height	18 in (46 cm)
Weight	33 lb (15 kg)
Country of origin	Hungary

One of the most distinctive dog breeds in the world, the Puli's corded coat is virtually unique—this characteristic is shared only with its larger relative, the Komondor. The Puli and Komondor worked together on the Hungarian plains where they were developed. The smaller Puli would act as a sheepdog, herding the flock, while the Komondor would be the flock guardian. Although, today, black-coated Pulix (the plural form of the breed's name) are generally seen in the show ring, these dogs occur in a wide range of colors. Black was favored originally, as it highlighted their presence among the sheep. Once corded, the Puli's coat needs no grooming, but it must be washed, and can be trimmed.

LIKES	NEEDS
✻ Splashing around in water	✻ Early training
✻ An outdoor life	✻ Focus on obedience
✻ Flyball competitions	✻ Socialization with people

Is this your perfect dog?

Teen living with parents
●●●●●●○○○○

Owner with physical disability
●●●●○○○○○○

Young single owner
●●●●●●○○○○

Allergy sufferers
●●●●●●●●●●

Young couple
●●●●●●●●○○

Trend-centric owner
●●●●●●●●○○

Family with young kids
●●●●●●○○○○

Individualist
●●●●●●●●●●

Family with teenagers
●●●●●●●●●●

Keen jogger
●●●●○○○○○○

Older single owner
●●●●●●●●○○

Enthusiastic hiker
●●●●●●●●○○

Older couple
●●●●●●●●○○

Countryside pursuits fan
●●○○○○○○○○

City dweller
●●●●○○○○○○

Beach lover
●●●●○○○○○○

Rural owner
●●●●●●●●●●

Canine sports competitor
●●●●●●●●○○

Hobby farmer
●●●●●●●●●●

AKC group: herding

Bouvier des Flandres

Height	27 in (69 cm)
Weight	88 lb (40 kg)
Country of origin	Belgium

The largest and best-known member of the Bouvier group, the Bouvier des Flandres is powerfully built and a versatile worker: "Bouvier" means "cattle drover." The advent of motorized transportation meant that these dogs were no longer needed to drive cattle to market. However, they are now used by the police instead, and have also proved very effective in search-and-rescue work and as guide dogs. Careful training is essential, as they are powerful and strong-willed dogs. In addition to regular brushing, their coats require trimming about once a month to stay at their best. The Bouvier des Flandres' high energy levels mean it is well suited to a home with teenagers.

LIKES

* Dog agility
* Plenty of exercise
* Human interaction

NEEDS

* Regular grooming
* Good training
* Early socialization

Bouvier des Flandres and Standard Poodle

Its coat usually turns out to be much shorter than that of the Bouvier, but the **Flandoodle**'s head is broader than that of a Poodle. Chocolate and black coat colors are most common.

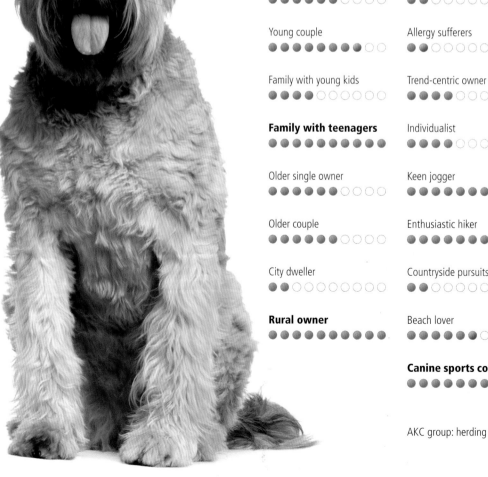

Is this your perfect dog?

Teen living with parents
●●●●●●○○○○

Hobby farmer
●●●●●●●●●●

Young single owner
●●●●●●○○○○

Owner with physical disability
●●○○○○○○○○

Young couple
●●●●●●●○○

Allergy sufferers
●●○○○○○○○○

Family with young kids
●●●●○○○○○○

Trend-centric owner
●●●●○○○○○○

Family with teenagers
●●●●●●●●●

Individualist
●●●●○○○○○○

Older single owner
●●●●●●○○○○

Keen jogger
●●●●●●●●○○

Older couple
●●●●●●○○○○

Enthusiastic hiker
●●●●●●●●○○

City dweller
●●○○○○○○○○

Countryside pursuits fan
●●○○○○○○○○

Rural owner
●●●●●●●●●

Beach lover
●●●●●●○○○○

Canine sports competitor
●●●●●●●●●●

AKC group: herding

Briard

Height	27 in (69 cm)
Weight	76 lb (35 kg)
Country of origin	France

This breed came to prominence outside its native country, France, when it was pressed into service carrying messages and performing other tasks during the First World War. Historically, the Briard had worked as a sheepdog, and it was a favorite of the French ruler, Napoleon Bonaparte. Even when compared with other stock-herding breeds, the Briard ranks as one of the most active members of the group. It is related to the Beauceron (page 162), but has a longer coat. A shared and distinctive feature of these breeds is the presence of double dewclaws on their hind feet, resembling additional toes. These have a functional significance, helping the dog to turn around quickly without losing its balance. Eye tests for breeding stock are recommended.

Briard and Poodle

The Poodle's influence means the **Bridoodle** has a shorter coat than the Briard, but it tends to hang down, rather than being curled. Puppies can be hypoallergenic.

LIKES
* Protecting the family
* Different environments
* Canine sports

NEEDS
* Considerable daily exercise
* Good training
* Socialization with people

Is this your perfect dog?

Teen living with parents
●●●●●●○○○○

Owner with physical disability
●●○○○○○○○○

Young single owner
●●●●●●○○○○

Allergy sufferers
●●○○○○○○○○

Young couple
●●●●●●●○○

Trend-centric owner
●●●●○○○○○○

Family with young kids
●●●●○○○○○○

Individualist
●●●●○○○○○○

Family with teenagers
●●●●●●●●●●

Keen jogger
●●●●●●●●○○

Older single owner
●●●●●●○○○○

Enthusiastic hiker
●●●●●●●●●●

Older couple
●●●●●●○○○○

Countryside pursuits fan
●●○○○○○○○○

City dweller
●●○○○○○○○○

Beach lover
●●●●●●○○○○

Rural owner
●●●●●●●●●●

Canine sports competitor
●●●●●●●●●●

Hobby farmer
●●●●●●●●●●

AKC group: herding

Pyrenean Shepherd

Height	21 in (53 cm)
Weight	32 lb (15 kg)
Country of origin	France

Also known as the Berger de Pyrénées, this breed has been working in the Pyrenean region between France and Spain for 1,000 years. Pyrenean Shepherds are the smallest of the French sheepdogs, watched over by the protective presence of the Great Pyrenees (opposite). There are two different recognized forms—the "rough-faced," or long-haired variant, and a shorter-coated, "smooth-faced" form. Pyrenean Shepherds display great stamina and pace, which you need to consider before getting one as a pet. They are ideal for people living on their own, as they form a strong attachment to an individual, but puppies need to be introduced to a wide social circle, so they do not grow up being shy with other people.

LIKES

* Training
* Canine sports
* Space at home

NEEDS

* Plenty of exercise
* Early socialization
* Moderate grooming

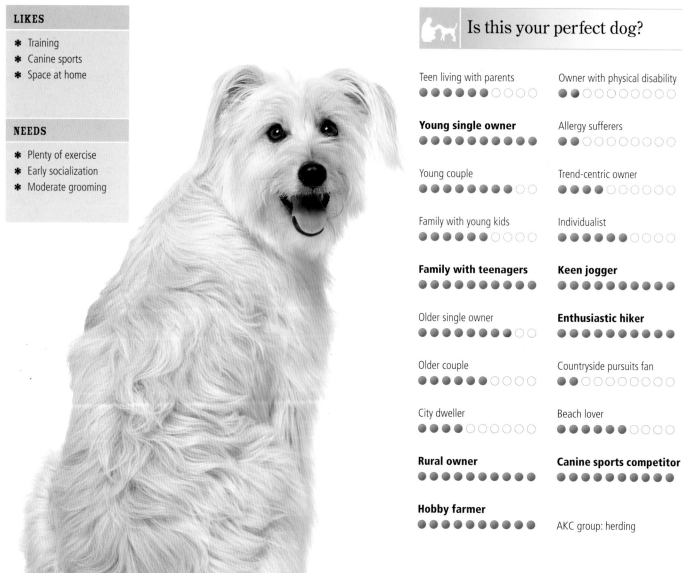

Is this your perfect dog?

Teen living with parents
●●●●●●○○○○

Owner with physical disability
●●○○○○○○○○

Young single owner
●●●●●●●●●●

Allergy sufferers
●●○○○○○○○○

Young couple
●●●●●●●●○○

Trend-centric owner
●●●●○○○○○○

Family with young kids
●●●●●●○○○○

Individualist
●●●●●●○○○○

Family with teenagers
●●●●●●●●●●

Keen jogger
●●●●●●●●●●

Older single owner
●●●●●●●●○○

Enthusiastic hiker
●●●●●●●●●●

Older couple
●●●●●●●○○○

Countryside pursuits fan
●●○○○○○○○○

City dweller
●●●●○○○○○○

Beach lover
●●●●●●○○○○

Rural owner
●●●●●●●●●●

Canine sports competitor
●●●●●●●●●●

Hobby farmer
●●●●●●●●●●

AKC group: herding

Great Pyrenees

Height	32 in (80 cm)
Weight	165 lb (75 kg)
Country of origin	France

Also known as the Pyrenean Mountain Dog, this large mastiff-type dog originally protected flocks from wolves and thieves, rather than undertaking herding duties. Unusually, the Great Pyrenees has also been involved in illicit activity, being tasked with smuggling goods in special backpacks across the border between France and Spain, avoiding customs posts by following mountain paths. Great Pyrenees are mostly white, allowing them to blend in with the sheep they were protecting. These dogs were traditionally equipped with sharp collars, created using protruding nails, which would protect their vulnerable throat area in the event of conflict. The decline of the wolf could have spelled the end of these giants, but their attractive appearance and surprisingly genial nature has ensured their future in the show ring and as companions.

LIKES

* Space to roam
* Family life
* Cool climates

NEEDS

* Early socialization
* Good control
* Breeding stock checked for hip dysplasia

Great Pyrenees and Border Collie

If both parents are short-coated, the puppies will be too. **Border Pyrenees** are likely to be black and white in color, with black areas being most prominent on the head.

Is this your perfect dog?

Teen living with parents
●●●●○○○○○○

Owner with physical disability
●●○○○○○○○○

Young single owner
●●●●●○○○○○

Allergy sufferers
●●○○○○○○○○

Young couple
●●●●●●●○○○

Trend-centric owner
●●●●○○○○○○

Family with young kids
●●○○○○○○○○

Individualist
●●●●●●○○○○

Family with teenagers
●●●●●●●●○○

Keen jogger
●●●●●●○○○○

Older single owner
●●●●●○○○○○

Enthusiastic hiker
●●●●●●●●○○

Older couple
●●●●●○○○○○

Countryside pursuits fan
●●○○○○○○○○

City dweller
●●○○○○○○○○

Beach lover
●●●●●●○○○○

Rural owner
●●●●●●●●○○

Canine sports competitor
●●●●●●○○○○

Hobby farmer
●●●●●●●●●●

AKC group: working

For another Great Pyrenees crossbreed, see page 166.

Finnish Lapphund

Height 20 in (51 cm)
Weight 53 lb (24 kg)
Country of origin Finland

Descended from ancestral stock from northern Scandinavia, the Finnish Lapphund was traditionally kept for herding reindeer, but has proved to be just as adept working with sheep and cattle. These lapphunds are well protected against the cold of their native climate by their dense double coat. There has been a divergence in their appearance in recent years on geographic lines. The Finnish form is parti-colored, typically with tan chest and underparts, with black on the upper parts of the body, whereas the Swedish form tends to be a dark solid color. The upright ears of these dogs may sometimes be curled over at their tips. Finnish Lapphunds make excellent companions, and although they will bark, they tend only to do so when concerned, and so make good watchdogs.

LIKES

* Cooler climates
* Plenty of exercise
* Sledding

NEEDS

* Good training
* Moderate grooming
* Activity

Is this your perfect dog?

Teen living with parents
●●●●●●●●○○

Owner with physical disability
●●○○○○○○○○

Young single owner
●●●●●●○○○○

Allergy sufferers
●●○○○○○○○○

Young couple
●●●●●●●●○○

Trend-centric owner
●●●●●●●○○○

Family with young kids
●●●●●●○○○○

Individualist
●●●●●●●○○○

Family with teenagers
●●●●●●●●●●

Keen jogger
●●●●●●●●○○

Older single owner
●●●●●●○○○○

Enthusiastic hiker
●●●●●●●●●●

Older couple
●●●●●●○○○○

Countryside pursuits fan
●●●●●●●●●○

City dweller
●●●●○○○○○○

Beach lover
●●●●●●○○○○

Rural owner
●●●●●●●●●●

Canine sports competitor
●●●●●●●●●●

Hobby farmer
●●●●●●●●●○

AKC group: herding

Norwegian Buhund

Height 18 in (46 cm)
Weight 57 lb (26 kg)
Country of origin Norway

Developed as a versatile farm dog and companion, the Norwegian Buhund is also an alert guardian. As it has an independent streak, training from an early age is important. These are incredibly active dogs and possess great stamina, so they are ideal sporting companions. They need adequate mental and physical exercise to avoid behavioral problems. The coat of the Norwegian Buhund is much shorter than that of other breeds from Scandinavia, and it seems to be more adaptable to hot climates than many Nordic dogs, with a thriving population in Australia. Paler wheaten shades are sought after, although brown and even black Norwegian Buhund puppies will crop up in some litters.

Is this your perfect dog?

LIKES	NEEDS
* Working and playing	* Plenty of exercise
* Family life	* Little grooming
* Activity	* Care around livestock

Teen living with parents
●●●●●●○○○○

Owner with physical disability
●●○○○○○○○○

Canine sports competitor
●●●●●●●●●●

Young single owner
●●●●●●●○○○

Allergy sufferers
●●○○○○○○○○

AKC group: herding

Young couple
●●●●●●●●○○

Trend-centric owner
●●●●○○○○○○

Family with young kids
●●●●●○○○○○

Family with teenagers
●●●●●●●●●●

Older single owner
●●●●●●○○○○

Individualist
●●●●●○○○○○

Older couple
●●●●●●●○○○

Keen jogger
●●●●●●●●○○

City dweller
●●●●○○○○○○

Enthusiastic hiker
●●●●●●●●●●

Rural owner
●●●●●●●●●●

Countryside pursuits fan
●●○○○○○○○○

Hobby farmer
●●●●●●●●●●

Beach lover
●●●●●●○○○○

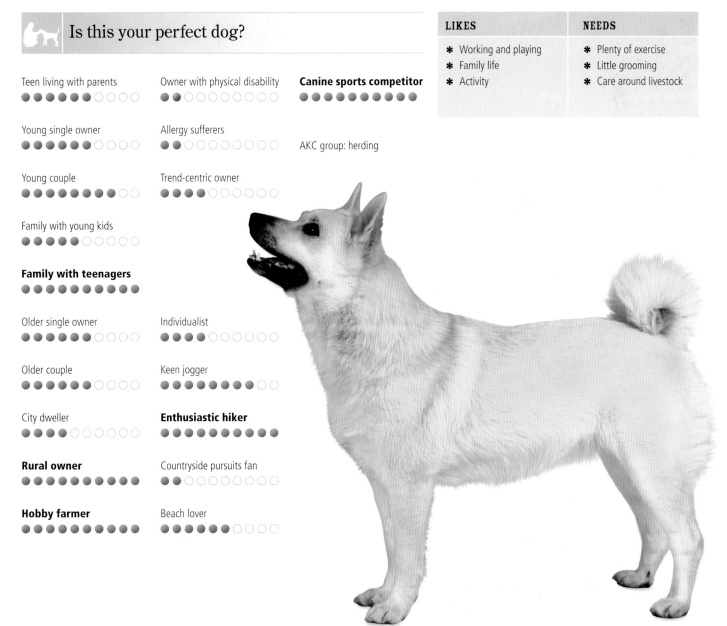

Icelandic Sheepdog

Height	16 in (41 cm)
Weight	57 lb (26 kg)
Country of origin	Iceland

Icelandic Sheepdogs were popular as early as 1650, when these dogs were recorded as being highly sought after by English shepherds. They traditionally worked on their own without close supervision, tracking down loose sheep that had wandered off, sometimes over large distances, and herding them to lower ground for the colder months. This role demanded stamina and determination, which are still characteristics of the breed, along with a friendly nature and a loud bark—which you may wish to bear in mind. Although it only gained full show recognition in the United States in June 2010, the Icelandic Sheepdog is becoming more widely known and appreciated.

Is this your perfect dog?

Teen living with parents
●●●●●●●○○○

Allergy sufferers
●●○○○○○○○○

Keen jogger
●●●●●●●●○○

Beach lover
●●●●●●●○○○

Young single owner
●●●●●●●●○○

Trend-centric owner
●●●●●●○○○○

Enthusiastic hiker
●●●●●●●●●●

Canine sports competitor
●●●●●●●●●●

Young couple
●●●●●●●●○○

Individualist
●●●●●●○○○○

Countryside pursuits fan
●●○○○○○○○○

AKC group: herding

Family with young kids
●●●●○○○○○○

Family with teenagers
●●●●●●●●●○

Older single owner
●●●●●●○○○○

Older couple
●●●●●●●○○○

City dweller
●●●●○○○○○○

Rural owner
●●●●●●●●●●

Hobby farmer
●●●●●●●●●○

Owner with physical disability
●●○○○○○○○○

LIKES
* Roaming
* Being active
* Family life

NEEDS
* Recall training
* Good socialization
* Moderate grooming

Swedish Vallhund

Height 14 in (36 cm)
Weight 33 lb (15 kg)
Country of origin Sweden

The area where this breed originated is revealed by its Swedish name, Västgötaspets, which literally translates as "spitz dog of the West Goths," while "vallhund" simply means "farm dog." Swedish Vallhunds were actually used as cattle herders, much like the Welsh Corgi breeds (pages 138 and 139), and it has been suggested that these corgis contributed to the breed's origins. Swedish Vallhunds may nip, so they are not an ideal choice if you have a young family, but they are loyal and delight in human company—even showing off for their owners. Like other herding breeds, the Swedish Vallhund needs to be active, and these dogs have proved effective competitors at a host of canine sports, ranging from flyball to obedience.

LIKES

* Plenty of exercise
* Playing games
* Hunting rats

NEEDS

* Little grooming
* Good socialization
* Training not to nip

Is this your perfect dog?

Teen living with parents
●●●●●●○○○○

Owner with physical disability
●●○○○○○○○○

Young single owner
●●●●●●○○○○

Allergy sufferers
●●○○○○○○○○

Young couple
●●●●●●○○○○

Trend-centric owner
●●●●○○○○○○

Family with young kids
●●○○○○○○○○

Individualist
●●●●○○○○○○

Family with teenagers
●●●●●●●●○○

Keen jogger
●●●●●○○○○○

Older single owner
●●●●●●○○○○

Enthusiastic hiker
●●●●●●●●●○

Older couple
●●●●●●●●○○

Countryside pursuits fan
●●○○○○○○○○

City dweller
●●●●○○○○○○

Beach lover
●●●●●●●○○○

Rural owner
●●●●●●●●●●

Canine sports competitor
●●●●●●●●●●

Hobby farmer
●●●●●●●●●●

AKC group: herding

Canaan Dog

Height 24 in (61 cm)
Weight 55 lb (25 kg)
Country of origin Israel

The Canaan Dog is an unusual breed, one of a group known as pariah dogs. This is a description given to dogs that were originally domesticated, but then reverted to a free-living existence. The Canaan Dog's ancestors were first caught in the 1930s, when they lived in a feral state in the Negev Desert in Israel, after which they started to be domesticated again. The puppies proved adaptable, and were soon used for various tasks including mine detecting, search-and-rescue work, and even as guide dogs. Careful pairings meant that a recognizable type of dog started to emerge, laying the foundations for the breed subsequently known as the Canaan Dog. Canaan Dogs still show traces of their past in some of their characteristic behavior, though, such as their urge to dig. These dogs are now found in many countries around the world.

LIKES

* Being active
* Family life
* Learning

NEEDS

* Early socialization
* Secure fencing
* Training not to dig

AKC group: herding

Is this your perfect dog?

Teen living with parents
●●●●●●●●○○

Family with young kids
●●●●●●○○○○

Older couple
●●●●●●●○○○

Trend-centric owner
●●●●●○○○○○

Young single owner
●●●●●●●●○○

Family with teenagers
●●●●●●●●●○

City dweller
●●●●○○○○○○

Individualist
●●●●●●●●●●

Young couple
●●●●●●●●○○

Older single owner
●●●●●●○○○○

Rural owner
●●●●●●●●●○

Keen jogger
●●●●●●●○○○

Hobby farmer
●●●●●●●●○○

Enthusiastic hiker
●●●●●●●●●●

Owner with physical disability
●●○○○○○○○○

Countryside pursuits fan
●●○○○○○○○○

Allergy sufferers
●●○○○○○○○○

Beach lover
●●●●●●○○○○

Canine sports competitor
●●●●●●●●●●

German Shepherd Dog

Height	26 in (66 cm)
Weight	88 lb (40 kg)
Country of origin	Germany

Better known for a time as the Alsatian, the German Shepherd Dog (or GSD) was created with the specific intention of creating an intelligent breed that would learn quickly. The breed has therefore been used in a wide variety of delicate working situations, ranging from search-and-rescue to police work. Most German Shepherds today are smooth coated, but the occasional long-coated individual crops up. There used to be a wire-haired form, which now appears to have become extinct. German Shepherd Dogs do suffer from some health problems, notably hip dysplasia, but screening of breeding stock has helped to reduce such problems. In recent years, the controversial white form has grown in popularity, and has become known as the White Shepherd Dog.

German Shepherd Dog and Pug

Tending to be short-coated and quite stocky, the **Shug** may retain the curled tail of its Pug ancestor, and is typically a medium-sized dog, with a much more pronounced nose than the Pug.

LIKES
* Training activities
* Working
* Familiar people

NEEDS
* Good socialization
* Moderate grooming
* Careful feeding

Is this your perfect dog?

Teen living with parents
●●●●●●○○○○

Young single owner
●●●●●●●●○○

Young couple
●●●●●●●●○○

Family with young kids
●●○○○○○○○○

Family with teenagers
●●●●●●●●●●

Older single owner
●●●●●●○○○○

Older couple
●●●●●●●○○○

City dweller
●●●●○○○○○○

Rural owner
●●●●●●●●●●

Hobby farmer
●●●●●●●●○○

Owner with physical disability
●●○○○○○○○○

Allergy sufferers
●●○○○○○○○○

Trend-centric owner
●●●●○○○○○○

Individualist
●●●●○○○○○○

Keen jogger
●●●●●○○○○○

Enthusiastic hiker
●●●●●●●●○○

Countryside pursuits fan
●●○○○○○○○○

Beach lover
●●●●●●○○○○

Canine sports competitor
●●●●●●●●●●

AKC group: herding

For other German Shepherd Dog crossbreeds, see pages 27, 51, and 167.

Belgian Malinois

Height	26 in (66 cm)
Weight	66 lb (30 kg)
Country of origin	Belgium

The classification of the Belgian shepherd breeds, which are lighter in build than their German counterparts, is quite confused. Although the four forms—Malinois, Belgian Sheepdog, Tervuren, and Laekenois—differ quite markedly in appearance, not all canine registries recognize them individually. The American Kennel Club, for example, refers to the Malinois as a breed in its own right—the Belgian Malinois—preferring to restrict the use of the name Belgian Sheepdog to the Groenendael. In their Belgian homeland, however, all four are simply considered as variants of a single breed, which is also the line of the Kennel Club in the United Kingdom. The reverse applies in Australia and New Zealand, however, where all four are recognized as separate breeds. The Malinois resembles the Tervuren in color, but is short coated. These dogs are lively, intelligent, and responsive to training.

LIKES

* Being energetic
* Playing games
* Being encouraged

NEEDS

* Good training
* Plenty of exercise
* Little grooming

Is this your perfect dog?

Teen living with parents
●●●●●●○○○○

City dweller
●●○○○○○○○○

Hobby farmer
●●●●●●●●●●

Allergy sufferers
●●●●○○○○○○

Young single owner
●●●●●●○○○○

Rural owner
●●●●●●●●●●

Owner with physical disability
●●○○○○○○○○

Trend-centric owner
●●●●●○○○○○

Young couple
●●●●●●●●○○

Individualist
●●●●○○○○○○

Family with young kids
●●●●○○○○○○

Keen jogger
●●●●●●●●○○

Family with teenagers
●●●●●●●●●●

Enthusiastic hiker
●●●●●●●●●●

Older single owner
●●●●●●○○○○

Countryside pursuits fan
●●●○○○○○○○

Older couple
●●●●●●○○○○

Beach lover
●●●●●●○○○○

Canine sports competitor
●●●●●●●●●●

AKC group: herding

Belgian Tervuren

Height 26 in (66 cm)
Weight 66 lb (30 kg)
Country of origin Belgium

The Belgian Tervuren is named after the region of Belgium where it was created. It has a dense double coat, which is a combination of mahogany mixed with black areas of hair, although the head should always be black. Bitches tend to be slightly smaller and more elegant overall. The feet of both sexes have an almost catlike appearance. Belgian Tervurens are highly intelligent and can easily become bored, particularly in puppyhood. This can lead them to become destructive and possibly even aggressive. More than with other breeds, you should consider that these dogs cannot be left alone for long periods, and need to be kept engaged.

LIKES

* Working with people
* Being active
* Being mentally stimulated

NEEDS

* Regular grooming
* Sensible training
* Plenty of exercise

Belgian Tervuren and Standard Poodle

Tervoodles tend predominantly to be black, thanks to the parent breeds, but other colors may be developed by using Poodles that are not black.

Is this your perfect dog?

Teen living with parents
●●●●●●○○○○

Owner with physical disability
●●○○○○○○○○

Young single owner
●●●●●●○○○○

Allergy sufferers
●●○○○○○○○○

Young couple
●●●●●●●●○○

Trend-centric owner
●●●●○○○○○○

Family with young kids
●●●●○○○○○○

Individualist
●●●●○○○○○○

Family with teenagers
●●●●●●●●●●

Keen jogger
●●●●●●●●○○

Older single owner
●●●●●●○○○○

Enthusiastic hiker
●●●●●●●●●●

Older couple
●●●●●●○○○○

Countryside pursuits fan
●●○○○○○○○○

City dweller
●●○○○○○○○○

Beach lover
●●●●●●○○○○

Rural owner
●●●●●●●●●●

Canine sports competitor
●●●●●●●●●●

Hobby farmer
●●●●●●●●●●

AKC group: herding

Laekenois

Height	26 in (66 cm)
Weight	66 lb (30 kg)
Country of origin	Belgium

In terms of appearance, the Laekenois is the most distinctive of the Belgian shepherd group, although it has yet to achieve full recognition in the United States. It was used for herding sheep around the castle at Laeken—now a suburb in northwest Brussels—and also as a guard dog, watching over linen put out in the fields to dry. It is considered to represent the oldest surviving lineage of the Belgian shepherd dogs. It has a tweed appearance, as a result of light brown and white hair being intermingled in its coat, with some darker areas. The coat has a tousled appearance—though a smooth-coated puppy may sometimes be born. It takes some time for a Laekenois puppies' ears to achieve their distinctive upright position, as can be seen in the pictures on this page.

LIKES

* Being active
* Watching for strangers
* Human company

NEEDS

* Relatively little grooming
* Good training
* Plenty of exercise

Is this your perfect dog?

Teen living with parents	**Hobby farmer**
●●●●●●○○○○	●●●●●●●●●●
Young single owner	Owner with physical disability
●●●●●●○○○○	●●○○○○○○○○
Young couple	Allergy sufferers
●●●●●●●○○	●●●●○○○○○○
Family with young kids	Trend-centric owner
●●●●○○○○○○	●●●●○○○○○○
Family with teenagers	Individualist
●●●●●●●●●●	●●●●○○○○○○
Older single owner	Keen jogger
●●●●●●○○○○	●●●●●●●●○○
Older couple	**Enthusiastic hiker**
●●●●●○○○○	●●●●●●●●●●
City dweller	Countryside pursuits fan
●●○○○○○○○○	●●○○○○○○○○
Rural owner	Beach lover
●●●●●●●●●●	●●●●●●●○○○
	Canine sports competitor
	●●●●●●●●●●

AKC group: not yet achieved full recognition in U.S.

Belgian Sheepdog

Height	26 in (66 cm)
Weight	66 lb (30 kg)
Country of origin	Belgium

The Belgian Sheepdog takes its alternative name, Groenendael, from a chateau south of Brussels, where it was first bred in 1885. It has distinctive coloration, being pure black—sometimes with a small white area on the chest. The coat on the body is quite smooth, but there is a distinctive ruff of longer hair framing the face, combined with an "apron" or "jabot" on the chest. These dogs also have a thick undercoat. This is shed particularly in the spring, when they will need more frequent grooming.

LIKES	NEEDS
✳ An active lifestyle	✳ Frequent grooming
✳ Canine sports	✳ Good training
✳ Family life	✳ Early socialization

Is this your perfect dog?

Teen living with parents
●●●●●●○○○○

Young single owner
●●●●●○○○○○

Young couple
●●●●●●●●○○

Family with young kids
●●●●○○○○○○

Family with teenagers
●●●●●●●●●●

Older single owner
●●●●●●○○○○

Older couple
●●●●●○○○○

City dweller
●●○○○○○○○○

Rural owner
●●●●●●●●●●

Hobby farmer
●●●●●●●●●●

Owner with physical disability
●●○○○○○○○○

Allergy sufferers
●●○○○○○○○○

Trend-centric owner
●●●●○○○○○○

Individualist
●●●●○○○○○○

Keen jogger
●●●●●●●●○○

Enthusiastic hiker
●●●●●●●●●●

Countryside pursuits fan
●●○○○○○○○○

Beach lover
●●●●●●○○○○

Canine sports competitor
●●●●●●●●●●

AKC group: herding

Beauceron

Height 28 in (71 cm)
Weight 88 lb (40 kg)
Country of origin France

This versatile guarding and herding dog was first used to watch over flocks of sheep in the Paris area over 500 years ago, where its name comes from. During the First World War, their strength and bravery under fire meant that Beaucerons were highly valued. After hostilities ended, the breed began a new career as a police dog. As with all large dogs, you will need to avoid feeding Beaucerons before exercise, as they are particularly susceptible to the potentially fatal condition of bloat. Black and tan is the coloring typically associated with these dogs, to the extent that they are also known as "bas rouge," literally meaning "red stockings," a reference to the markings on their legs. There is also a rare harlequin form.

LIKES

* Learning
* Family life
* Playing games

NEEDS

* Plenty of exercise
* Good training
* Regular clipping of double hind dewclaws

Beauceron and Standard Poodle

The use of the Standard Poodle ensures that **Beauceroodle** puppies are likely to grow up to be similar in size to a small Beauceron. Their coat length is longer than that of their Beauceron parents.

Is this your perfect dog?

Teen living with parents
●●●●●●○○○○

Hobby farmer
●●●●●●●●●●

Young single owner
●●●●●●○○○○

Owner with physical disability
●●○○○○○○○○

Young couple
●●●●●●●○○

Allergy sufferers
●●○○○○○○○○

Family with young kids
●●●●○○○○○○

Trend-centric owner
●●●○○○○○○○

Family with teenagers
●●●●●●●●●●

Individualist
●●●●○○○○○○

Older single owner
●●●●●●○○○

Keen jogger
●●●●●●●●●○

Older couple
●●●●●●●○○○

Enthusiastic hiker
●●●●●●●●●●

City dweller
●●○○○○○○○○

Countryside pursuits fan
●●○○○○○○○○

Rural owner
●●●●●●●●●○

Beach lover
●●●●○○○○○○

Canine sports competitor
●●●●●●●●●○

AKC group: herding

Anatolian Shepherd Dog

Height	32 in (80 cm)
Weight	141 lb (64 kg)
Country of origin	Turkey

The Anatolian Shepherd Dog is an ancient and industrious breed that acted as a sheepdog and guardian on the plains of what is now Turkey. Though a loyal companion, potential owners should remember that the ancestors of these dogs have been roaming for centuries, rather than being confined in a home. They are tough campaigners, instinctively suspicious of strangers, and possess an independent streak. This can make training difficult, because although your dog may respond most of the time, there is always the possibility that it will decide to ignore you at some stage. Anatolian Shepherd Dogs vary noticeably in color and size in their homeland, although they are becoming increasingly standardized for show purposes. These dogs can be prone to becoming overweight, as you can see in the picture on the right.

LIKES	NEEDS
* Families	* Secure fencing
* Space at home	* Good socialization
* Plenty of exercise	* Experienced owners

Is this your perfect dog?

Teen living with parents
●●○○○○○○○○

Owner with physical disability
●●○○○○○○○○

Young single owner
●●○○○○○○○○

Allergy sufferers
●●○○○○○○○○

Young couple
●●●○○○○○○○

Trend-centric owner
●●○○○○○○○○

Family with young kids
●●○○○○○○○○

Individualist
●●○○○○○○○○

Family with teenagers
●●●●●●●●○○

Keen jogger
●●●●●●●●○○

Older single owner
●●○○○○○○○○

Enthusiastic hiker
●●●●●●●●●●

Older couple
●●○○○○○○○○

Countryside pursuits fan
●●○○○○○○○○

City dweller
●●○○○○○○○○

Beach lover
●●●●○○○○○○

Rural owner
●●●●●●●●●●

Canine sports competitor
●●●●●●○○○○

Hobby farmer
●●●●●●●●●●

AKC group: working

For an Anatolian Shepherd Dog crossbreed, see page 174.

American Eskimo Dog

Height	15 in (38 cm)
Weight	35 lb (16 kg)
Country of origin	Germany

Better known in Europe as the German Spitz, the breed's name was changed in North America following anti-German feeling arising from the First World War. This had critical commercial significance back then, as these adaptable dogs were popular circus performers of the period, and a number of today's bloodlines can trace their origins back to ancestors who enchanted audiences in such shows. An Eski will be a great choice if you are looking for a dog to develop into a talented agility performer. American Eskimo Dogs have extrovert temperaments, and there are three sizes of this breed to choose from—toy, miniature, and standard. As their name suggests, they are not very popular outside the United States.

LIKES	NEEDS
✽ Learning tricks	✽ Regular grooming
✽ Exploring on walks	✽ Strict feeding
✽ Playing with toys	✽ Discouragement from barking

American Eskimo Dog and Jack Russell Terrier

Eskijacks have relatively short coats, normally with longer hair around the ears. They are similarly colored to Jack Russells, and are full of personality—but they can be noisy.

 ## Is this your perfect dog?

Teen living with parents
●●●●●●●○○○

Owner with physical disability
●●●●●●○○○○

Young single owner
●●●●●●●○○○

Allergy sufferers
●●○○○○○○○○

Young couple
●●●●●●●●○○

Trend-centric owner
●●●●●●●●○○

Family with young kids
●●●●●●○○○○

Individualist
●●●●●○○○○○

Family with teenagers
●●●●●●●●●○

Keen jogger
●●●●●●○○○○

Older single owner
●●●●●●●●○○

Enthusiastic hiker
●●●●●●●○○○

Older couple
●●●●●●●●○○

Countryside pursuits fan
●●○○○○○○○○

City dweller
●●●●●●●●○○

Beach lover
●●●●●●○○○○

Rural owner
●●●●●●●●○○

Canine sports competitor
●●●●●●●●●●

Hobby farmer
●●●●●●○○○○

AKC group: non-sporting

Samoyed

Height 22 in (56 cm)
Weight 66 lb (30 kg)
Country of origin Siberia

The stunning, pure white coloration is just one of a number of attractive traits in the Samoyed, although other colors, including black and white, have been seen in the past. The breed is named after the Samoyed people, whose tents its ancestors used to share. This living arrangement meant that, unlike many sled dogs and reindeer herders, Samoyeds were instinctively used to people of all ages: today, the breed has a reputation for being child friendly. All Samoyeds seen in the West are descended from a dozen dogs that were brought to England in the late 1800s. They immediately caused a sensation, with their stunning appearance that was so different from existing breeds of the time. Samoyeds also helped on polar expeditions during this era, pulling sleds in the Antarctic.

LIKES	NEEDS
✳ Human contact	✳ Activity to prevent boredom
✳ Canine sports	✳ Considerable grooming
✳ Being a watchdog	✳ Consistent training

Is this your perfect dog?

Teen living with parents	Hobby farmer
●●●●●●●●○○	●●●●●●●●○○
Young single owner	Owner with physical disability
●●●●●●○○○○	●●○○○○○○○○
Young couple	Allergy sufferers
●●●●●●●●○○	●●○○○○○○○○
Family with young kids	Trend-centric owner
●●●●●●●●●●	●●●●●●●●○○
	Individualist
	●●●●○○○○○○
	Keen jogger
	●●●●●●●●○○
Family with teenagers	**Enthusiastic hiker**
●●●●●●●●●●	●●●●●●●●●●
Older single owner	Countryside pursuits fan
●●●●●●○○○○	●●○○○○○○○○
Older couple	Beach lover
●●●●●●●○○○	●●●●●●○○○○
City dweller	**Canine sports competitor**
●●●●○○○○○○	●●●●●●●●●●
Rural owner	
●●●●●●●●●●	AKC group: working

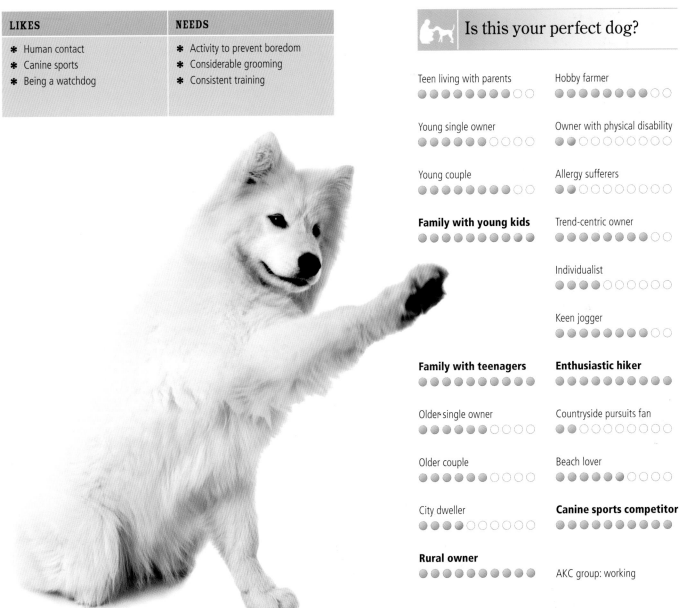

Siberian Husky

Height	24 in (61 cm)
Weight	60 lb (27 kg)
Country of origin	Siberia

Northern tribes developed their own distinctive breeds as a means of transport, such as the Alaskan Malamute (opposite). The Siberian Husky represents one of the oldest of all canine bloodlines, having existed in a purebred form for over 3,000 years. Powerfully built in spite of their relatively small size, these are genuine sled dogs, capable of great endurance as well as speed. Siberian Huskies have helped to foster sled-dog racing as a year-round sport, even in the absence of snow. Teams of dogs pull special carts with their handler or "musher" riding on the back. They are very active and social dogs, preferring to live alongside other Siberian Huskies, rather than on their own.

Siberian Husky and Great Pyrenees

Although smaller than Great Pyrenees, **Siberian Pyrenees** are still large and powerful dogs, with tremendous stamina—so they are not for everyone. Their fur is typically tricolored.

LIKES
* An active lifestyle
* Competing in sled-racing
* Communal howling

NEEDS
* Consistent training
* Plenty of space
* Moderate grooming

Is this your perfect dog?

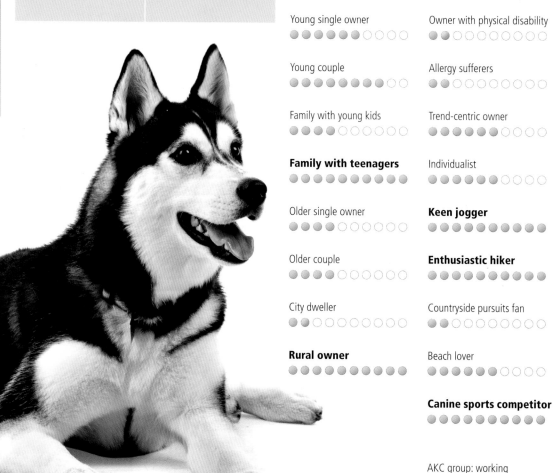

Teen living with parents ●●●●●●●○○○	Hobby farmer ●●●●●●●●○○
Young single owner ●●●●●●●○○○	Owner with physical disability ●●○○○○○○○○
Young couple ●●●●●●●●○○	Allergy sufferers ●●○○○○○○○○
Family with young kids ●●●●○○○○○○	Trend-centric owner ●●●●●○○○○○
Family with teenagers ●●●●●●●●●●	Individualist ●●●●●●●○○○
Older single owner ●●●●○○○○○○	**Keen jogger** ●●●●●●●●●●
Older couple ●●●●○○○○○○	**Enthusiastic hiker** ●●●●●●●●●●
City dweller ●●○○○○○○○○	Countryside pursuits fan ●●●●●●●●●○
Rural owner ●●●●●●●●●●	Beach lover ●●●●●●○○○○
	Canine sports competitor ●●●●●●●●●●

AKC group: working

Alaskan Malamute

Height	26 in (66 cm)
Weight	86 lb (39 kg)
Country of origin	United States

Strong, powerful, and confident by nature, the Alaskan Malamute is named after the Alaskan people known as the Mahlemuts, who relied on these dogs in the frozen wastelands of the far north, long before the advent of motorized transportation in the region. Alaskan Malamutes are pack dogs, with a defined social structure and any dog-meet-dog introductions should be carried out on neutral territory, particularly between intact (not neutered) males, to reduce the risk of fighting. Puppies also need to be taught not to chase cats. It ranks among the oldest breeds in the world. Individuals can have a very striking appearance, thanks to their light blue eyes, which is a trait seen in a number of similar breeds, such as the Siberian Husky (opposite).

LIKES
* Lots of activity
* A close association with people
* Colder weather

NEEDS
* Plenty of exercise
* Careful socialization
* Frequent grooming

Is this your perfect dog?

Teen living with parents ●●●●○○○○○○

Family with teenagers ●●●●●●●●○○

City dweller ●●○○○○○○○○

Hobby farmer ●●●●●●○○○○

Young single owner ●●●●○○○○○○

Older single owner ●●●●○○○○○○

Rural owner ●●●●●●●●●●

Owner with physical disability ●●○○○○○○○○

Young couple ●●●●●●○○○○

Older couple ●●●●○○○○○○

Allergy sufferers ●●○○○○○○○○

Family with young kids ●●●●○○○○○○

Trend-centric owner ●●●●○○○○○○

Individualist ●●●●○○○○○○

Keen jogger ●●●●●●●●○○

Enthusiastic hiker ●●●●●●●●●○

Countryside pursuits fan ●●○○○○○○○○

Beach lover ●●●●○○○○○○

Canine sports competitor ●●●●●●●●●○

AKC group: working

Alaskan Malamute and German Shepherd Dog
Raised ears are a characteristic of these dogs, but their coloration is subdued, with fewer white areas than the Alaskan Malamute. Blue-eyed **Alaskan Shepherds** look particularly striking.

Norwegian Lundehund

Height   15 in (38 cm)
Weight   14 lb (6.5 kg)
Country of origin   Norway

The Norwegian Lundehund is a very unusual and highly specialized spitz breed that was kept for hunting puffins on cliffs in its native Norway when they came ashore to breed. It was a very dangerous task, requiring great agility. The dogs also needed to be quite small, to be able to grab young puffins from their underground burrows. One feature that hints at the breed's past is the presence of extra toes on its feet. These helped to anchor it to the cliffs, lessening the risk of a fatal fall. The Norwegian Lundehund's forelegs can extend out at an angle of 90 degrees, and its double-jointed neck is also incredibly flexible. These are inquisitive dogs, and responsive by nature.

LIKES

* Climbing
* Being a household pet
* Agility competitions

NEEDS

* Weight monitoring
* Moderate grooming
* Careful house-training

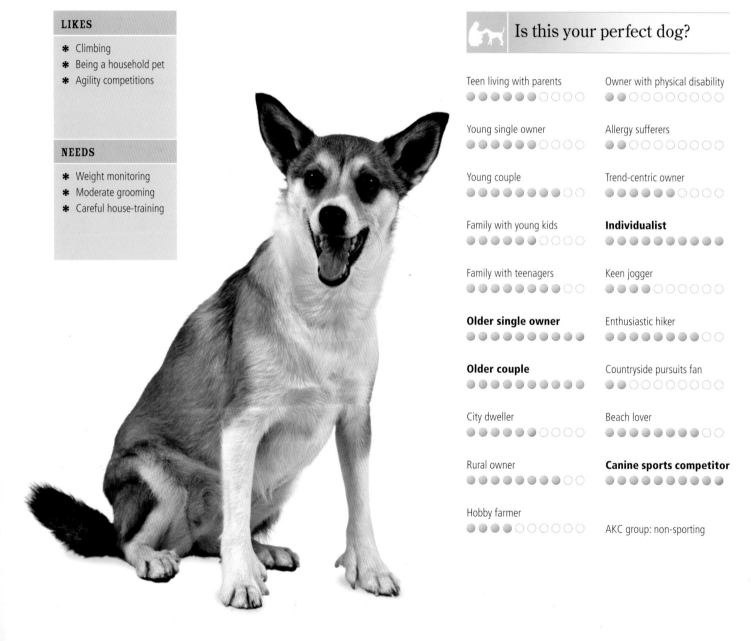

Is this your perfect dog?

Teen living with parents	Owner with physical disability
Young single owner	Allergy sufferers
Young couple	Trend-centric owner
Family with young kids	**Individualist**
Family with teenagers	Keen jogger
Older single owner	Enthusiastic hiker
Older couple	Countryside pursuits fan
City dweller	Beach lover
Rural owner	**Canine sports competitor**
Hobby farmer	AKC group: non-sporting

Dalmatian

Height	24 in (61 cm)
Weight	66 lb (30 kg)
Country of origin	Croatia

This breed is supposedly named after the Dalmatian coast, where it may have been developed. What is certain is that the breed became sought-after in the 1800s as a stylish carriage dog, running alongside horse-drawn vehicles to guard against attacks from highwaymen. Today's Dalmatians still have great stamina, and make lively and genial companions for people with active lifestyles. Do be aware that some Dalmatians suffer from kidney and bladder stones. These beautiful dogs are often chosen for their characteristic, highly individual black or chocolate spotted coat patterning. Puppies are born with white coats, and subsequently develop their spots around three weeks later.

LIKES

* Plenty of exercise
* Running alongside a cyclist
* Being with people

NEEDS

* Checking for deafness
* Little grooming
* Good training

Dalmatian and Labrador Retriever

Stocky and well-built, the coloration of **Dalmadors** is influenced by that of their parents. Puppies tend to be quite solid in color, with only small white areas showing spotted markings.

Is this your perfect dog?

Teen living with parents
●●●●●●●○○

Family with teenagers
●●●●●●●●●

Rural owner
●●●●●●●●●

Owner with physical disability
●●○○○○○○○

Young single owner
●●●●●●●○○

Older single owner
●●●●●○○○○

Hobby farmer
●●●●●●○○○

Allergy sufferers
●●●●●●○○○

Young couple
●●●●●●●○○

Older couple
●●●●○○○○○

Trend-centric owner
●●●●●●●○○

Family with young kids
●●●●●●○○○

City dweller
●●○○○○○○○

Individualist
●●●●●●●●○

Keen jogger
●●●●●●●●●

Enthusiastic hiker
●●●●●●●●●

Countryside pursuits fan
●●○○○○○○○

Beach lover
●●●●●●○○○

Canine sports competitor
●●●●●●●●●

AKC group: non-sporting

Saint Bernard

Height	36 in (91 cm)
Weight	260 lb (120 kg)
Country of origin	Switzerland

One of the genial giants of the dog world, the Saint Bernard was developed at a monastery high in the Swiss Alps, where its ancestors were used to search for missing travelers in the winter snow. One of the most famous Saint Bernards, a dog called Barry, saved over 200 lives. The popular image of the breed, based on a painting by Sir Edwin Landseer, shows a Saint Bernard carrying a miniature keg of brandy around its neck to revive those it rescued. This was simply artistic interpretation though—these dogs were never equipped in this way. The size of the Saint Bernard means they can be cumbersome in the home, and they often drool, which will not suit the house-proud. These placid dogs make very easy-going pets.

LIKES	NEEDS
* Space outdoors	* Early training
* An uncluttered home	* Careful exercise while growing
* Lots of attention	* Breeding stock checked for hip dysplasia

Is this your perfect dog?

Teen living with parents
●●●●○○○○○○

Owner with physical disability
●●○○○○○○○○

Young single owner
●●●●●●○○○○

Allergy sufferers
●●○○○○○○○○

Young couple
●●●●●●●○○

Trend-centric owner
●●●●●●○○○○

Family with young kids
●●○○○○○○○○

Individualist
●●●●●●○○○○

Family with teenagers
●●●●●●●●○

Keen jogger
●●●●●●○○○○

Older single owner
●●●●●●●○○

Enthusiastic hiker
●●●●●●●●●

Older couple
●●●●●●○○○

Countryside pursuits fan
●●○○○○○○○○

City dweller
●●○○○○○○○○

Beach lover
●●●●●●●●○○

Rural owner
●●●●●●●●●

Canine sports competitor
●●●●●●○○○○

Hobby farmer
●●●●●●○○○

AKC group: working

Greater Swiss Mountain Dog

Height 28 in (71 cm)
Weight 135 lb (61 kg)
Country of origin Switzerland

The Greater Swiss Mountain Dog is the largest and oldest of the four breeds of Swiss mountain dog—Greater Swiss Mountain Dog, Entlebucher, Bernese, and Appenzeller—also known as Sennenhunds. They all display similar coloration, having a tricolored coat with red (rust), black, and white areas. The Greater Swiss Mountain Dog was developed as a multipurpose farm dog, not just working with livestock, but also pulling distinctive carts used as a means of transportation. As with all large dogs, Greater Swiss Mountain Dogs mature quite slowly. House-training can be a particular issue, with bitches sometimes suffering urinary incontinence. As long as you are prepared for the issues that come with keeping such a large dog, they make great family companions.

Is this your perfect dog?

Teen living with parents
●●●●●●○○○○

Rural owner
●●●●●●●●●●

Keen jogger
●●●●●●●○○○

Beach lover
●●●●●●○○○○

Young single owner
●●●●●●●○○○

Hobby farmer
●●●●●●●●●○

Enthusiastic hiker
●●●●●●●●●○

Canine sports competitor
●●●●●●●●●●

Young couple
●●●●●●●●○○

Owner with physical disability
●●○○○○○○○○

Countryside pursuits fan
●●○○○○○○○○

AKC group: working

Family with young kids
●●●●○○○○○○

Allergy sufferers
●●●●○○○○○○

Family with teenagers
●●●●●●●●●●

Trend-centric owner
●●●●○○○○○○

Older single owner
●●●●●●○○○○

Individualist
●●●●○○○○○○

Older couple
●●●●●●○○○○

City dweller
●●○○○○○○○○

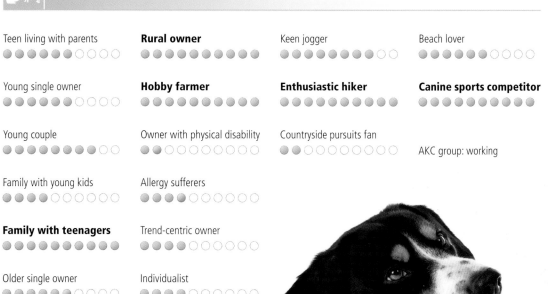

Entlebucher Mountain Dog

Height	20 in (51 cm)
Weight	66 lb (30 kg)
Country of origin	Switzerland

A close relative of the Greater Swiss Mountain Dog (page 171), this breed is named after the Entlen mountains where it was first developed, primarily as a cattle herder. It is the smallest of the Sennenhunds, but displays the typical coloration associated with the group, with rust-colored fur on the head and the lower part of the legs. Some individuals are born with a bobtail. Be aware that potential parents should be checked for hip dysplasia, as their puppies may be affected, too. This tends to be an issue with many breeds, such as the Swiss Mountain Dogs. Careful screening helps to control the problem and should ensure that you start with a healthy dog.

LIKES

* Canine sports
* An active lifestyle
* Being with people

NEEDS

* Minimal grooming
* Good socialization
* Plenty to do

Is this your perfect dog?

Teen living with parents
●●●●●●●●○○

Owner with physical disability
●●○○○○○○○○

Young single owner
●●●●●●●●○○

Allergy sufferers
●●●●○○○○○○

Young couple
●●●●●●●○○○

Trend-centric owner
●●●●○○○○○○

Family with young kids
●●●●●●○○○○

Individualist
●●●●●○○○○○

Family with teenagers
●●●●●●●●●○

Keen jogger
●●●●●●○○○○

Older single owner
●●●●●●●○○○

Enthusiastic hiker
●●●●●●●●●●

Older couple
●●●●●●●○○○

Countryside pursuits fan
●●○○○○○○○○

City dweller
●●●●○○○○○○

Beach lover
●●●●●●○○○○

Rural owner
●●●●●●●●●●

Canine sports competitor
●●●●●●●●●●

Hobby farmer
●●●●●●●●●○

AKC group: herding

Bernese Mountain Dog

Height 28 in (71 cm)
Weight 100 lb (45 kg)
Country of origin Switzerland

The best known of the Swiss mountain dogs, the Bernese Mountain Dog is named after the canton of Bern. It is a powerful, muscular dog, and has proved to be a versatile working companion in the past. These affectionate dogs are now popular as family pets, particularly as they get along well with children, but their working background should not be forgotten, as they have high energy levels. If they become bored, this may lead to behavioral problems, such as persistent barking. Unfortunately, Bernese Mountain Dogs are vulnerable to various mobility issues, so ask a veterinarian to check for joint problems. The final member of the mountain dog group is the Appenzeller, which is instantly recognizable by its curled tail.

LIKES

* Being active
* Working with people
* A family lifestyle

NEEDS

* Positive training
* Moderate grooming
* Plenty of exercise

AKC group: working

Bernese Mountain Dog and Border Collie

Intelligent, easy to train, and active by nature, **Borderneses** tend to be tricolored, with white patterning mainly on the chest and underparts, although some are just black and white.

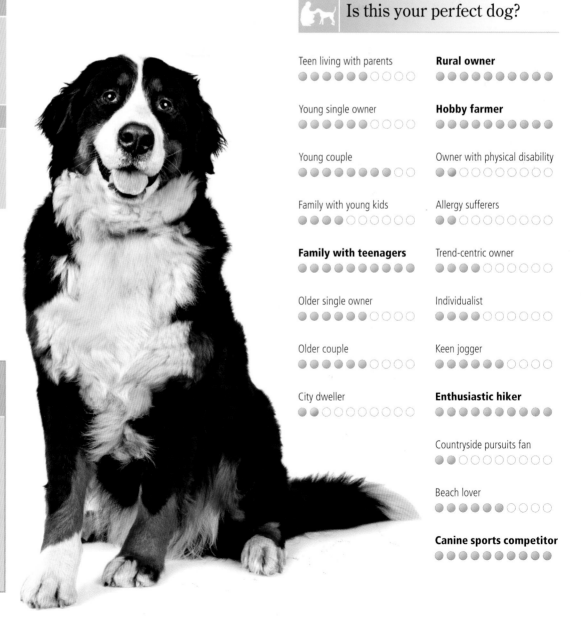

Is this your perfect dog?

Teen living with parents ●●●●●●○○○○	**Rural owner** ●●●●●●●●●●
Young single owner ●●●●●●○○○○	**Hobby farmer** ●●●●●●●●●●
Young couple ●●●●●●●●○○	Owner with physical disability ●●○○○○○○○○
Family with young kids ●●●●○○○○○○	Allergy sufferers ●●○○○○○○○○
Family with teenagers ●●●●●●●●●●	Trend-centric owner ●●●●●○○○○○
Older single owner ●●●●●●○○○○	Individualist ●●●●●○○○○○
Older couple ●●●●●●●●○○	Keen jogger ●●●●●●●○○○
City dweller ●●○○○○○○○○	**Enthusiastic hiker** ●●●●●●●●●●
	Countryside pursuits fan ●●○○○○○○○○
	Beach lover ●●●●●●○○○○
	Canine sports competitor ●●●●●●●●●●

Great Dane

Height	36 in (91 cm)
Weight	176 lb (80 kg)
Country of origin	Germany

Ranking as the tallest breed in the world, the Great Dane will tower over young children, and its physical presence can be intimidating, though it is not normally aggressive. Within the home, though, they will occupy a lot of space simply by stretching out, so you will need a fairly large area to accommodate this breed. As with other giant breeds, it is particularly important that Great Danes are never fed before exercise, as this leaves them vulnerable to the potentially fatal condition of bloat. Great Dane puppies should be exercised often and in short sessions, rather than taken on occasional marathon hikes, so as not to risk damage to their developing skeletal systems—they grow relatively slowly.

LIKES

* Family life
* Playing
* Running off the leash

NEEDS

* Early socialization
* Little grooming
* A lot of food

Great Dane and Anatolian Shepherd Dog

Combining two giants of the dog world unsurprisingly results in correspondingly large offspring. Space and adequate training are vital for **Plush Danois.** The coat is typically short, but plush.

Is this your perfect dog?

Teen living with parents	Owner with physical disability
●●●●●●○○○○	●●○○○○○○○○
Young single owner	Allergy sufferers
●●●●●●○○○○	●●●●○○○○○○
Young couple	Trend-centric owner
●●●●●●●○○○	●●●●●●○○○○
Family with young kids	Individualist
●●●●○○○○○○	●●●●●○○○○○
Family with teenagers	Keen jogger
●●●●●●●●●○	●●●●○○○○○○
Older single owner	Enthusiastic hiker
●●●●○○○○○○	●●●●●○○○○○
Older couple	Countryside pursuits fan
●●●●○○○○○○	●●○○○○○○○○
City dweller	Beach lover
●●○○○○○○○○	●●●●●●●○○○
Rural owner	Canine sports competitor
●●●●●●●●●○	●●●●○○○○○○
Hobby farmer	
●●●●●●○○○○	AKC group: working

Tibetan Mastiff

Height 28 in (71 cm)
Weight 180 lb (82 kg)
Country of origin Tibet

The Tibetan Mastiff represents a link with the early days of canine domestication. In common with wolves—but unlike most domestic dogs—the Tibetan Mastiff has just a single period of heat each year, so a bitch will only produce one litter a year, rather than the more usual two. It is a large, powerfully built breed that was originally used to warn of the approach of strangers, and to intimidate unwanted visitors. Today's Tibetan Mastiffs may appear large, but they were even bigger in the past. The breed retains a strong protective streak. Tibetan Mastiffs require considerable space, and are not suitable for an urban lifestyle. You should also think carefully about the cost implications of keeping such a large dog.

LIKES

* Playing
* Family life
* Guarding property

NEEDS

* Good early socialization
* Sound training
* Moderate grooming

Is this your perfect dog?

Teen living with parents
●●○○○○○○○○

Owner with physical disability
●●○○○○○○○○

Young single owner
●●●●○○○○○○

Allergy sufferers
●●○○○○○○○○

Young couple
●●●●●●○○○○

Trend-centric owner
●●●●○○○○○○

Family with young kids
●●○○○○○○○○

Individualist
●●●●○○○○○○

Family with teenagers
●●●●●●●●●○

Keen jogger
●●●●●●●●●○

Older single owner
●●●●○○○○○○

Enthusiastic hiker
●●●●●●●●●●

Older couple
●●●●○○○○○○

Countryside pursuits fan
●●○○○○○○○○

City dweller
●●○○○○○○○○

Beach lover
●●●●●●○○○○

Rural owner
●●●●●●●●●●

Canine sports competitor
●●●●○○○○○○

Hobby farmer
●●●●●●●●○○

AKC group: working

Portuguese Water Dog

Height	22 in (56 cm)
Weight	55 lb (25 kg)
Country of origin	Portugal

For many years, this native Portuguese breed languished in obscurity, and was facing an uncertain future, its numbers having fallen to as few as 50 individuals. In recent years, however, efforts to conserve the breed received a major boost when it was chosen as a family pet by the Obamas to live with them at the White House, guaranteeing worldwide publicity. Part of the reason for this decision was the hope that their puppy would be hypoallergenic. The original task of the Portuguese Water Dog was to assist fishermen pulling in their nets off the country's Algarve coast. Their coat is styled like that of a Poodle, to help them swim more effectively. Portuguese Water Dogs make good companions and they respond well to training.

LIKES

* Jumping into water
* A coastal lifestyle
* Being with people

NEEDS

* Plenty of physical exercise
* Mental stimulation
* Toys to retrieve

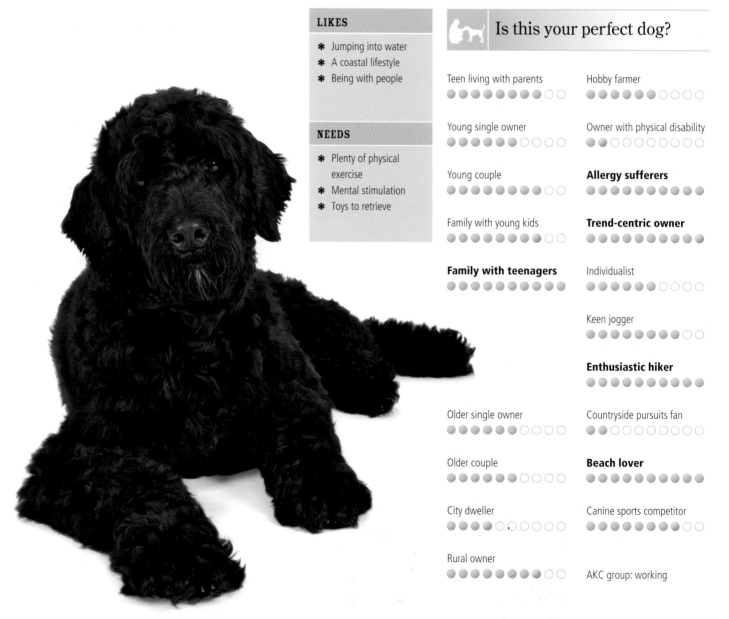

Is this your perfect dog?

Teen living with parents	Hobby farmer
Young single owner	Owner with physical disability
Young couple	**Allergy sufferers**
Family with young kids	**Trend-centric owner**
Family with teenagers	Individualist
	Keen jogger
	Enthusiastic hiker
Older single owner	Countryside pursuits fan
Older couple	**Beach lover**
City dweller	Canine sports competitor
Rural owner	AKC group: working

Newfoundland

Height	28 in (71 cm)
Weight	150 lb (68 kg)
Country of origin	Canada

This breed was originally developed to help fishermen at sea, like the Portuguese Water Dog (opposite). The Newfoundland is a gentle giant, which uses its strength to help haul nets of fish onto land, and pull carts to transport the fish to market. It can swim very well, even in choppy water, assisted by its webbed feet, and even today Newfoundlands like to plunge into water if the opportunity presents itself. They are known to have been lifesavers, pulling drowning people from the water to safety. However, alongside their power and strength is a strong desire to build a bond with members of its family. They are most commonly jet black or sometimes brown, with the black-and-white variant being recognized separately as the Landseer.

LIKES

* Going into water
* A family existence
* Being around children

NEEDS

* Lots of food
* Plenty of grooming
* Sound training

Is this your perfect dog?

Teen living with parents
●●●●●●●●○○

Hobby farmer
●●●●●●○○○○

Young single owner
●●●●●●○○○○

Owner with physical disability
●●○○○○○○○○

Young couple
●●●●●●●●○○

Allergy sufferers
●●○○○○○○○○

Family with young kids
●●●●●●○○○○

Trend-centric owner
●●●●○○○○○○

Family with teenagers
●●●●●●●●●●

Individualist
●●●●○○○○○○

Older single owner
●●●●●●○○○○

Keen jogger
●●●●●●●●○○

Older couple
●●●●●●●○○○

Enthusiastic hiker
●●●●●●●●●●

City dweller
●●○○○○○○○○

Countryside pursuits fan
●●○○○○○○○○

Rural owner
●●●●●●●●●●

Beach lover
●●●●●●●●●●

Canine sports competitor
●●●●●●○○○○

AKC group: working

Xoloitzcuintli

Height	22 in (56 cm)
Weight	31 lb (14 kg)
Country of origin	Mexico

Also known as the Mexican Hairless Dog, the native name of this breed is pronounced *sholo-its-quintli*, and is often shortened to Xolo. As well as the standard variety, there are also miniature and toy forms. There is even a fully coated form, known as the powderpuff, which crops up regularly in litters. Even a typical Xolo does possess some hair on its body, usually on its extremities—around the head, feet, and the tip of the tail. Not everyone likes their appearance, but Xolos are intelligent by nature, and may induce less of an allergic response in vulnerable people than a dog with a full coat. The Xoloitzcuintli tends not to suffer badly with fleas.

LIKES	NEEDS
* A stable temperature	* A coat for colder months
* "Wipe-over" grooming	* Sunblock in warm weather
* Sleeping alongside its owner	* Exercise indoors

Is this your perfect dog?

Teen living with parents
●●●●●●●●○○

Owner with physical disability
●●●●○○○○○○

Young single owner
●●●●●●○○○○

Allergy sufferers
●●●●●●●●●●

Young couple
●●●●●●●●○○

Trend-centric owner
●●●●●●●●●●

Family with young kids
●●●●●●●○○○

Individualist
●●●●●●●●●●

Family with teenagers
●●●●●●●●○○

Keen jogger
●●●●○○○○○○

Older single owner
●●●●●●●●●○

Enthusiastic hiker
●●●●○○○○○○

Older couple
●●●●●●●●●○

Countryside pursuits fan
●●○○○○○○○○

City dweller
●●●●●●○○○○

Beach lover
●●○○○○○○○○

Rural owner
●●●●●●○○○○

Canine sports competitor
●●●●●●●●○○

Hobby farmer
●●●●●●○○○○

AKC group: non-sporting

Leonberger

Height	32 in (80 cm)
Weight	165 lb (75 kg)
Country of origin	Germany

The Leonberger's origins are unique—it is the only breed that has ever been created purely for a political purpose. During the 1800s, the mayor of the German town of Leonberg decided that he wanted to have a specific breed that would look suitably imposing on the town's coat of arms. The aim was to have a dog with a leonine appearance and the Leonberger was bred, on this basis, from a variety of other large breeds, including the Newfoundland (page 177) and Saint Bernard (page 170). The Leonberger is a dependable guardian, in addition to being used to pull carts in some areas, thereby revealing its strength. Do bear in mind that Leonbergers may be quite short-lived, and are susceptible to some cancers. Despite their huge size, they make friendly and responsive pets.

LIKES

* Swimming
* Playing games
* Family life

NEEDS

* Early socialization
* Moderate grooming
* Obedience training

Is this your perfect dog?

Teen living with parents	Older couple	Hobby farmer	Trend-centric owner
Young single owner	City dweller	Owner with physical disability	Individualist
Young couple	**Rural owner**	Allergy sufferers	Keen jogger
Family with young kids			Enthusiastic hiker
Family with teenagers			Countryside pursuits fan
Older single owner			Beach lover
			Canine sports competitor

AKC group: working

Schipperke

Height	13 in (33 cm)
Weight	18 lb (8 kg)
Country of origin	Belgium

These medium-sized spitz-type dogs are black in color, and are sometimes referred to as Belgian barge dogs. Schipperkes were once a common sight on the barges that plied their trade on the canal network in Europe. Their purpose was really to act as watchdogs, alerting those on the boat to the presence of strangers in the vicinity, and, as a result, they have a justified reputation for being alert and sometimes noisy dogs. The Schipperke's lively nature means that it tends not to relax, and it can get bored easily in the home. They need the stimulus of going out for regular walks, which gives them the opportunity to explore and employ their natural curiosity. The shape of the tail may vary in appearance.

LIKES

* Being active
* Playing games
* Chasing rodents

NEEDS

* Moderate grooming
* Socialization with people
* Discouragement from barking

Is this your perfect dog?

Teen living with parents
●●●●●●●○○○

Owner with physical disability
●●●●○○○○○○

Young single owner
●●●●●●○○○○

Allergy sufferers
●●○○○○○○○○

Young couple
●●●●●●●●○○

Trend-centric owner
●●●●○○○○○○

Family with young kids
●●●●○○○○○○

Individualist
●●●●●○○○○○

Family with teenagers
●●●●●●●●●○

Keen jogger
●●●●●○○○○○

Older single owner
●●●●●●●●●○

Enthusiastic hiker
●●●●●●●○○○

Older couple
●●●●●●●●●○

Countryside pursuits fan
●●○○○○○○○○

City dweller
●●●●●●●●○○

Beach lover
●●●●●○○○○○

Rural owner
●●●●●●●○○○

Canine sports competitor
●●●●●●●●○○

Hobby farmer
●●●●●●●●○○

AKC group: non-sporting

Keeshond

Height	18 in (46 cm)
Weight	45 lb (20 kg)
Country of origin	The Netherlands

Typically wolf-gray in color, the Keeshond was traditionally kept on barges operating from the Netherlands. The canals were major trading routes when the breed was created, in the eighteenth century. The Keeshond had to be adaptable, being expected to live in a cramped area on the barge. These dogs undertook a wide variety of tasks, acting as guards and serving as rodent controllers, but their most unusual role was helping to guide the barge through the fog, barking to indicate the correct course for the bargeman to follow. Today, Keeshonden (the plural form of the breed's name) are valued for being good companions and keen watchdogs, although, perhaps unsurprisingly, they are inclined to be quite noisy. Bear in mind that these dogs can develop epilepsy, usually a treatable condition.

LIKES

* Being with people
* Urban life
* A watchdog role

NEEDS

* Regular grooming
* Moderate exercise
* Sensitive training

Is this your perfect dog?

Teen living with parents
●●●●●●○○○○

Owner with physical disability
●●○○○○○○○○

Young single owner
●●●●●●○○○○

Allergy sufferers
●●○○○○○○○○

Young couple
●●●●●●●○○○

Trend-centric owner
●●●●○○○○○○

Family with young kids
●●●○○○○○○○

Individualist
●●●●○○○○○○

Family with teenagers
●●●●●●●●●●

Keen jogger
●●●●●○○○○○

Older single owner
●●●●●●●●●●

Enthusiastic hiker
●●●●●●●●○○

Older couple
●●●●●●●●●●

Countryside pursuits fan
●●○○○○○○○○

City dweller
●●●●●●●○○

Beach lover
●●●●●●○○○○

Rural owner
●●●●●●●○○○

Canine sports competitor
●●●●●●●●○○

Hobby farmer
●●●●●●○○○○

AKC group: non-sporting

Shiba Inu

Height 16 in (41 cm)
Weight 24 lb (11 kg)
Country of origin Japan

The Shiba Inu is the smallest of Japan's native spitz breeds, and tends to be pale in color, usually found in shades of cream to red, although you may see black-and-tan individuals. It is a very old breed—skeletal remains dating back over 2,500 years, matching those of the Shiba Inu of today, have been discovered in Japan, where the breed was primarily used to hunt birds. These dogs have become much more popular in the West in recent years. They are very clean, grooming themselves frequently, and they are also remarkably easy to house-train. A very unusual feature is the call uttered by these dogs, which has been nicknamed the "Shiba scream," because of its sound. They are otherwise quiet though, and rarely bark.

LIKES

* Close family
* Exploring off the leash
* Playing

NEEDS

* Early socialization
* Minimal grooming
* Daily exercise

Is this your perfect dog?

Teen living with parents ●●●●●●●●○○	Family with young kids ●●●●●●●○○○	**Older couple** ●●●●●●●●●○	Allergy sufferers ●●●●●●●●○○
Young single owner ●●●●●●●○○○	**Family with teenagers** ●●●●●●●●●●	City dweller ●●●●●●●●○○	Trend-centric owner ●●●●●●●○○○
Young couple ●●●●●●●●○○	**Older single owner** ●●●●●●●●●●	Rural owner ●●●●●●●●○○	Individualist ●●●●●●●●○○
		Hobby farmer ●●●●●●○○○○	Keen jogger ●●●●●●●●○○
		Owner with physical disability ●●●●○○○○○○	Enthusiastic hiker ●●●●●●●●○○
			Countryside pursuits fan ●●●●●●○○○○
			Beach lover ●●●●●●○○○○
			Canine sports competitor ●●●●●●●●○○

AKC group: non-sporting

Shiba Inu and Cocker Spaniel

Stocky, with a broad head and quite a wide, short muzzle, the **Shocker** is often smooth coated. The influence of the Shiba Inu tends to dominate in such crosses.

Akita

Height	28 in (71 cm)
Weight	110 lb (50 kg)
Country of origin	Japan

This ancient Japanese breed is renowned for its loyalty, although in its early days it was used for dogfighting. The best-known Akita, called Hachikō, was kept by a Japanese professor who traveled into work by train every day. Hachikō always walked with his owner to the station and then returned to greet him when he traveled home each afternoon. One day in May 1925, Professor Ueno died at work and Hachikō returned from the station alone. The faithful dog returned every day to greet the train for the rest of his life, always hoping to see the professor again. Akitas are not especially well-disposed toward other dogs, so encouraging them to mix well from an early age is important.

Is this your perfect dog?

Teen living with parents
●●●●○○○○○○

Young single owner
●●●●●●○○○○

Young couple
●●●●●●○○○○

Family with young kids
●●●●○○○○○○

Family with teenagers
●●●●●●●●●●

Older single owner
●●●●○○○○○○

Older couple
●●●●○○○○○○

City dweller
●●●●●●○○○○

Rural owner
●●●●●●●●●●

Hobby farmer
●●●●●●○○○○

Owner with physical disability
●●○○○○○○○○

Allergy sufferers
●●●●●○○○○○

Trend-centric owner
●●●●○○○○○○

Individualist
●●●●○○○○○○

Keen jogger
●●●●●●●●○○

Enthusiastic hiker
●●●●●●●●○○

Countryside pursuits fan
●●○○○○○○○○

Beach lover
●●●●●○○○○○

Canine sports competitor
●●●●○○○○○○

AKC group: working

LIKES
* A single dog household
* Plenty of exercise
* Being a guardian

NEEDS
* Early socialization
* Effective leash training
* Relatively little grooming

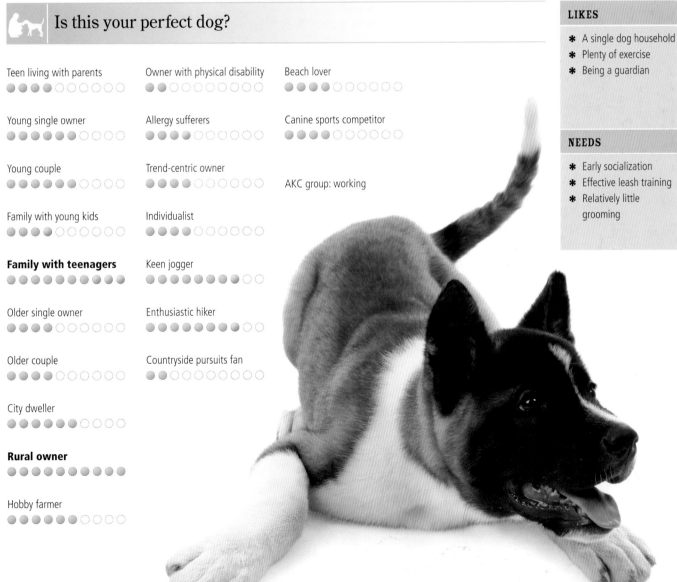

Chinese Shar-pei

Height	20 in (51 cm)
Weight	60 lb (27 kg)
Country of origin	China

This ancient breed was on the verge of extinction in the mid-1970s, when a Hong Kong dog enthusiast raised the plight of the Chinese Shar-pei in a dog magazine. Breeders around the world responded, and these interesting dogs are being kept in many countries, with their future now secured. Their skin is heavily wrinkled, and is loose on the body—an advantage for a dog that was used in organized dogfighting contests, ensuring it was difficult for an opponent to grab. Although the aggressive traits of the Chinese Shar-pei have been significantly diluted, always remember that these dogs are not inclined to back down if they feel threatened. They must therefore be well trained so they always return when called.

LIKES	NEEDS
* Acting independently	* Ears cleaned
* Working as a guardian	* Checks of skin folds for possible infection
* Being the only dog at home	* Socialization

Chinese Shar-pei and Dalmatian

Not all **Sharmatian** puppies from a litter will display spotted patterning, which is often muted when present. They may inherit the Shar-pei's blue tongue, and the Dalmatian's tail.

Is this your perfect dog?

Teen living with parents
●●●●○○○○○○

Owner with physical disability
●●○○○○○○○○

Young single owner
●●●●●●○○○○

Allergy sufferers
●●●●○○○○○○

Young couple
●●●●●●●○○○

Trend-centric owner
●●●●●●●○○

Family with young kids
●●●●○○○○○○

Individualist
●●●●●●○○○○

Family with teenagers
●●●●●●●●○○

Keen jogger
●●●●●●●○○

Older single owner
●●●●●●○○○○

Enthusiastic hiker
●●●●●●●●●○

Older couple
●●●●●●●○○○

Countryside pursuits fan
●●○○○○○○○○

City dweller
●●●●○○○○○○

Beach lover
●●●●○○○○○○

Rural owner
●●●●●●●○○○

Canine sports competitor
●●●●○○○○○○

Hobby farmer
●●●●○○○○○○

AKC group: non-sporting

Chow Chow

Height	22 in (56 cm)
Weight	70 lb (32 kg)
Country of origin	China

The Chow Chow is thought to be one of the oldest of all dog breeds, based on DNA analysis. Both this breed and the Chinese Shar-pei are believed to be descended from the same ancestral stock. One of the less evident but most revealing signs of the two breeds' relationship is the distinctive pigmentation of their tongues, which is bluish in both cases. With an appearance likened to that of a small bear, the Chow Chow has a justified reputation for being stubborn, and—unlike most dogs—is often disinclined to play. These dogs have fulfilled a number of roles in their Chinese homeland, including pulling carts and guarding property, as well as hunting. Chow Chows can suffer from problems with their eyelashes, which may irritate the eye. This may require surgical correction.

LIKES	NEEDS
✳ Guarding its family	✳ Patient training
✳ Being groomed	✳ Encouragement to play
✳ A moderately active lifestyle	✳ Socialization with people

 Is this your perfect dog?

Teen living with parents	Owner with physical disability
●●●●○○○○○○	●●○○○○○○○○
Young single owner	Allergy sufferers
●●●●○○○○○○	●●○○○○○○○○
Young couple	Trend-centric owner
●●●●●●○○○○	●●●●○○○○○○
Family with young kids	Individualist
●●○○○○○○○○	●●●●○○○○○○
Family with teenagers	Keen jogger
●●●●○○○○○○	●●●●●●○○○○
Older single owner	Enthusiastic hiker
●●●●●●○○○○	●●●●●●●○○○
Older couple	Countryside pursuits fan
●●●●●●●●●●	●●○○○○○○○○
City dweller	Beach lover
●●●●●●○○○○	●●○○○○○○○○
Rural owner	Canine sports competitor
●●●●●●○○○○	●●○○○○○○○○
Hobby farmer	
●●●●○○○○○○	AKC group: non-sporting

Standard Schnauzer

Height	20 in (51 cm)
Weight	50 lb (23 kg)
Country of origin	Germany

Schnauzers have a reputation for being intelligent dogs and are able to work closely with people. The standard is the ancestral form, bred in the traditional colors of either black or "salt-and-pepper," which looks predominantly grayish. The coat has a wiry texture, and can be hand stripped or clipped to maintain its appearance; the beard should be trimmed regularly as well. Like most working breeds, the Standard Schnauzer is a very active dog, and without adequate exercise and mental stimulation, it can become bored and destructive around the home. Try not to stick to the same route when out walking, but vary your walks to provide more interest. Standard Schnauzers are quick learners, and are not difficult to train.

Standard Schnauzer and Kerry Blue Terrier

The physical similarity between these breeds means that **Sherry** puppies are not likely to differ very significantly in appearance, although the defining coloration of the Kerry Blue may be missing.

LIKES	NEEDS
✳ Opportunities to explore	✳ Lots of grooming
✳ Being outdoors	✳ Plenty of exercise
✳ Family life	✳ Consistent training

Is this your perfect dog?

Teen living with parents
●●●●●●○○○

Owner with physical disability
●●○○○○○○○○

Young single owner
●●●●●●○○○○

Allergy sufferers
●●●●●●○○○○

Young couple
●●●●●●●○○

Trend-centric owner
●●●●○○○○○○

Family with young kids
●●●○○○○○○

Individualist
●●●●●●○○○○

Family with teenagers
●●●●●●●●●

Keen jogger
●●●●●●○○○○

Older single owner
●●●●●●●○○

Enthusiastic hiker
●●●●●●●●○○

Older couple
●●●●●●○○○

Countryside pursuits fan
●●○○○○○○○○

City dweller
●●●●○○○○○

Beach lover
●●●●●●○○○○

Rural owner
●●●●●●●●●

Canine sports competitor
●●●●●●●●●●

Hobby farmer
●●●●●●●○○

AKC group: working

Giant Schnauzer

Height 28 in (71 cm)
Weight 77 lb (35 kg)
Country of origin Germany

This is the largest of the three schnauzer breeds—giant, standard (opposite), and miniature (page 109). The distinctive "salt-and-pepper" coloring is often seen, with this gray coloration being the result of the mixed white, black, and gray hairs in the coat. Bear in mind that Schnauzer puppies—irrespective of the size—are often surprisingly dark in color at first, and may show markings later. Their appearance will soon change, and a dark stripe down the back of "salt-and-pepper" individuals will vanish as well. Black is also a common color for Giant Schnauzers. These dogs are highly adaptable, and acted as herding dogs in the past—taking farm stock to market—as well as guardians, and more recently police dogs. Giant Schnauzers are generally quiet by nature, not given to barking.

LIKES
* Being active
* Playing
* Family life

NEEDS
* Socialization with people
* Beard trimming
* Regular grooming

Is this your perfect dog?

Teen living with parents
●●●●●●○○○○

Owner with physical disability
●●○○○○○○○○

Young single owner
●●●●●●○○○○

Allergy sufferers
●●●●●●○○○○

Young couple
●●●●●●●●○○

Trend-centric owner
●●●●●○○○○○

Family with young kids
●●●●○○○○○○

Individualist
●●●●○○○○○○

Family with teenagers
●●●●●●●●●○

Keen jogger
●●●●●●●○○○

Older single owner
●●●●●●○○○○

Enthusiastic hiker
●●●●●●●●○○

Older couple
●●●●●●○○○○

Countryside pursuits fan
●●○○○○○○○○

City dweller
●●●●○○○○○○

Beach lover
●●●●●●○○○○

Rural owner
●●●●●●●●●●

Canine sports competitor
●●●●●●●●●●

Hobby farmer
●●●●●●●●○○

AKC group: working

Boxer

Height	25 in (64 cm)
Weight	70 lb (32 kg)
Country of origin	Germany

The Boxer has a playful, exuberant nature. It settles well as a household pet and makes a loyal guardian. However, it does need adequate exercise or it may become bored and destructive around the home, and it may start to dig in the yard. Boxers occur in two recognized color forms: fawn and brindle, typically with a white area on the chest, and sometimes on the muzzle, too. White boxers—where a quarter or more of the coat is white—cannot be shown in the show ring, but make good pets. Boxers with this pale coat will be more vulnerable to skin cancer though, and boxers are generally more susceptible to cancer than most other breeds. Its short coat means this breed needs very little grooming.

Boxer and Beagle

Enthusiastic and friendly, the **Bogle** could become very popular. Puppies tend to grow larger than Beagles. Black and shades of red tend to dominate, broken by smaller areas of white.

LIKES

* Chasing toys
* Plenty of exercise
* Children

NEEDS

* Minimal grooming
* Awareness of heatstroke
* Consistent training

 ## Is this your perfect dog?

Teen living with parents
●●●●●●●●●●

Owner with physical disability
●●○○○○○○○○

Young single owner
●●●●●●●●○○

Allergy sufferers
●●●●●○○○○○

Young couple
●●●●●●●●●○

Trend-centric owner
●●●●●●●○○○

Family with young kids
●●●●●●○○○○

Individualist
●●●●●○○○○○

Family with teenagers
●●●●●●●●●○

Keen jogger
●●●●●●●●○○

Older single owner
●●●●●●●○○○

Enthusiastic hiker
●●●●●●●●●○

Older couple
●●●●●●○○○○

Countryside pursuits fan
●●○○○○○○○○

City dweller
●●●●●●○○○○

Beach lover
●●●●●●●●○○

Rural owner
●●●●●●●●●○

Canine sports competitor
●●●●●●●●○○

Hobby farmer
●●●●○○○○○○

AKC group: working

Dogue de Bordeaux

Height 27 in (69 cm)
Weight 120 lb (54.5 kg)
Country of origin France

This French mastiff has become increasingly popular in recent years. Dogues de Bordeaux are fawn in color, but individuals vary, with more reddish varieties being preferred. There may be a restricted area of white on the chest. The powerfully built Dogue de Bordeaux has been trained to pull carts in the past, and this breed is said to have the largest head of all dogs, relative to its body size, with its upper lips hanging down over the lower jaw. The arrangement of the lips helps to explain why these mastiffs tend to drool, particularly in hot weather. In common with other short-nosed (or "brachycephalic") breeds, they should not be exercised in very hot weather, because they are susceptible to breathing problems.

LIKES	NEEDS
✳ Being the only dog at home	✳ Good training
✳ Acting as a guardian	✳ Careful feeding
✳ Tug toys	✳ Minimal grooming

Is this your perfect dog?

Teen living with parents
●●●●○○○○○○

Owner with physical disability
●●○○○○○○○○

Young single owner
●●●●●●●●○○

Allergy sufferers
●●●●●○○○○○

Young couple
●●●●●●●●●●

Trend-centric owner
●●●●○○○○○○

Family with young kids
●●○○○○○○○○

Individualist
●●●●●○○○○○

Family with teenagers
●●●●●●●●●○

Keen jogger
●●●●●○○○○○

Older single owner
●●●●●●○○○○

Enthusiastic hiker
●●●●●●●●○○

Older couple
●●●●●●○○○○

Countryside pursuits fan
●●○○○○○○○○

City dweller
●●●●○○○○○○

Beach lover
●●●●●●○○○○

Rural owner
●●●●●●●●●●

Canine sports competitor
●●●●○○○○○○

Hobby farmer
●●●●○○○○○○

AKC group: working

Neapolitan Mastiff

Height	30 in (76 cm)
Weight	165 lb (75 kg)
Country of origin	Italy

Neapolitan Mastiffs are gigantic dogs, and may have an ancestry stretching back to the days of ancient Rome, around 2,000 years ago. They make formidable guardians, and are very powerful. This means they can be a potential liability even when on the leash, unless they are well trained and easily controllable. Puppies often do not appreciate their own strength. The loose skin of the Neapolitan Mastiff hangs in folds, indicating the breed's fighting ancestry, and you need to be aware that infections may develop in these skin folds. These dogs are not generally fast, but can have sudden bursts of speed. The size and power of the Neapolitan Mastiff mean that this breed is neither suitable for a home with young children, nor for an inexperienced owner.

LIKES

* Space to exercise
* Acting as a guardian
* Patroling its territory

NEEDS

* Lots of food
* Positive training
* Good socialization

Is this your perfect dog?

Teen living with parents
●●●●○○○○○○

Young single owner
●●●●●●○○○○

Young couple
●●●●●●●●●○

Family with young kids
●●○○○○○○○○

Family with teenagers
●●●●●●●○○○

Older single owner
●●●●○○○○○○

Older couple
●●●●○○○○○○

City dweller
●●○○○○○○○○

Rural owner
●●●●●●●●●○

Hobby farmer
●●●●●●○○○○

Owner with physical disability
●●○○○○○○○○

Allergy sufferers
●●○○○○○○○○

Trend-centric owner
●●○○○○○○○○

Individualist
●●●●○○○○○○

Keen jogger
●●○○○○○○○○

Enthusiastic hiker
●●●●○○○○○○

Countryside pursuits fan
●●○○○○○○○○

Beach lover
●●○○○○○○○○

Canine sports competitor
●●○○○○○○○○

AKC group: working

Cane Corso

Height	27 in (69 cm)
Weight	110 lb (50 kg)
Country of origin	Italy

Another breed of Italian mastiff, the Cane Corso can be easily distinguished from the Neapolitan Mastiff by the absence of heavily wrinkled skin. The Cane Corso is a very powerful breed, and although once widely kept across modern-day Italy, it had become quite localized in southern areas, before more recently becoming sought after overseas. Its name—pronounced *kahnay korso*—indicates a breed that actually catches quarry such as wild boar, rather than just signaling its presence to a huntsman. These dogs tend to be either black or fawn in coloration. Although Cane Corsos tend not to bark excessively, they are likely to be instinctively suspicious of visitors, and good socialization is therefore important from an early age.

Is this your perfect dog?

LIKES	NEEDS
✳ Being trained	✳ Socialization with
✳ Bonding with its owner	people
✳ Watching for danger	✳ Good control
	✳ Minimal grooming

Teen living with parents
●●●●○○○○○○

Owner with physical disability
●●○○○○○○○○

Enthusiastic hiker
●●●●●●●●○○

Young single owner
●●●●●●●●○○

Allergy sufferers
●●●●○○○○○○

Countryside pursuits fan
●●●●○○○○○○

Young couple
●●●●●●●●○○

Trend-centric owner
●●●●○○○○○○

Beach lover
●●●●○○○○○○

Family with young kids
●●○○○○○○○○

Individualist
●●●●○○○○○○

Canine sports competitor
●●●●●●○○○○

Family with teenagers
●●●●●●●●○○

Keen jogger
●●●●●●○○○○

AKC group: working

Older single owner
●●●●○○○○○○

Older couple
●●●●○○○○○○

City dweller
●●○○○○○○○○

Rural owner
●●●●●●●●●○

Hobby farmer
●●●●●●○○○○

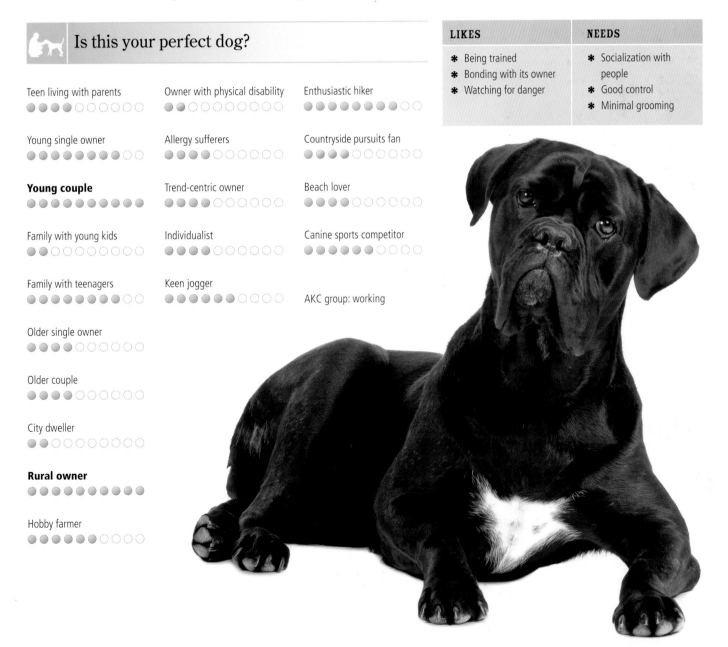

Bullmastiff

Height	27 in (69 cm)	
Weight	130 lb (59 kg)	
Country of origin	United Kingdom	

In Victorian Britain, gamekeepers faced an escalating battle to control poachers on large estates, and these conflicts could often become violent. As a result, the gamekeeping fraternity developed a larger, more powerful breed of dog to accompany them on their rounds—the Bullmastiff. The Bullmastiff was created from crossings of the existing Mastiff (opposite) with the now essentially extinct Old English Bulldog. The type of bulldog used in this cross was quite different from today's bulldogs—it was much longer in the leg, and more powerful overall. Bullmastiffs can be fawn, red, or brindle in color, with only a restricted amount of white (if any) present on the chest. They are quiet dogs, disinclined to bark. As is the case with many mastiff breeds, bitches grow to a smaller size than male dogs. These dogs make loyal pets, but are very strong.

LIKES

* Being outdoors
* Plenty of exercise
* Being a guardian

NEEDS

* Minimal grooming
* Good training
* Breeding stock checked for hip dysplasia

 ## Is this your perfect dog?

Teen living with parents	Owner with physical disability
●●●●○○○○○○	●●○○○○○○○○
Young single owner	Allergy sufferers
●●●●●●●●○○	●●●●○○○○○○
Young couple	Trend-centric owner
●●●●●●●●●○	●●○○○○○○○○
Family with young kids	Individualist
●●○○○○○○○○	●●●●●●○○○○
Family with teenagers	Keen jogger
●●●●●●●●○○	●●●●○○○○○○
Older single owner	Enthusiastic hiker
●●○○○○○○○○	●●●●●●●○○○
Older couple	Countryside pursuits fan
●●○○○○○○○○	●●○○○○○○○○
City dweller	Beach lover
●●○○○○○○○○	●●●●●●○○○○
Rural owner	Canine sports competitor
●●●●●●●●●●	●●●●●○○○○○
Hobby farmer	AKC group: working
●●●●●●○○○○	

 # Mastiff

Height	30 in (76 cm)
Weight	250 lb (113 kg)
Country of origin	United Kingdom

The ancestors of this breed—also known as the English Mastiff—can trace their lineage back more than 2,000 years. Mastiffs have long been valued as guardians, and they will still perform this role today, within the home. They are large but not particularly athletic dogs. It is important to remember, as with other large breeds, that Mastiff puppies develop slowly and must be exercised cautiously for the first couple of years of life, in order to minimize joint or skeletal damage. Brief, frequent periods of exercise are recommended. Mastiffs tend to be a relatively pale, fawnlike color, with a dark mask, though this is less obvious in brindle examples of this breed.

LIKES

* Plenty of food
* Being watchful
* A soft bed

NEEDS

* Minimal grooming
* A strong owner
* Good training

Is this your perfect dog?

Teen living with parents	Owner with physical disability
●●●●○○○○○○	●●○○○○○○○○
Young single owner	Allergy sufferers
●●●●●●●●○○	●●●●○○○○○○
Young couple	Trend-centric owner
●●●●●●●●●○	●●●●○○○○○○
Family with young kids	Individualist
●●○○○○○○○○	●●●●○○○○○○
Family with teenagers	Keen jogger
●●●●●●●●○○	●●●●●●○○○○
Older single owner	Enthusiastic hiker
●●○○○○○○○○	●●●●●●●○○○
Older couple	Countryside pursuits fan
●●○○○○○○○○	●●○○○○○○○○
City dweller	Beach lover
●●○○○○○○○○	●●●●●●○○○○
Rural owner	Canine sports competitor
●●●●●●●●●●	●●○○○○○○○○
Hobby farmer	
●●●●●●○○○○	AKC group: working

For a Mastiff crossbreed, see page 99.

Rottweiler

Height	27 in (69 cm)
Weight	110 lb (50 kg)
Country of origin	Germany

The powerfully built Rottweiler used to act as a herding dog, taking cattle to market. Since then, the breed has been employed by various police forces, and even used in search-and-rescue work. Rottweilers are an intelligent and responsive breed in terms of training, but can also be highly territorial, and may attack in the absence of their owner. The breed's relative lack of patience also means that it is probably not the ideal choice for a home with young children. In terms of coloration, the majority of the coat is a glossy black, with tan markings above the eyes, around the mouth, and on the shoulders and lower limbs. Male dogs generally grow larger than bitches.

LIKES

* Consistent training
* Playing games
* Working with cattle

NEEDS

* Minimal grooming
* Good socialization
* Plenty of exercise

Is this your perfect dog?

Teen living with parents ●●○○○○○○○○	Hobby farmer ●●●●●●●●○○
Young single owner ●●●●●●●●●●	Owner with physical disability ●●○○○○○○○○
Young couple ●●●●●●●●●●	Allergy sufferers ●●●○○○○○○○
Family with young kids ●●○○○○○○○○	Trend-centric owner ●●○○○○○○○○
Family with teenagers ●●●●●●●●○○	Individualist ●●○○○○○○○○
Older single owner ●●●●○○○○○○	Keen jogger ●●●●●●●○○○
Older couple ●●●●○○○○○○	Enthusiastic hiker ●●●●●●●●○○
City dweller ●●●○○○○○○○	Countryside pursuits fan ●●○○○○○○○○
Rural owner ●●●●●●●●●●	Beach lover ●●●●●○○○○○
	Canine sports competitor ●●●●●●○○○○

AKC group: working

Doberman Pinscher

Height 28 in (71 cm)
Weight 88 lb (40 kg)
Country of origin Germany

Although sometimes confused with the Rottweiler (opposite), it is easy to recognize a Doberman, thanks to its lighter build, and longer and relatively narrow muzzle. It was developed as a guarding breed—working closely with its handler in a variety of situations—and retains strong protective instincts, remaining particularly suspicious of visitors. Although their short, sleek fur contributes to their good looks, Doberman Pinschers can be vulnerable to various skin ailments. Once typical causes such as fleas are eliminated, it may turn out to be a food allergy, which will need further investigation by a veterinarian.

Is this your perfect dog?

Teen living with parents
●●●●●○○○○○

Older couple
●●●●●○○○○○

Trend-centric owner
●●●●●○○○○○

Countryside pursuits fan
●●○○○○○○○○

Young single owner
●●●●●●●●●●

City dweller
●●○○○○○○○○

Individualist
●●●●●○○○○○

Beach lover
●●●●●●○○○○

Young couple
●●●●●●●●●○

Rural owner
●●●●●●●●●●

Keen jogger
●●●●●●●●○○

Canine sports competitor
●●●●●●○○○○

Family with young kids
●●○○○○○○○○

Hobby farmer
●●●●●●○○○○

Enthusiastic hiker
●●●●●●●●○○

AKC group: working

Family with teenagers
●●●●●●●●○○

Owner with physical disability
●●○○○○○○○○

Older single owner
●●●●○○○○○○

Allergy sufferers
●●●●●○○○○○

LIKES
* Plenty of activity
* A standard diet
* Human company

NEEDS
* Positive training
* Good socialization
* Minimal grooming

Doberman Pinscher and Standard Poodle

Typically tousled in appearance, reflecting the Poodle's input into their ancestry, **Doodleman Pinschers** are intelligent by nature. Their coloration is very variable, but some puppies have a typical Doberman patterning.

Kuvasz

Height	30 in (76 cm)
Weight	200 lb (90 kg)
Country of origin	Hungary

The whitish fur of the Kuvasz contrasts beautifully with its black nose and dark eyes. Their pale coat allowed these flock guardians to blend in with the sheep that they were protecting from wolves. Dogs tended to work alone, and this gave the Kuvasz an independent side to its nature—this enduring independent streak can make training difficult, although patient persistence should ultimately pay off. The key to successful training of this breed is to start in puppyhood. It is also a good idea to let your puppy meet a range of people and other dogs, too, once its vaccinations are complete. In the past, the Kuvasz's coat could be either straight or wavy, although Kuvaszs all tend to have straight coats today.

LIKES

* Being outdoors
* An active lifestyle
* Long walks

NEEDS

* A fit owner
* Space in the home
* Moderate grooming

Is this your perfect dog?

Teen living with parents
●●●●●○○○○○

Owner with physical disability
●●○○○○○○○○

Young single owner
●●●●●●●○○

Allergy sufferers
●●○○○○○○○○

Young couple
●●●●●●●●○

Trend-centric owner
●●●●●○○○○

Family with young kids
●●○○○○○○○○

Individualist
●●●●○○○○○○

Family with teenagers
●●●●●●●●●

Keen jogger
●●●●●●●○○○

Older single owner
●●●●●○○○○○

Enthusiastic hiker
●●●●●●●●●

Older couple
●●●●○○○○○○

Countryside pursuits fan
●●○○○○○○○○

City dweller
●●○○○○○○

Beach lover
●●●●○○○○○○

Rural owner
●●●●●●●●●

Canine sports competitor
●●●●○○○○○○

Hobby farmer
●●●●●●●○○

AKC group: working

Komondor

Height	32 in (80 cm)
Weight	132 lb (60 kg)
Country of origin	Hungary

Traditionally seen working with the Puli (page 147), the Komondor acted as a flock guardian, ready to combat attacks on sheep by wolves, other dogs, or rustlers. As a working dog in the United States, the breed has adapted well to defending sheep in its care from unfamiliar predators, including coyotes and pumas. The Komondor's very distinctive, heavy, matted coat is weather-resistant, as befits a breed developed to spend its time working outdoors. Puppies, however, have soft, fluffy coats.

Komondorok (the plural form of the breed's name) are remarkably quick-moving if roused, but generally, around the home, they make quite placid companions, while remaining suspicious of strangers. They do have an independent side to their nature, so adequate training is very important.

LIKES

* An active lifestyle
* Family life
* Being outdoors

NEEDS

* Plenty of exercise
* Space
* Positive training

Is this your perfect dog?

Teen living with parents
●●●●●●○○○○

Family with teenagers
●●●●●●●●●●

City dweller
●●○○○○○○○○

Hobby farmer
●●●●●●●●●●

Young single owner
●●●●●●●○○○

Older single owner
●●●●●○○○○○

Rural owner
●●●●●●●●●●

Owner with physical disability
●●○○○○○○○○

Young couple
●●●●●●●●●○

Older couple
●●●●○○○○○○

Allergy sufferers
●●●●○○○○○○

Family with young kids
●●●●○○○○○○

Trend-centric owner
●●●●●●○○○○

Individualist
●●●●●●●●○○

Keen jogger
●●●●●●○○○○

Enthusiastic hiker
●●●●●●●●●●

Countryside pursuits fan
●●○○○○○○○○

Beach lover
●●○○○○○○○○

Canine sports competitor
●●●●●●○○○○

AKC group: working

3Your Perfect Dogs

Here, you will find a list of all the dogs that are a perfect match for each profile. If you are tracking more than one set of recommendations through the book, this section should help you narrow down your choices. For more help deciding between different breeds, ask the experts: a veterinarian, knowledgeable breeder, or the staff at your local shelter.

The dogs listed as a perfect match, such as this Pyrenean Shepherd, are the dogs that are truly perfect for each profile, but you can find more choices by expanding your profile to include your other interests or more elements of your lifestyle.

What Does Perfect Mean?

The dogs rated a perfect ten for a profile have been judged very tightly to help narrow down your choices while using this book. They are also related to how perfect the owner is to the dog (from the dog's perspective). For example, a young single owner is assumed to be by far the person most likely to be able to control the medium-sized, active dogs—such as a Pyrenean Shepherd—that have been matched to them. If you don't think any of the dogs listed in your profile are right for you, it will help to look at additional profiles to add more potential criteria to your selection. For example, if you are a young single owner who also likes jogging, you will find more choices recommended.

In contrast, some profiles have several dogs listed—nearly all dogs will be happy in the countryside with a rural owner, for example. In this case, by adding another profile, you will be able to narrow down your perfect match.

It is also worth remembering that the difference between an eight or ten match is not highly significant, but comparing a two with a ten does represent a marked difference in terms of suitability. Dogs rated eight out of ten will also fit very well with your profile.

Perfect dogs	Page	Also matches
TEEN LIVING WITH PARENTS (TP)		
Mutt	23	YC, FT, TI, CS
Whippet	74	FT, OS, OC, RO, CS
Bedlington Terrier	83	FT, OS, OC
Toy Fox Terrier	84	OS, OC, HF
Norfolk Terrier	92	YC, OS, OC, CD, HF
Norwich Terrier	93	YC, OS, OC, CD, HF
Boston Terrier	97	YC, FT, OS, OC, CD
Pug	125	OS, OC, CD
Shetland Sheepdog	146	OS, OC, RO, HF, CS
Boxer	188	YC, FT, RO
YOUNG SINGLE OWNER (YS)		
Pyrenean Shepherd	150	FT, RO, HF, KJ, EH, CS
Rottweiler	194	YC, RO
Doberman Pinscher	195	YC, RO
YOUNG COUPLE (YC)		
Mutt	23	TP, FT, TI, CS
Irish Water Spaniel	25	RO, HF, CP
Greyhound	70	RO, CP
Border Terrier	91	FT, RO, CS
Norfolk Terrier	92	TP, OS, OC, CD, HF
Norwich Terrier	93	TP, OS, OC, CD, HF
Boston Terrier	97	TP, FT, OS, OC, CD
Bull Terrier	101	FT, EH
Miniature Bull Terrier	102	FT, RO, EH
Miniature Schnauzer	109	FT, RO, HF, CS
Italian Greyhound	121	OS, OC, CD
Miniature Pinscher	127	OS, OC
Pomeranian	133	OS, OC, CD
Boxer	188	TP, FT, RO
Dogue de Bordeaux	189	RO
Neapolitan Mastiff	190	RO
Cane Corso	191	RO
Bullmastiff	192	RO
Mastiff	193	RO
Rottweiler	194	YS, RO
Doberman Pinscher	195	YS, RO
Kuvasz	196	FT, RO, EH
Komondor	197	FT, RO, HF, EH
FAMILY WITH YOUNG KIDS (FY)		
Beagle	54	FT, RO, EH, CP
Basset Hound	56	FT, RO, EH, CP
English Toy Spaniel	118	OS, OC, CD
Cavalier King Charles Spaniel	119	OS, OC, CD
Samoyed	165	FT, RO, EH, CS
FAMILY WITH TEENAGERS (FT)		
Mutt	23	TP, YC, TI, CS
Welsh Springer Spaniel	26	RO, HF, CP
English Springer Spaniel	27	RO, HF, CP

Perfect dogs	Page	Also matches
Sussex Spaniel	28	RO, HF, CP
English Cocker Spaniel	30	RO, CP
Cocker Spaniel	31	RO, CP
Field Spaniel	32	RO, HF, CP
Brittany	33	RO, HF, EH, CP
English Setter	34	RO, HF, EH, CP
Irish Setter	36	RO, HF, TC, EH, CP
Irish Red-and-White Setter	37	RO, HF, TI, EH, CP
Spinone Italiano	39	RO, HF, EH, CP
Flat-coated Retriever	40	RO, HF, EH, CP
Curly-coated Retriever	41	RO, HF, EH, CP, BL
Golden Retriever	42	RO, HF, PD, EH, CP, BL
Labrador Retriever	43	RO, HF, PD, EH, CP, BL
Chesapeake Bay Retriever	45	RO, HF, EH, CP, BL
Standard Poodle	46	RO, HF, AS, TC
Wire-haired Pointing Griffon	47	RO, HF, EH, CP
German Pointers	48	RO, HF, EH, CP
Pointer	49	RO, HF, EH, CP
Vizsla	50	RO, HF, EH, CP
Weimaraner	51	RO, HF, EH, CP
Portuguese Podengo Pequeno	53	RO, HF
Beagle	54	FY, RO, EH, CP
Basset Hound	56	FY, RO, EH, CP
Petit Basset Griffon Vendéen	57	RO, HF, EH, CP
Harrier	59	RO, HF, EH, CP
Treeing Walker Coonhound	60	RO, HF, EH, CP
Bluetick Coonhound	61	RO, HF, KJ, EH, CP
American English Coonhound	62	RO, HF, EH, CP
Black-and-Tan Coonhound	63	RO, HF, KJ, EH, CP
Bloodhound	64	RO, HF, KJ, EH, CP
Otterhound	65	RO, HF, KJ, EH
Pharaoh Hound	66	RO, TC
Ibizan Hound	67	RO, TC, TI
Saluki	68	RO, TC, KJ, EH
Scottish Deerhound	72	RO, HF, EH
Irish Wolfhound	73	RO, HF
Whippet	74	TP, OS, OC, RO, CS
Plott Hound	75	RO, HF, KJ, EH, CP
Norwegian Elkhound	76	RO, HF, EH, CP
Rhodesian Ridgeback	77	RO, HF, KJ, EH
Bedlington Terrier	83	TP, OS, OC
Soft-coated Wheaten Terrier	88	RO, HF, EH, CS
Kerry Blue Terrier	89	RO, HF, EH
Border Terrier	91	YC, RO, CS
Sealyham Terrier	96	CD, RO, HF
Boston Terrier	97	TP, YC, OS, OC, CD
Bull Terrier	101	YC, EH
Miniature Bull Terrier	102	YC, RO, EH
Welsh Terrier	106	RO, HF, EH, CS
Miniature Schnauzer	109	YC, RO, HF, CS
Black Russian Terrier	111	RO, EH
Löwchen	120	OS, OC, CD
Tibetan Terrier	130	HF, EH, CS

Perfect dogs	Page	Also matches
Australian Shepherd	137	RO, HF, CS
Bearded Collie	140	RO, HF, EH, CS
Old English Sheepdog	141	RO, HF, EH, CS
Border Collie	142	RO, HF, CS
Puli	147	RO, HF, AS, TI
Bouvier des Flandres	148	RO, HF, CS
Briard	149	RO, HF, EH, CS
Pyrenean Shepherd	150	YS, RO, HF, KJ, EH, CS
Great Pyrenees	151	RO, HF
Finnish Lapphund	152	RO, HF, EH, CS
Norwegian Buhund	153	RO, HF, EH, CS
Icelandic Sheepdog	154	RO, HF, EH, CS
Canaan Dog	156	RO, HF, TI, EH, CS
German Shepherd Dog	157	RO, CS
Belgian Malinois	158	RO, HF, EH, CS
Belgian Tervuren	159	RO, HF, EH, CS
Laekenois	160	RO, HF, EH, CS
Belgian Sheepdog	161	RO, HF, EH, CS
Beauceron	162	RO, HF, EH, CS
American Eskimo Dog	164	OC, CS
Samoyed	165	FY, RO, EH, CS
Siberian Husky	166	RO, KJ, EH, CS
Alaskan Malamute	167	RO, KJ, EH, CS
Dalmatian	169	RO, KJ, EH, CS
Saint Bernard	170	RO, EH
Greater Swiss Mountain Dog	171	RO, HF, EH, CS
Entlebucher Mountain Dog	172	RO, HF, EH, CS
Bernese Mountain Dog	173	RO, HF, EH, CS
Great Dane	174	RO
Tibetan Mastiff	175	FT, EH
Portuguese Water Dog	176	AS, TC, EH, BL
Newfoundland	177	RO, EH, CP
Leonberger	179	RO
Schipperke	180	OS, OC
Keeshond	181	OS, OC
Shiba Inu	182	OS, OC
Akita	183	RO
Chinese Shar-pei	184	EH
Standard Schnauzer	186	RO, CS
Giant Schnauzer	187	RO, CS
Boxer	188	T, YC, RO
Kuvasz	196	YC, RO, EH
Komondor	197	YC, RO, HF, EH

OLDER SINGLE OWNER (OS)

Perfect dogs	Page	Also matches
Dachshund	52	OC
Whippet	74	TP, FT, OC, RO, CS
West Highland White Terrier	78	OC
Cairn Terrier	79	OC
Skye Terrier	81	OC
Dandie Dinmont Terrier	82	OC
Bedlington Terrier	83	TP, FT, OC
Toy Fox Terrier	84	TP, OC, HF

Perfect dogs	Page	Also matches
Glen of Imaal Terrier	86	OC, RO, HF
Manchester Terrier	90	OC, CD, HF
Norfolk Terrier	92	TP, YC, OC, CD, HF
Norwich Terrier	93	TP, YC, OC, CD, HF
Boston Terrier	97	TP, YC, FT, OC, CD
Yorkshire Terrier	103	OC, CD
Australian Terrier	104	OC
Silky Terrier	105	OC, AS
Brussels Griffon	112	OC, CD
Affenpinscher	113	OC, CD
Shih Tzu	114	OC, CD
Bichon Frisé	115	OC, CD, AS
Maltese	116	OC, CD, AS
Havanese	117	OC, CD, AS
English Toy Spaniel	118	FY, OC, CD
Cavalier King Charles Spaniel	119	FY, OC, CD
Löwchen	120	FT, OC, CD
Italian Greyhound	121	YC, OC, CD
Chihuahua	122	OC, CD, TC
Chinese Crested	123	OC, CD, TI
Pekingese	124	OC, CD, PD
Pug	125	TP, OC, CD
Miniature and Toy Poodles	126	OC, AS, CS
Miniature Pinscher	127	YC, OC
Lhasa Apso	128	OC, CD
Tibetan Spaniel	129	OC, CD
Papillon	131	OC, CD
Japanese Chin	132	OC, CD, PD
Pomeranian	133	YC, OC, CD
English Bulldog	134	OC, CD
French Bulldog	135	OC, CD
Shetland Sheepdog	146	TP, OC, RO, HF, CS
Norwegian Lundehund	168	OC, TI, CS
Xoloitzcuintli	178	OC, AS, TC, TI
Schipperke	180	FT, OC
Keeshond	181	FT, OC
Shiba Inu	182	FT, OC

OLDER COUPLE (OC)

Perfect dogs	Page	Also matches
Dachshund	52	OS
Whippet	74	TP, FT, OS, RO, CS
West Highland White Terrier	78	OS
Cairn Terrier	79	OS
Skye Terrier	81	OS
Dandie Dinmont Terrier	82	OS
Bedlington Terrier	83	TP, FT, OC
Toy Fox Terrier	84	TP, OS, HF
Glen of Imaal Terrier	86	OS, RO, HF
Manchester Terrier	90	OS, CD, HF
Norfolk Terrier	92	TP, YC, OS, CD, HF
Norwich Terrier	93	TP, YC, OS, CD, HF
Boston Terrier	97	TP, YC, FT, OS, CD
Yorkshire Terrier	103	OS, CD

Perfect dogs	Page	Also matches
Australian Terrier	104	OS
Silky Terrier	105	OS, AS
Brussels Griffon	112	OS, CD
Affenpinscher	113	OS, CD
Shih Tzu	114	OS, CD
Bichon Frisé	115	OS, CD, AS
Maltese	116	OS, CD, AS
Havanese	117	OS, CD, AS
English Toy Spaniel	118	FY, OS, CD
Cavalier King Charles Spaniel	119	FY, OS, CD
Löwchen	120	FT, OS, CD
Italian Greyhound	121	YC, OS, CD
Chihuahua	122	OS, CD, TC
Chinese Crested	123	OS, CD, TI
Pekingese	124	OS, CD, PD
Pug	125	TP, OS, CD
Miniature and Toy Poodles	126	OS, AS, CS
Miniature Pinscher	127	YC, OS
Lhasa Apso	128	OS, CD
Tibetan Spaniel	129	OS, CD
Papillon	131	OS, CD
Japanese Chin	132	OS, CD, PD
Pomeranian	133	YC, OS, CD
English Bulldog	134	OS, CD
French Bulldog	135	OS, CD
Shetland Sheepdog	146	TP, OS, RO, HF, CS
American Eskimo Dog	164	FT, CS
Norwegian Lundehund	168	OS, TI, CS
Xoloitzcuintli	178	OS, AS, TC, TI
Schipperke	180	FT, OS
Keeshond	181	FT, OS
Shiba Inu	182	FT, OS
Chow Chow	185	

CITY DWELLER (CD)

Perfect dogs	Page	Also matches
Manchester Terrier	91	OS, OC, HF
Norfolk Terrier	92	TP, YC, OS, OC, HF
Norwich Terrier	93	TP, YC, OS, OC, HF
Sealyham Terrier	96	FT, RO, HF
Boston Terrier	97	TP, YC, FT, OS, OC
Yorkshire Terrier	103	OS, OC
Brussels Griffon	112	OS, OC
Affenpinscher	113	OS, OC
Shih Tzu	114	OS, OC
Bichon Frisé	115	OS, OC, AS
Maltese	116	OS, OC, AS
Havanese	117	OS, OC, AS
English Toy Spaniel	118	FY, OS, OC
Cavalier King Charles Spaniel	119	FY, OS, OC
Löwchen	120	FT, OS, OC
Italian Greyhound	121	YC, OS, OC
Chihuahua	122	OS, OC, TC
Chinese Crested	123	OS, OC, TI

Perfect dogs	Page	Also matches
Pekingese	124	OS, OC, PD
Pug	125	TP, OS, OC
Lhasa Apso	128	OS, OC
Tibetan Spaniel	129	OS, OC
Papillon	131	OS, OC
Japanese Chin	132	OS, OC, PD
Pomeranian	133	YC, OS, OC
English Bulldog	134	OS, OC
French Bulldog	135	OS, OC

RURAL OWNER (RO)

Perfect dogs	Page	Also matches
American Water Spaniel	24	EH, CP
Irish Water Spaniel	25	YC, HF, CP
Welsh Springer Spaniel	26	FT, HF, CP
English Springer Spaniel	27	FT, HF, CP
Sussex Spaniel	28	FT, HF, CP
Clumber Spaniel	29	HF, CP
English Cocker Spaniel	30	FT, CP
Cocker Spaniel	31	FT, CP
Field Spaniel	32	FT, HF, CP
Brittany	33	FT, HF, EH, CP
English Setter	34	FT, HF, EH, CP
Gordon Setter	35	HF, EH, CP
Irish Setter	36	FT, HF, TC, EH, CP
Irish Red-and-White Setter	37	FT, HF, TI, EH, CP
Finnish Spitz	38	HF, EH, CP
Spinone Italiano	39	FT, HF, EH, CP
Flat-coated Retriever	40	FT, HF, EH, CP
Curly-coated Retriever	41	FT, HF, EH, CP, BL
Golden Retriever	42	FT, HF, PD, EH, CP, BL
Labrador Retriever	43	FT, HF, PD, EH, CP, BL
Nova Scotia Duck Tolling Retriever	44	HF, EH, CP, BL
Chesapeake Bay Retriever	45	FT, HF, EH, CP, BL
Standard Poodle	46	FT, HF, AS, TC
Wire-haired Pointing Griffon	47	FT, HF, EH, CP
German Pointers	48	FT, HF, EH, CP
Pointer	49	FT, HF, EH, CP
Vizsla	50	FT, HF, EH, CP
Weimaraner	51	FT, HF, EH, CP
Portuguese Podengo Pequeno	53	FT, HF
Beagle	54	FY, FT, EH, CP
Basenji	55	TI
Basset Hound	56	FY, FT, EH, CP
Petit Basset Griffon Vendéen	57	FT, HF, EH, CP
American Foxhound	58	HF, KJ, EH, CP
Harrier	59	FT, HF, EH, CP
Treeing Walker Coonhound	60	FT, HF, EH, CP
Bluetick Coonhound	61	FT, HF, KJ, EH, CP
American English Coonhound	62	FT, HF, EH, CP
Black-and-Tan Coonhound	63	FT, HF, KJ, EH, CP
Bloodhound	64	FT, HF, KJ, EH, CP
Otterhound	65	FT, HF, KJ, EH
Pharaoh Hound	66	FT, TC

Perfect dogs	Page	Also matches
Ibizan Hound	67	FT, TC, TI
Saluki	68	FT, TC, KJ, EH
Afghan Hound	69	TC, KJ, EH
Greyhound	70	YC, CP
Borzoi	71	TC, EH
Scottish Deerhound	72	FT, HF, EH
Irish Wolfhound	73	FT, HF
Whippet	74	TP, FT, OS, OC, CS
Plott Hound	75	FT, HF, KJ, EH, CP
Norwegian Elkhound	76	FT, HF, EH, CP
Rhodesian Ridgeback	77	FT, HF, KJ, EH
Scottish Terrier	80	HF
Fox Terrier	85	HF
Glen of Imaal Terrier	86	OS, OC, HF
Irish Terrier	87	HF, EH, CS
Soft-coated Wheaten Terrier	88	FT, HF, EH, CS
Kerry Blue Terrier	89	FT, HF, EH
Border Terrier	91	YC, FT, CS
Parson Jack Russell Terrier	94	HF, EH, CS
Jack Russell Terriers	95	HF, EH, CS
Sealyham Terrier	96	FT, CD, HF
German Pinscher	98	HF, EH, CS
American Staffordshire Bull Terrier	99	HF
Staffordshire Bull Terrier	100	HF, EH
Miniature Bull Terrier	102	YC, FT, EH
Welsh Terrier	106	FT, HF, EH, CS
Lakeland Terrier	107	HF
Cesky Terrier	108	HF
Miniature Schnauzer	109	YC, FT, HF, CS
Airedale Terrier	110	HF, EH
Black Russian Terrier	111	FT, EH
Australian Cattle Dog	136	HF, EH, CS
Australian Shepherd	137	FT, HF, CS
Cardigan Welsh Corgi	138	HF
Pembroke Welsh Corgi	139	HF
Bearded Collie	140	FT, HF, EH, CS
Old English Sheepdog	141	FT, HF, EH, CS
Border Collie	142	FT, HF, CS
Polish Lowland Sheepdog	143	HF, BL
Rough Collie	144	HF, EH
Smooth Collie	145	HF, EH
Shetland Sheepdog	146	TP, OS, OC, HF, CS
Puli	147	FT, HF, AS, TI
Bouvier des Flandres	148	FT, HF, CS
Briard	149	FT, HF, EH, CS
Pyrenean Shepherd	150	YS, FT, HF, KJ, EH, CS
Great Pyrenees	151	FT, HF
Finnish Lapphund	152	FT, HF, EH, CS
Norwegian Buhund	153	FT, HF, EH, CS
Icelandic Sheepdog	154	FT, HF, EH, CS
Swedish Vallhund	155	HF, CS
Canaan Dog	156	FT, HF, TI, EH, CS

Perfect dogs	Page	Also matches
German Shepherd Dog	157	FT, CS
Belgian Malinois	158	FT, HF, EH, CS
Belgian Tervuren	159	FT, HF, EH, CS
Laekenois	160	FT, HF, EH, CS
Belgian Sheepdog	161	FT, HF, EH, CS
Beauceron	162	FT, HF, EH, CS
Anatolian Shepherd Dog	163	HF, EH
Samoyed	165	FY, FT, EH, CS
Siberian Husky	166	FT, KJ, EH, CS
Alaskan Malamute	167	FT, KJ, EH, CS
Dalmatian	169	FT, KJ, EH, CS
Saint Bernard	170	FT, EH
Greater Swiss Mountain Dog	171	FT, HF, EH, CS
Entlebucher Mountain Dog	172	FT, HF, EH, CS
Bernese Mountain Dog	173	FT, HF, EH, CS
Great Dane	174	FT
Tibetan Mastiff	175	FT, EH
Newfoundland	177	FT, EH, CP
Leonberger	179	FT
Akita	183	FT
Standard Schnauzer	186	FT, CS
Giant Schnauzer	187	FT, CS
Boxer	188	TP, YC, FT
Dogue de Bordeaux	189	YC
Neapolitan Mastiff	190	YC
Cane Corso	191	YC
Bullmastiff	192	YC
Mastiff	193	YC
Rottweiler	194	YS, YC
Doberman Pinscher	195	YS, YC
Kuvasz	196	YC, FT, EH
Komondor	197	YC, FT, HF, EH

HOBBY FARMER (HF)

Perfect dogs	Page	Also matches
Irish Water Spaniel	25	YC, RO, CP
Welsh Springer Spaniel	26	FT, RO, CP
English Springer Spaniel	27	FT, RO, CP
Sussex Spaniel	28	FT, RO, CP
Clumber Spaniel	29	RO, CP
Field Spaniel	32	FT, RO, CP
Brittany	33	FT, RO, EH, CP
English Setter	34	FT, RO, EH, CP
Gordon Setter	35	RO, EH, CP
Irish Setter	36	FT, RO, TC, EH, CP
Irish Red-and-White Setter	37	FT, RO, TI, EH, CP
Finnish Spitz	38	RO, EH, CP
Spinone Italiano	39	FT, RO, EH, CP
Flat-coated Retriever	40	FT, RO, EH, CP
Curly-coated Retriever	41	FT, RO, EH, CP, BL
Golden Retriever	42	FT, RO, PD, EH, CP, BL
Labrador Retriever	43	FT, RO, HF, PD, EH, CP, BL
Nova Scotia Duck Tolling Retriever	44	RO, EH, CP, BL

Perfect dogs	Page	Also matches
Chesapeake Bay Retriever	45	FT, RO, EH, CP, BL
Standard Poodle	46	FT, RO, AS, TC
Wire-haired Pointing Griffon	47	FT, RO, EH, CP
German Pointers	48	FT, RO, EH, CP
Pointer	49	FT, RO, EH, CP
Vizsla	50	FT, RO, EH, CP
Weimaraner	51	FT, RO, EH, CP
Portuguese Podengo Pequeno	53	FT, RO
Petit Basset Griffon Vendéen	57	FT, RO, EH, CP
American Foxhound	58	RO, KJ, EH, CP
Harrier	59	FT, RO, EH, CP
Treeing Walker Coonhound	60	FT, RO, EH, CP
Bluetick Coonhound	61	FT, RO, KJ, EH, CP
American English Coonhound	62	FT, RO, EH, CP
Black-and-Tan Coonhound	63	FT, RO, KJ, EH, CP
Bloodhound	64	FT, RO, KJ, EH, CP
Otterhound	65	FT, RO, KJ, EH
Scottish Deerhound	72	FT, RO, EH
Irish Wolfhound	73	FT, RO
Plott Hound	75	FT, RO, KJ, EH, CP
Norwegian Elkhound	76	FT, RO, EH, CP
Rhodesian Ridgeback	77	FT, RO, KJ, EH
Scottish Terrier	80	RO
Toy Fox Terrier	84	TP, OS, OC
Fox Terrier	85	RO
Glen of Imaal Terrier	86	OS, OC, RO
Irish Terrier	87	RO, EH, CS
Soft-coated Wheaten Terrier	88	FT, RO, EH, CS
Kerry Blue Terrier	89	FT, RO, EH
Manchester Terrier	90	OS, OC, CD
Norfolk Terrier	92	TP, YC, OS, OC, CD
Norwich Terrier	93	TP, YC, OS, OC, CD
Parson Jack Russell Terrier	94	RO, EH, CS
Jack Russell Terriers	95	RO, EH, CS
Sealyham Terrier	96	FT, CD, RO
German Pinscher	98	RO, EH, CS
American Staffordshire Bull Terrier	99	RO
Staffordshire Bull Terrier	100	RO, EH
Welsh Terrier	106	FT, RO, EH, CS
Lakeland Terrier	107	RO
Cesky Terrier	108	RO
Miniature Schnauzer	109	YC, FT, RO, CS
Airedale Terrier	110	RO, EH
Tibetan Terrier	130	FT, EH, CS
Australian Cattle Dog	136	RO, EH, CS
Australian Shepherd	137	FT, RO, CS
Cardigan Welsh Corgi	138	RO
Pembroke Welsh Corgi	139	RO
Bearded Collie	140	FT, RO, EH, CS
Old English Sheepdog	141	FT, RO, EH, CS
Border Collie	142	FT, RO, CS
Polish Lowland Sheepdog	143	RO, BL

Perfect dogs	Page	Also matches
Rough Collie	144	RO, EH
Smooth Collie	145	RO, EH
Shetland Sheepdog	146	TP, OS, OC, RO, CS
Puli	147	FT, RO, AS, TI
Bouvier Des Flandres	148	FT, RO, CS
Briard	149	FT, RO, EH, CS
Pyrenean Shepherd	150	YS, FT, RO, KJ, EH, CS
Great Pyrenees	151	FT, RO
Finnish Lapphund	152	FT, RO, EH, CS
Norwegian Buhund	153	FT, RO, EH, CS
Icelandic Sheepdog	154	FT, RO, EH, CS
Swedish Vallhund	155	RO, CS
Canaan Dog	156	FT, RO, TI, EH, CS
Belgian Malinois	158	FT, RO, EH, CS
Belgian Tervuren	159	FT, RO, EH, CS
Laekenois	160	FT, RO, EH, CS
Belgian Sheepdog	161	FT, RO, EH, CS
Beauceron	162	FT, RO, EH, CS
Anatolian Shepherd Dog	163	RO, EH
Greater Swiss Mountain Dog	171	FT, RO, EH, CS
Entlebucher Mountain Dog	172	FT, RO, EH, CS
Bernese Mountain Dog	173	FT, RO, EH, CS
Komondor	197	YC, FT, RO, EH

OWNER WITH PHYSICAL DISABILITY (PD)

Perfect dogs	Page	Also matches
Golden Retriever	42	FT, RO, HF, EH, CP, BL
Labrador Retriever	43	FT, RO, HF, EH, CP, BL
Pekingese	124	OS, OC, CD
Japanese Chin	132	OS, OC, CD

ALLERGY SUFFERERS (AS)

Perfect dogs	Page	Also matches
Standard Poodle	46	FT, RO, HF, TC
Silky Terrier	105	OS, OC
Bichon Frisé	115	OS, OC, CD
Maltese	116	OS, OC, CD
Havanese	117	OS, OC, CD
Miniature and Toy Poodles	126	OS, OC, CS
Puli	147	FT, RO, HF, TI
Portuguese Water Dog	176	FT, TC, EH, BL
Xoloitzcuintli	178	OS, OC, TC, TI

TREND-CENTRIC OWNER (TC)

Perfect dogs	Page	Also matches
Irish Setter	36	FT, RO, HF, EH, CP
Standard Poodle	46	FT, RO, HF, AS
Pharaoh Hound	66	FT, RO
Ibizan Hound	67	FT, RO, TI
Saluki	68	FT, RO, KJ, EH
Afghan Hound	69	RO, KJ, EH
Borzoi	71	RO, EH
Chihuahua	122	OS, OC, CD
Portuguese Water Dog	176	FT, AS, EH, BL
Xoloitzcuintli	178	OS, OC, AS, TI

Perfect dogs	Page	Also matches
THE INDIVIDUALIST (TI)		
Designer dogs generally	22	
Mutt	23	TP, YC, FT, CS
Irish Red-and-White Setter	37	FT, RO, HF, EH, CP
Basenji	55	RO
Ibizan Hound	67	FT, RO, TC
Chinese Crested	123	OS, OC, CD
Puli	147	FT, RO, HF, AS
Canaan Dog	156	FT, RO, HF, EH, CS
Norwegian Lundehund	168	OS, OC, CS
Xoloitzcuintli	178	OS, OC, AS, TC
KEEN JOGGER (KJ)		
American Foxhound	58	RO, HF, EH, CP
Bluetick Coonhound	61	FT, RO, HF, EH, CP
Black-and-Tan Coonhound	63	FT, RO, HF, EH, CP
Bloodhound	64	FT, RO, HF, EH, CP
Otterhound	65	FT, RO, HF, EH
Saluki	68	FT, RO, TC, EH
Afghan Hound	69	RO, TC, EH
Plott Hound	75	FT, RO, HF, EH, CP
Rhodesian Ridgeback	77	FT, RO, HF, EH
Pyrenean Shepherd	150	YS, FT, RO, HF, EH, CS
Siberian Husky	166	FT, RO, EH, CS
Alaskan Malamute	167	FT, RO, EH, CS
Dalmatian	169	FT, RO, EH, CS
ENTHUSIASTIC HIKER (EH)		
American Water Spaniel	24	RO, CP
Brittany	33	FT, RO, HF, CP
English Setter	34	FT, RO, HF, CP
Gordon Setter	35	RO, HF, CP
Irish Setter	36	FT, RO, HF, TC, CP
Irish Red-and-White Setter	37	FT, RO, HF, TI, CP
Finnish Spitz	38	RO, HF, CP
Spinone Italiano	39	FT, RO, HF, CP
Flat-coated Retriever	40	FT, RO, HF, CP
Curly-coated Retriever	41	FT, RO, HF, CP, BL
Golden Retriever	42	FT, RO, HF, PD, CP, BL
Labrador Retriever	43	FT, RO, HF, PD, CP, BL
Nova Scotia Duck Tolling Retriever	44	RO, HF, CP, BL
Chesapeake Bay Retriever	45	FT, RO, HF, CP, BL
Wire-haired Pointing Griffon	47	FT, RO, HF, CP
German Pointers	48	FT, RO, HF, CP
Pointer	49	FT, RO, HF, CP
Vizsla	50	FT, RO, HF, CP
Weimaraner	51	FT, RO, HF, CP
Beagle	54	FY, FT, RO, CP
Basset Hound	56	FY, FT, RO, CP
Petit Basset Griffon Vendéen	57	FT, RO, HF, CP
American Foxhound	58	RO, HF, KJ, CP
Harrier	59	FT, RO, HF, CP

Perfect dogs	Page	Also matches
Treeing Walker Coonhound	60	FT, RO, HF, CP
Bluetick Coonhound	61	FT, RO, HF, KJ, CP
American English Coonhound	62	FT, RO, HF, CP
Black-and-Tan Coonhound	63	FT, RO, HF, KJ, CP
Bloodhound	64	FT, RO, HF, KJ, CP
Otterhound	65	FT, RO, HF, KJ
Saluki	68	FT, RO, TC, KJ
Afghan Hound	69	RO, TC, KJ
Borzoi	71	RO, TC
Scottish Deerhound	72	FT, RO, HF
Plott Hound	75	FT, RO, HF, KJ, CP
Norwegian Elkhound	76	FT, RO, HF, CP
Rhodesian Ridgeback	77	FT, RO, HF, KJ
Irish Terrier	87	RO, HF, CS
Soft-coated Wheaten Terrier	88	FT, RO, HF, CS
Kerry Blue Terrier	89	FT, RO, HF
Parson Jack Russell Terrier	94	RO, HF, CS
Jack Russell Terriers	95	RO, HF, CS
German Pinscher	98	RO, HF, CS
Staffordshire Bull Terrier	100	RO, HF
Bull Terrier	101	YC, FT
Miniature Bull Terrier	102	YC, FT, RO
Welsh Terrier	106	FT, RO, HF, CS
Airedale Terrier	110	RO, HF
Black Russian Terrier	111	FT, RO
Tibetan Terrier	130	FT, HF, CS
Australian Cattle Dog	136	RO, HF, CS
Bearded Collie	140	FT, RO, HF, CS
Old English Sheepdog	141	FT, RO, HF, CS
Rough Collie	144	RO, HF
Smooth Collie	145	RO, HF
Briard	149	FT, RO, HF, CS
Pyrenean Shepherd	150	YS, FT, RO, HF, KJ, CS
Finnish Lapphund	152	FT, RO, HF, CS
Norwegian Buhund	153	FT, RO, HF, CS
Icelandic Sheepdog	154	FT, RO, HF, CS
Canaan Dog	156	FT, RO, HF, TI, CS
Belgian Malinois	158	FT, RO, HF, CS
Belgian Tervuren	159	FT, RO, HF, CS
Laekenois	160	FT, RO, HF, CS
Belgian Sheepdog	161	FT, RO, HF, CS
Beauceron	162	FT, RO, HF, CS
Anatolian Shepherd Dog	163	RO, HF
Samoyed	165	FY, FT, RO, CS
Siberian Husky	166	FT, RO, KJ, CS
Alaskan Malamute	167	FT, RO, KJ, CS
Dalmatian	169	FT, RO, KJ, CS
Saint Bernard	170	FT, RO
Greater Swiss Mountain Dog	171	FT, RO, HF, CS
Entlebucher Mountain Dog	172	FT, RO, HF, CS
Bernese Mountain Dog	173	FT, RO, HF, CS
Tibetan Mastiff	175	FT, RO

Perfect dogs	Page	Also matches
Portuguese Water Dog	176	FT, AS, TC, BL
Newfoundland	177	FT, RO, CP
Chinese Shar-pei	184	FT
Kuvasz	196	YC, FT, RO
Komondor	197	YC, FT, RO, HF

COUNTRYSIDE PURSUITS FAN (CP)

Perfect dogs	Page	Also matches
American Water Spaniel	24	RO, EH
Irish Water Spaniel	25	YC, RO, HF
Welsh Springer Spaniel	26	FT, RO, HF
English Springer Spaniel	27	FT, RO, HF
Sussex Spaniel	28	FT, RO, HF
Clumber Spaniel	29	RO, EH
English Cocker Spaniel	30	FT, RO
Cocker Spaniel	31	FT, RO
Field Spaniel	32	FT, RO, HF
Brittany	33	FT, RO, HF, EH
English Setter	34	FT, RO, HF, EH
Gordon Setter	35	RO, HF, EH
Irish Setter	36	FT, RO, HF, TC, EH
Irish Red-and-White Setter	37	FT, RO, HF, TI, EH
Finnish Spitz	38	RO, HF, EH
Spinone Italiano	39	FT, RO, HF, EH
Flat-coated Retriever	40	FT, RO, HF, EH
Curly-coated Retriever	41	FT, RO, HF, EH, BL
Golden Retriever	42	FT, RO, HF, PD, EH, BL
Labrador Retriever	43	FT, RO, HF, PD, EH, BL
Nova Scotia Duck Tolling Retriever	44	RO, HF, EH, BL
Chesapeake Bay Retriever	45	FT, RO, HF, EH, BL
Wire-haired Pointing Griffon	47	FT, RO, HF, EH
German Pointers	48	FT, RO, HF, EH
Pointer	49	FT, RO, HF, EH
Vizsla	50	FT, RO, HF, EH
Weimaraner	51	FT, RO, HF, EH
Beagle	54	FY, FT, RO, EH
Basset Hound	56	FY, FT, RO, EH
Petit Basset Griffon Vendéen	57	FT, RO, HF, EH
American Foxhound	58	RO, HF, KJ, EH
Harrier	59	FT, RO, HF, EH
Treeing Walker Coonhound	60	FT, RO, HF, EH
Bluetick Coonhound	61	FT, RO, HF, KJ, EH
American English Coonhound	62	FT, RO, HF, KJ, EH
Black-and-Tan Coonhound	63	FT, RO, HF, KJ, EH
Bloodhound	64	FT, RO, HF, KJ, EH
Greyhound	70	YC, RO
Plott Hound	75	FT, RO, HF, KJ, EH
Norwegian Elkhound	76	FT, RO, HF, EH

BEACH LOVER (BL)

Perfect dogs	Page	Also matches
Curly-coated retriever	41	FT, RO, HF, EH, CP
Golden Retriever	42	FT, RO, HF, PD, EH, CP
Labrador Retriever	43	FT, RO, HF, PD, EH, CP

Perfect dogs	Page	Also matches
Nova Scotia Duck Tolling Retriever	44	RO, HF, EH, CP
Chesapeake Bay Retriever	45	FT, RO, HF, EH, CP
Portuguese Water Dog	176	FT, AS, TC, EH
Newfoundland	177	FT, RO, EH

CANINE SPORTS COMPETITOR (CS)

Perfect dogs	Page	Also matches
Mutt	23	TP, YC, FT, TI
Whippet	74	TP, FT, OS, OC, RO
Irish Terrier	87	RO, HF, EH
Soft-coated Wheaten Terrier	88	FT, RO, HF, EH
Border Terrier	91	YC, FT, RO
Parson Jack Russell Terrier	94	RO, HF, EH
Jack Russell Terriers	95	RO, HF, EH
German Pinscher	98	RO, HF, EH
Welsh Terrier	106	FT, RO, HF, EH
Miniature Schnauzer	109	YC, FT, RO, HF
Miniature and Toy Poodles	126	OS, OC, AS
Tibetan Terrier	130	FT, HF, EH
Australian Cattle Dog	136	RO, HF, EH
Australian Shepherd	137	FT, RO, HF
Bearded Collie	140	FT, RO, HF, EH
Old English Sheepdog	141	FT, RO, HF, EH
Border Collie	142	FT, RO, HF
Polish Lowland Sheepdog	143	RO, HF
Shetland Sheepdog	146	TP, OS, OC, RO, HF
Bouvier des Flandres	148	FT, RO, HF
Briard	149	FT, RO HF, EH
Pyrenean Shepherd	150	YS, FT, RO, HF, KJ, EH
Finnish Lapphund	152	FT, RO, HF, EH
Norwegian Buhund	153	FT, RO, HF, EH
Icelandic Sheepdog	154	FT, RO HF, EH
Swedish Vallhund	155	RO, HF
Canaan Dog	156	FT, RO, HF, TI, EH
German Shepherd Dog	157	FT, RO
Belgian Malinois	158	FT, RO, HF, EH
Belgian Tervuren	159	FT, RO, HF, EH
Laekenois	160	FT, RO, HF, EH
Belgian Sheepdog	161	FT, RO, HF, EH
Beauceron	162	FT, RO, HF, EH
American Eskimo Dog	164	FT, OC
Samoyed	165	FY, FT, RO, EH
Siberian Husky	166	FT, RO, KJ, EH
Alaskan Malamute	167	FT, RO, KJ, EH
Norwegian Lundehund	168	OS, OC, TI
Dalmatian	169	FT, RO, KJ, EH
Greater Swiss Mountain Dog	171	FT, RO, HF, EH
Entlebucher Mountain Dog	172	FT, RO, HF, EH
Bernese Mountain Dog	173	FT, RO, HF, EH
Standard Schnauzer	186	FT, RO
Giant Schnauzer	187	FT, RO

Index

Number in **bold** indicates main entry.

Acknowledgments

The publisher wishes to thank U.S. consultant Caroline Coile.
For editorial: Donna Gregory, Liz Jones, Etty Payne. Indexing: Diana LeCore.
For design: Yumiko Tahata, Paul Turner. Additional thanks to Gareth Butterworth, Tania Field, Sue Pressley, and Geoff Windram.

Author David Alderton is very grateful to Sorrel, Philippa, and Lucy for all their invaluable input, and for making this such an enjoyable project, as well as to Stonecastle Graphics.

Marshall Editions would like to thank the following agencies for supplying images for inclusion in this book:

Key: t = top b = bottom c = center r = right l = left. Main directory images indicated in **bold**.

Animal Photography
Alex Grace 32; Eva-Maria Kramer 59t, 86t; Julie Poole 61, 62, 62t; Sally Anne Thompson 25t, 57t; Tara Gregg 24t; Tetsu Yamazaki 25, 28, 28t, 41, 58, 67, 68, 72, 76, 81, 82, 88, 93, 107, 120; Tracy Morgan 113, 113t.

Getty Images
Dan Burn-Forti 53; Michael Duva 84; Tracy Morgan 24, 37, 59, 65, 75, 86, 108, 153, 154, 155, 156, 168, 197.

Shutterstock.com
Ado6 15t; Alexia Khruscheva 122; Andreas Gradin 40, 44, 44t, 104, 104t; Anke van Wky 77t; Anna Hoychuk 8; Anna Hudorozkova 66t, 93t; Anna Kucherova 175t; Anna Tyurina 178; Art_man 124t; Barbara O'Brien 164; Chantal Ringuette 176; Christian Mueller 65t; Cynoclub 34t, 85, 127, 158, 195t; David Huntley Creative 174t; Dien 103, 132t; Dmitry Kalinovsky 110; Dorottya Mathe 6, 9bl, 117, 117t; Ekaterina Nikitina 91t; Eric Isselee 9cr, 11c, 11bl, 12tr, 17b, 20b, 21t, 21c, 21b, 27t, 29, 31t, 33, 33t, 35t, 46t, 47, 47t, 48, 48t, 49, 49t, 51, 51t, 56, 57, 67t, 69, 69t, 70t, 72t, 73t, 74t, 78t, 79, 82t, 83t, 85t, 88t, 94, 94t, 95t, 97, 97t, 98, 99, 99t, 100, 101t, 106, 111, 112t, 115, 116, 116t, 119t, 120t, 122t, 123, 123t, 127t, 128, 128t, 130, 132, 135, 135t, 137, 137t, 140, 141, 142t, 143, 148, 149, 149t, 150, 150t, 151, 151t, 152, 157, 159, 162, 162t, 163, 167, 169, 169t, 172, 174, 175, 177t, 179t, 180, 180t, 181t, 183t, 186, 187, 191, 193t, 196, 196t, 198; Erik Lam 2-3, 4, 9tr, 10tr, 11tr, 11cl, 20t, 22l, 23t, 35, 36, 40t, 45, 50t, 52, 64, 64t, 91, 95, 100t, 101, 110t, 114t, 118, 118t, 119, 124, 129, 129t, 138, 139t, 141t, 142, 143t, 144t, 148t, 152t, 157t, 159t, 160, 160t, 161, 161t, 170, 171, 171t, 177, 184, 185t, 190, 191t, 192; Fesus Robert 147t; Foaloce 68t;

Gelpi JM 34, 43; Gleb Semenjuk 154t; GLYPHstock 181; Greenfire 63, 63t; GVictoria 146t; Ilja Generalov 10tl, 125; Ingvald Kaldhussater 179; Irina oxilixo Danilova 9tl, 42; Jagodka 10cl, 10br, 14b, 20c, 26, 27, 38, 38t, 66, 71, 71t, 73, 74, 83, 109t, 126, 126t, 133t, 146, 173, 182t, 186t, 188, 193; Jeff Banke 187t; Jody 26t; JP Chretien 131t; Julia Remezova 114, 139; Kazlouski Siarhei 158t; Konstantin Gushcha 19tr, 103t; Kuznetsov Alexey 167t, 178t; L. Nagy 37t; Lenkadan 29t; Liliya Kulianionak 52t, 185; Linn Currie 80, 96; Lipowski Milan 87, 87t; Makarova Viktoria 172t; Margo Harrison 136t; Marina Jay 55t, 133; Mark Herreid 168t; Marlonneke Willemsen 89, 89t; Mila Atkovska 30; Misti Hymas 60; Nancy dressel 30t; Nata Sdobnikova 166; Neil Lockhart 61t; NickOmanPhoto 164t; Nikolai Tsvetkov 55, 109, 122; Nixx Photography 1; Oksix 42t; Otsphoto 102, 102t, 108t; PardoY 54; Paul Cotney 130t; Paul Cotney 192t; Pavel Hlystov 145, 145t; Pelevina Ksinia 77; Perry Harmon 79t; Petr Jilek 173t; Phil Date 105, 105t; Picture-Pets 22r; Quayside 39, 39t; Richard Chaff 195; Richard Peterson 188t; Robynrg 80t, 106t; Sergey Lavrentev 16tr, 131; SergiyN 78; Steamroller_blues 121, 144, 165, 165t, 182, 183; Stefan Petru Andronache 36t; Steve Heap 58t; Susan Schmitz 23bl, 46, 56t, 136, 176t, 194; Tatiana Gass 138t; Tobkatrina 111t, 170t; TonyB 107t; Touloubaev Stanislav 81t; Ulrich Willmunder 98t; Utekhina Anna 96t, 121t, 125t, 166t, 197t; Violetblue 92, 92t; Viorel Sima 43t, 50, 54t, 115t, 140t, 189t; Vitaly Titov & Maria Sidelnikova 184t, 189; Vladimir Sklyarov 194t; Vladyslav Starozhylov 70; Willee Cole 31, 41t, 90t, 134, 134t, 147; Zuzule 45t.

The publisher would also like to thank the following for contributing images to the book: Creative Commons/Eget bildearkiv/Plotthund 75t; Creative Commons/Jon-Eric Melsæter 153t; Creative Commons/Marilyn Piurek 53t; Creative Commons/Pitke 84t; Creative Commons/psmithy 32t; Creative Commons/Roger Ahlbrand 90; Creative Commons/Samorodokhanaana http://www.ruscanaan.ru 156t; Creative Commons/TS Eriksson 155t; Public Domain/Dmitry Guskov 76t; Public Domain/Kingkong954 60t.

While every effort has been made to credit contributors, Marshall Editions would like to apologize should there have been any omissions or errors and would be pleased to make the appropriate correction to future editions of the book.